A Poetics of
Women's
Autobiography

A Poetics of Women's Autobiography

Marginality and the Fictions
of Self-Representation

SIDONIE SMITH

INDIANA UNIVERSITY PRESS
Bloomington and Indianapolis

This book was brought to publication
with the assistance of a grant from the
Andrew W. Mellon Foundation.

Library of Congress Cataloging-in-Publication Data

Smith, Sidonie.
A poetics of women's autobiography.

Bibliography: p.
Includes index.
1. English prose literature—Women authors—
History and criticism.   2. Autobiography—Women authors.
3. Women—Great Britain—Biography—History and
criticism.   4. Self in literature.   5. Marginality,
Social, in literature.   6. Women and literature—
Great Britain.   7. Kingston, Maxine Hong. Woman
warrior.
PR756.A9S65   1987   820'.9'492   86-45990
ISBN 0-253-34505-7
ISBN 0-253-20443-7 (pbk.)

for Greg

CONTENTS

Acknowledgments

This book has been a long time coming. It marks the culmination of a decade spent rethinking literature, the canon, and the woman writer. It has been a decade rich in ideas, professional opportunities, personal growth, and especially friendships. And so I want here to express my sororal appreciation for those women whose friendships have constituted a large part of my life during the last ten years. My commitment to Women's Studies dates back to the hot afternoons of the Tucson spring in 1974 when Myra Dinnerstein and I pieced together the proposal for a Women's Studies program at the University of Arizona. Throughout the last thirteen years Myra has always been there, a kind of "mother [or sister] of us all," promoting our professional, intellectual, and personal lives. Others—Pat Mac-Corquodale, Sherri O'Donnell, Mary Thornberry, Donna Guy, Susan Hardy Aiken, Maureen Turim, Laurel Wilkening, Eliana Rivera—have provided a rich and diverse set of voices through and against which to discover my own feminist perspective and practice. And so have those feminist critics who, during the last decade, have made of literary criticism a vital, provocative, and challenging arena of debate and creativity.

I also want to express appreciation to Marcus Billson, who worked through with me the early stages of theoretical thinking about autobiography. And appreciation also to David Gitlitz, who as a colleague and mentor has supported my scholarly interests in the midst of my administrative life.

I thank also my son, Anthony, who spent his fifth through tenth years accommodating his mother's need to spend weekends, evenings, early mornings writing her book. Finally, I thank my husband, Greg, for his fierce commitment to the integrity of ideas and his critical support of my intellectual and professional life.

A Poetics of
Women's
Autobiography

I

Theoretical Considerations

ONE

Autobiography Criticism and the Problematics of Gender

> We may safely assert that the knowledge
> men acquire of women, even as they have
> been and are, without reference to what
> they might be, is wretchedly imperfect and
> superficial and will always be so until
> women themselves have told all they have
> to tell.
>
> —John Stuart Mill, *The Subjection of Women*

Suddenly everyone in the universe of literary critics and theorists seems to be talking about autobiography, a genre critics described until recently as a kind of flawed biography at worst, and at best a historiographical document capable of capturing the essence of a nation or the spirit of an age. Ironically, or inevitably, as more and more critics talk about autobiography, the sense of its generic conventions, even its very definition, has begun to blur, until some now question whether autobiography exists at all. "Autobiography," suggests James Olney, "is not so much a mode of literature as literature is a mode of autobiography—and not by any means the only possible mode."[1] This genre, apparently so simple, so self-evident, so readily accessible to the reader, is ultimately as complex as the subject it seeks to capture in its representation and as various as the rhetorical expressions through which, with the mediation of language, that subjectivity reads itself into the world.

During the last thirty years, and more particularly during the last ten, books and articles about autobiography have appeared at an increasing rate. Recently two bibliographical essays have attempted to capture the history and shifting preoccupations of that criticism: the essay appended to William C. Spengemann's *Forms of Autobiography* and the introductory essay in Olney's anthology, *Autobiography: Essays Theoretical and Critical*.[2] Spengemann, situating the first surge of critical interest in autobiography in the

3

late nineteenth and early twentieth centuries, cites three contributing phenomena: the increasing number of autobiographies reaching an interested
public; the increasing number of critical essays focusing on autobiography;
and the influence of Wilhelm Dilthey's call for a writing of history grounded
in autobiographical documents.[3] But I would add that prior cultural influences must have motivated those three expressions of a general interest,
among them the revolutionary movements of the late eighteenth century,
with their pressure for greater democratization of society; the preoccupations of an individualism privileged by romanticism and, later, by Victorian
notions of evolutionary progress; the Industrial Revolution and its informing myth of the self-made man; the historiographical elaboration of the
"great man" thesis; Darwinism, most particularly social Darwinism, with its
emphasis on the survival of the fittest; Freudianism and the analytical
methods psychoanalysis brought to bear on self-reflection; and the great
outburst of literary activity and of literacy that attended those developments.

Interest in autobiography continued to intensify through the early twentieth century with the work of such individuals as Dilthey's student and son-
in-law, Georg Misch, whose *History of Autobiography in Antiquity* argues, in
Carlylian fashion, that the progressive unfolding of Western history can be
read in the representative lives of the people who participated in its unfolding and that the particular types of Western Man can be read in the hermeneutics of each successive manifestation of self-representation.[4] But Misch,
whose work was long in coming and then for years remained unavailable in
translation, did not greatly influence the criticism of autobiography until
mid-century, when a new interest coalesced. Olney traces this second surge
to 1956 and the publication of Georges Gusdorf's article "Conditions and
Limits of Autobiography." Spengemann traces it to 1970 and the publication of Francis R. Hart's essay "Notes for an Anatomy of Modern Autobiography," arguing that much of the work done before 1970, including
Gusdorf's seminal article, remained generally unknown. For both critics the
importance of the essays they cite lies in their attempt to subject autobiography to a systematic literary analysis.[5]

This more recent critical interest emerged from the rejection by a second
generation of the earlier generation's preoccupation with the *bios* of the
autobiographer, a critical focus that derived from the conceptualization of
autobiography as a subcategory of biography. From that earlier perspective
"truthfulness" in autobiography was a matter of biographical facticity. Any
textual inconsistency seemed easily resolvable by recourse to the historical
record for confirmation or refutation since the assumption was that "there
was nothing problematical about the *autos*, no agonizing questions of identity, self-definition, self-existence, or self-deception—at least none the

reader need attend to—and therefore the fact that the individual was himself narrating the story of himself had no troubling philosophical, psychological, literary, or historical implications."[6] A kind of moralist, the autobiography critic evaluated the quality of life as it was lived and the veracity
of the autobiographer as he or she narrated the story of that life.

By contrast, the second generation of critics has attuned itself to the
"agonizing questions" inherent in self-representation. For these critics,
truthfulness becomes a much more complex and problematic phenomenon. Since autobiography is understood to be a process through which the
autobiographer struggles to shape an "identity" out of amorphous subjectivity, the critic becomes a psychoanalyst of sorts, interpreting the truth of
an autobiography in its psychological dimensions rather than in its factual
or moral ones. Moreover, once the autobiographical act is conceived as
creative or interpretative, autobiography can be read as one generic possibility among many within the institution of literature, with the result that
critics and theorists do with it what they have done with other genres.
Wayne Shumaker, Margaret Bottrall, Paul Delaney, Daniel B. Shea, and
other historians of the form have charted the course of its historical and
thematic development; Francis R. Hart and Roy Pascal have postulated its
generic conventions and poetics; Spengemann and William L. Howarth
have defined its paradigmatic patterns.[7] And others have explored individual works or groups of works from a variety of critical scenarios. Most
particularly they have attempted to define the genre and to categorize its
manifold expressions in a hierarchy of types.[8]

Whatever the critical agenda, two underlying assumptions motivate these
approaches to autobiography—confidence in the referentiality of language
and a corollary confidence in the authenticity of the self.[9] But a third
generation of critics, the structuralists and poststructuralists, has challenged the notion of referentiality and undermined comfortable assumptions about an informing "I." These theorists suggest that the *unitas*, shattered by the influence of the unconscious and structured by linguistic configurations beyond any single mind, may be nothing more, and certainly
nothing less, than a convention of time and space where symbolic systems,
existing as infinite yet always structured possibility, speak themselves in the
utterance of a *parole*.[10] The autobiographical text becomes a narrative artifice, privileging a presence, or identity, that does not exist outside language. Given the very nature of language, embedded in the text lie alternative or deferred identities that constantly subvert any pretensions of truthfulness. As one critic would argue, "no autobiography can take place except
within the boundaries of a writing where concepts of subject, self, and
author collapse into the act of producing a text."[11] Such challenges both to
the concept of a speaking subject and to the belief in language's trans-

parency have shattered the epistemological certainties and ontological legitimacy of what French theorists call the "master narratives" of the West,
autobiography among them. As notions of an authoritative speaker, inten-
tionality, truth, meaning, and generic integrity are rejected, the former
preoccupations of autobiography critics—the nature of its truth, the emergence of its formal structures, the struggle with identity, even the assumption of a motivating self—are displaced by a new concern for the *graphia*,
"the careful teasing out of warring forces of signification within the text
itself."[12]

Certain implications of structuralist and poststructuralist theories have
led critics once again to shift focus and to look to the "reader" of autobiography, a preoccupation that moves in a variety of directions. For those
who assert that "writing is an inscription within an existing literary code,
either in the form of an appropriation or a rejection," autobiography becomes a manifestation of a prior act of reading on the part of the author
who rereads literary and cultural conventions.[13] For those who assert that
the self inscribed in autobiography is a rhetorical construct, the "fictive"
reader created by the autobiographer to help bring that self into existence
assumes prominence. These critics attend to the multitudinous strategies
autobiographers use as they manipulate and are in turn manipulated by an
implied reader. Still others consider the actual reader, you and me, before
the text. The textual critic holds that, since words in the autobiography
point to more than their referential meaning, which can never be recovered
anyway, readers become the actual creators of the text, bringing their own
cultural codes to a confrontation with the author's. Even more complicating, for the Lacanian critic "you" and "me" are always subjects in process,
always products of language, therefore not stable or stationary "selves";
thus there can be no "actual reader" before (in both senses) the text. Such
complexities inherent in a preoccupation with the reader may account for
the fact that after attempting to articulate a definition of autobiography in
his *L'Autobiographie en France*, Philip Lejeune rejected his earlier belief in
normative or essentialist definitions and argued instead for a conception of
autobiography as a *"mode of reading"* as well as a "mode of writing."[14] More
recently, Janet Varner Gunn has situated her theory of autobiography in
both moments of reading—"by the autobiographer who, in effect, is 'reading' his or her life; and by the reader of the autobiographical text," who is
also, in the encounter with the text, rereading his or her own life by association.[15]

Of course, such a brief summary must necessarily oversimplify in its
schematization the history of autobiography criticism. It cannot do justice
to the individual theories motivating the critical foci of that criticism and
that history. At best, it remains a critical fiction, since there has been, as

Spengemann reminds us, no such unilinear progression "from facticity, to psychology, to textuality."[16] Currently all these approaches to autobiography coexist. But such a summary does serve to set the context for a consideration of autobiography written by women.

For where in the maze of proliferating definitions and theories, in the articulation of teleologies and epistemologies, in the tension between poetics and historiography, in the placement and displacement of the "self" is there any consideration of woman's *bios*, woman's *autē*, woman's *graphia*, or woman's hermeneutics? Spengemann, alluding to Virginia Woolf's essay, "The Lives of the Obscure," places autobiographies by women under the rubric "Classes of People," those "certain sorts of people who might otherwise remain unknown."[17] Olney discusses autobiographies by women in relation to various "studies"—American, Afro-American, and African— and suggests that autobiography offers a means of exploring an experience.[18] Thus while both critics note the importance of autobiography in gaining information about woman's *bios*, neither goes beyond that acknowledgment to comment on the larger and more complex issues of woman's *autē*, woman's *graphia*, and woman's reading. In fact, until the last few years, the impact of gender on the autobiographical project has not been a serious focus of critical or theoretical inquiry.

Consider Misch's work on autobiography. Both his theory and his methodology have had a profound impact on subsequent studies of the genre. Here, then, are two introductory passages from his *History of Autobiography in Antiquity*, which, taken together, reveal his critical stance:

> Among the special relationships in life it is chiefly the self-assertion of the political will and the relation of the author to his work and to the public that show themselves to be normative in the history of autobiography.[19]

> Though essentially representations of individual personalities, autobiographies are bound always to be representative of their period, within a range that will vary with the intensity of the authors' participation in contemporary life and with the sphere in which they moved.[20]

For Misch, the "normative" definition of autobiography and the criteria used to evaluate the success of any particular autobiography lie in the relationship of the autobiographer to the arena of public life and discourse. Yet patriarchal notions of woman's inherent nature and consequent social role have denied or severely proscribed her access to the public space; and male distrust and consequent repression of female speech have either condemned her to public silence or profoundly contaminated her relationship to the pen as an instrument of power. If she presumes to claim a fully

human identity by seeking a place in the public arena, therefore, she trans-
gresses patriarchal definitions of female nature by enacting the scenario of
male selfhood.[21] As she does so, she challenges cultural conceptions of the
nature of woman and thereby invites public censure for her efforts. If she
bows to the discursive pressure for anonymity, however, she denies her
desire for a voice of her own.

Misch also emphasizes the "representative" nature of autobiography. Yet
if we attend to his definition of its "supreme example"—"the contemporary
intellectual outlook revealed in the style of an eminent person who has
himself played a part in the forming of the spirit of his time"—we recognize
how even so apparently unobjectionable a term as "representative" becomes problematic when considered from the perspective of woman's experience. What precisely would it signify for a woman's life and her narrative
to be "representative" of a period? Very few women have achieved the
status of "eminent person"; and those who have done so have more com-
monly been labeled "exceptional" rather than "representative" women. Perhaps such women and their autobiographies would more accurately be
"unrepresentative" of their period. Or perhaps such life stories, while unrepresentative of women's lives, might be representative of men's lives.
What would it mean for such autobiographers to be representative men,
and how might that tension between the representative and the unrepresentative manifest itself in their autobiographies? Or to ask the question in
slightly different terms: How might the tension between the ideal woman
and the ideal man manifest itself in women's autobiography? What impact
might that double identification have on women's readings of their lives—
readings that are done in public before a reader who "represents" the
patriarchal order? And what about the idea of "representation" itself?
Problematized, representation has become contaminated as the sign of an
earlier discursive dispensation, has been "denounced as complicitous with a
violence as old as Western History itself"—that is, with the imperialistic
designs of a speaking subject intent on "naming, controlling, remembering,
understanding."[22]

Autobiography critics who bring to their readings of women's texts the
assumptions so clearly embodied in Misch's work will attend only to a rare
autobiography by a woman, for instance, to the *Life* of St. Teresa of Avila.
The autobiographies of vocationless women might be locally interesting,
even delightful to read, as Anne Lady Halkett's is, but not culturally significant because the *bios* is not culturally significant and because the self-representation is not aesthetically significant by androcentric criteria. By such
criteria, then, the mass of women's lives seem doomed to remain silent, their
autobiographies to remain unwritten or, when written and read, to be misread and labeled inferior because they do not conform to Misch's normative

prescription of theme and structure. Falling in that zone Elaine Showalter characterizes, via Shirley and Edwin Ardener, as "wild," women's texts lie outside the dominant culture's boundaries in a spatial, experiential, and metaphysical "no-man's-land."[23] Moreover, to the degree that such critics assume a transparency to language as well as its ideological neutrality, they ignore the implications for the woman autobiographer of moving from the margins of culture toward the center in order to engage in a "master narrative" that defines the speaking subject as always male.

Ultimately, criteria such as Misch's are restrictive, prescriptive, and inappropriate to a reading of women's autobiographies; and yet critics certainly have continued to read from similar assumptions. In *The Value of the Individual*, the historian Karl Joachim Weintraub, influenced by Dilthey and Misch, traces in a series of texts the comparative value given by the autobiographer to "individuality" and to "pursuit of the typical and the model." Weintraub comments in his introduction:

> This heuristic device posits, on the one hand, the adherence of men to great personality ideals in which their culture tends to embody its values and objectives—and, on the other hand, a commitment to a self for which there is no model. The ideal which most clearly expresses the view that the task of life and of self-formation rests on the imitation of a lofty model is the ideal contained in the *Imitatio Christi*. An ideal form of being beckons men and women to model their lives upon it. There existed, and continue to exist, many such model conceptions of the personality in our tradition: the ideal of the Homeric Hero, the Germanic hero, the truly "polis-minded" man, the Roman *pater familias*, of Aristotle's "great-minded man," of the unshakable Stoic, the ideal monk, the ideal knight, the ideal gentleman, the ideal teacher, and so on.[24]

Clearly, all the model types are male models, a fact that suggests once again the degree to which Western discourse has conflated "male" norms and "human," or universal, norms. Moreover, Weintraub opposes to the model conception of personality a conception of individuality that privileges singularity and autonomy: "When the belief in individuality reaches its full force, this individual difference is seen to be a matter of great value in itself. . . . When this conception dominates man's awareness, it becomes his life's task to actualize the one mode of being which only he can be."[25] This valorization of autonomous selfhood demands the individual's willingness to challenge cultural expectations and to pursue uniqueness at the price of social ostracism. Yet even the rebel whose text projects a hostile society against which he struggles to define himself, if he is male, takes himself seriously because he and his public assume his significance within the dominant order: Only in the fullness of that membership can the fullness of his rebellion unfold.[26] For women, on the other hand, rebellious pursuit is

potentially catastrophic. To call attention to her distinctiveness is to become
"unfeminine." To take a voice and to authorize a public life are to risk loss
of reputation. Hence distinctiveness may never be attractive in and of itself.
Because of Weintraub's failure to acknowledge such issues, both polarities
of his dialectical schema derive from and reinscribe a male-identified paradigm.

It is through that androcentric paradigm that Weintraub reads two
women autobiographers, St. Teresa of Avila and Madame Guyon, both of
whom were mystics struggling to achieve the *Imitatio Christi*. Not surpris-
ingly, he fails to consider St. Teresa's identity as a woman, nay, a woman
mystic, in the patriarchal culture of sixteenth-century Spain. He fails also to
consider the value of the nun's life as an alternative to married life for
women of the period and therefore neglects the opportunities such a life
offered to women for pursuing "individuality" and "the model." He does
comment on the facts that she was charged by her confessor to write and to
rewrite her life story and that she describes herself as an "unwilling author"; and he even goes so far as to note that "she consistently insists that as
an unlearned woman she ought not to be writing."[27] While he calls that
theme a "deliberate" one, however, he does not find it necessary to explore
the rhetorical utility of self-abnegation for a woman who would dare to
speak, even to instruct, in a church and a culture that suspected and rigidly
proscribed such individualistic and atypical activities in women. When he
discusses the autobiography of Madame Guyon, Weintraub misses an opportunity to consider the impact of her experience as a married, rather
than virginal, woman on the kind of mysticism she so emphatically pursued
and defended.[28] Her profession of an antirational, antihistorical, utterly
selfless absorption in Christ and her projection of herself as proud and
powerful in the willing victimization she suffers for that love reveal much
about the complex attraction of mysticism for women of the period. For
Madame Guyon, ruthlessly tyrannized in a patriarchally enforced and loveless marriage, mysticism offered the promise of unique empowerment in its
exaggeration of the quintessential model of the feminine. And for both
women, as for a good many others during the period, mysticism itself
provided a nonscholarly engagement with religious experience to those
who were denied access to the realm of formalized theological discourse.
Weintraub prefers the more judicious and less histrionic St. Teresa. But in
either case he fails to account for his own scheme when he analyzes the
autobiographies of the two women. The typical and model script of a
woman's life is very much a convention of patriarchal culture, one that
women autobiographers must and do attend to; and their struggle for
individuality is complicated by the power of those culturally prescribed
norms of female identity. As a historian of ideas Weintraub reads and

writes, in the end, the history of a male idea because he does not attend to the historical specificities of women's lives or speculate on the relationship of woman's experience to her linguistic and discursive alternatives.

But what about those literary historians who would write the history of autobiography? How have women fared in their readings? In his exploration of sacred and secular autobiography in the seventeenth century, Delany does consider "female" autobiographers; but he relegates his discussion of them to the final chapter, noting that "Englishwomen of the seventeenth century lacked, because of their subservient social position, that firm identification with profession or occupation which was typical of their male counterparts."[29] He does recognize that women tended to express "a wider range of emotional responses" and "more awareness of concrete realities," concerns that would make the female autobiographers "less likely to be satisfied with a simple record of *res gestae*."[30] Yet while he manifests sensitivity to the cultural and historical phenomena influencing women's actual and textual lives and acknowledges, however cursorily, their contribution to the development of the genre, he cannot really place them, limited as he is by his association of the form with a specifically defined content and perspective. Because Delany is ultimately committed to androcentric paradigms of self-representation, he cannot grasp the challenge, the significance, and the vitality of the works by women that he discusses.

Nor can Shumaker, who makes interesting claims for women autobiographers but makes them fleetingly and in moralistic terms. Of the eighteenth-century "scandalous apologies" by Laetitia Pilkington, Constantia Phillips, and Lady Vane—all influenced by the nascent psychological novel—he writes: "Since before the publication of these three amorous confessions secular lives regularly ignored the feelings, whereas afterward they often did not, there is at least a possibility that three dishonest and libertine women did autobiography a lasting service."[31] Having made that claim for literary influence on generic development and then having offered a conventional indictment of the authors' lives in one sentence, Shumaker passes on, in effect silencing their works. Elsewhere he calls Anne Lady Halkett's autobiography "a charming narrative of her involved romantic adventures."[32] Here "charming" connotes a narrative appropriately, rather than reprehensibly, "feminine." Yet such appreciative language reveals certain assumptions about "feminine" narratives: They may be witty, skillful, polished, and yet they remain narrow in scope and limited in impact, generically neither profound nor significant.[33] While interested in exploring historical complexities of autobiography, Shumaker, from his patriarchal perspectives, ignores the complexities of women's public self-disclosure.

When we move from historiography to an ahistorical poetics concerned about the *autē*, or constitution of "self," in narrative, we seem to enter the realm of unbiased critical discourse. An essay such as Hart's, which so effectively anatomizes autobiography, does not open itself to the questions raised thus far about historical approaches to the genre. Apparently Hart's anatomy is applicable to all autobiographies; but looking more closely at it, we can locate certain definitions of the autobiographical situation that become especially problematic with reference to women's self-representation. For Hart, the "truth" of an autobiography emerges from "the relation between the autobiographer and his personal, historical subject." In order to understand that relationship, the reader must attend to the selected "I," which "is made and remade according to such criteria as naturalness, originality, essentiality, continuousness, integrity, and significance."[34] Hart appropriately exposes the constructive nature of the autobiographical project in which the "I" is made and remade. Yet for him the "I" is made and remade according to specific criteria. In other words, as a theorist Hart assumes a certain ideology of selfhood grounded in the metaphysical notion of the essential self, one that privileges individuality and separateness over connectedness. That conception of individuality may not motivate the most informed reading of women's autobiographical texts.

For instance, the ideology of individuality may, as Nancy Chodorow's revisionist psychoanalytic theory would suggest, derive from a decidedly male resolution of the tension between individuation and dependency. Indeed, as Chodorow, Dorothy Dinnerstein, and Jane Flax argue, the configuration of identity and the process of individuation differ for men and women to the extent that the relationship of the male and the female child to the mother during the pre-Oedipal stage differs. Because of the nature of the daughter's pre-Oedipal attachment to the mother, "feminine personality," suggests Chodorow, "comes to be based less on repression of inner objects, and fixed and firm splits in the ego, and more on retention and continuity of external relationships."[35] The daughter does not experience the same repression of desire for the mother that the son experiences since "a girl's libidinal turning to her father is not at the expense of, or a substitute for, her attachment to her mother."[36] Thus her experience of self is characterized by "more flexible and permeable ego boundaries."[37] In contrast, the young boy must repress desire for the mother as he turns to the world of the fathers and their power. And so "the basic feminine sense of self is connected to the world, the basic masculine sense of self is separate."[38] Since the boy comes to speak with the authority of the father and all fathers before him, those figures of public power who control the discourse and its economy of selfhood, the male experience is identified as the normative human paradigm. From this ideological perspective the girl comes to speak tentatively from outside the prevailing framework of individuality: She brings a different kind of voice to her narrative. To be sure, the difference in experience is culturally rather than biologically based, reproduced by the familial and cultural structures of power constitutive of patriarchy.

While French theorists of writing and sexual difference—Luce Irigaray, Julia Kristeva, and Hélène Cixous among them—approach the relationship between mothers and daughters from a different point of departure than do Anglo-American feminists, they also interrogate the complacency with which Western discourse has described and valued sexual difference in male and female writing. Specifically, French feminists seek to subvert the ideological assumptions of phallogocentrism by challenging the power and authority of the fathers to control any longer those master discourses of the West that privilege the word and thus the logical argumentation and causal narrative characterized as "masculine" writing. "Feminine" writing, identi-fied with the pre-Oedipal realm of the semiotic that, with the mother, is repressed on entry into the symbolic, they characterize as plural, contin-uous, interdependent, nonsensical, roundabout, a narrative of ruptures, gaps, wordplay, and *jouissance* fundamentally different from the forward drive of logocentric certitude and individuality. Breaking up logocentric discourse, *jouissance* signals the rupture of the semiotic, the erotic, the un-knowable and unrepresentable, the "feminine." The female subject thus enters the self-representational contract as an unrepresentable silence and evidences herself through what Cixous and Madeleine Gagnon describe as woman's milk, her different ink.[39] Seemingly silent and repressed, woman comes to speak loudly as she intervenes in the phallic drive of masculine discourse with her alternative language of fluid, plural subjectivity.

Theories of sexual and textual difference have an impact on theories of narrative, particularly autobiographical narrative. It may be that, as theo-rists of language and literature suggest, woman's subjectivity and therefore her text unfold narratively in patterns tied to her different psychosexual development. It may be that, as certain social-science researchers argue, "males represent experiences of self, others, space, and time in individualis-tic, objective, and distant ways, while females represent experiences in rela-tively interpersonal, subjective, immediate ways."[40] It may be that woman's relationship to representation itself is radically different from her brother's since, to the degree that she is closer to the mother and the mother's pre-Oedipal language, she is closer to the experience of language as presence rather than as absence. As Margaret Homans argues in her provocative fusing of the theories of Chodorow and Irigaray, woman "has the positive experience of never having given up entirely the presymbolic communica-tion that carries over, with the bond to the mother, beyond the preoedipal period. The daughter therefore speaks two languages at once. Along with symbolic language, she retains the literal or presymbolic language that the son represses at the time of his renunciation of his mother."[41] The doubled

languages of her experience as woman then would inform her self-representational project. Or it may be that the making and remaking of the
female self in autobiography emerges from the dialogic engagement with
the ideology of sexual difference promoted in the discourse of her time,
that her making and remaking is at once imitative and disruptive of the
criteria of selfhood promoted by Hart.

Now, we do not know how Hart would read works by women because, of
the forty works on which he bases his analysis, he cites only one by a woman
(Anaïs Nin), and the *only* comment he makes is that she was advised by
friends (men) to discontinue writing it (an interesting situation in itself).
Hart does not, then, misread autobiographies written by women so much as
he ignores them, omitting them from his applications of theory. Yet the
absence of women's autobiographies in his essay points to their earlier
absence from theoretical speculation about the genre. The theories seem to
derive from certain underlying assumptions: that men's and women's ways
of experiencing the world and the self and their relationship to language
and to the institution of literature are identical; or that women's autobiographies, because they emanate from lives of culturally insignificant people,
are themselves culturally insignificant; or that women's autobiographies,
because they may not inscribe an androcentric paradigm of selfhood, are
something other than real autobiography; or that autobiography is fundamentally a male generic contract, a point to which I will return in the
following chapter.

Other theorists who explore the poetics of autobiography look to psychoanalytic theory for critical framing. Willis R. Buck, Jr., for instance, in an
essay on Gibbon's Memoir B, elaborates a deconstructionist reading of autobiography grounded in Lacanian psychoanalysis.[42] While considering only
one autobiography, he proposes a general poetics of autobiographical signification, so that we may question the implications of that theory for wom-
en's autobiographies. Lacan's rereading of Freud posits sexual difference as
dependent on the relationship of the subject to the phallus, that "transcen-
dental signifier" representing the play of absence and presence inherent in
language. The Oedipal stage thus promotes the child's entrance into the
symbolic realm. Embracing the Law-of-the-Father—the prohibition of incest
(the *non*) and the signifying system of language (the *nom*, or naming, that
becomes possible only with the recognition of difference and absence)—the
child internalizes the cultural codes "engendered" by the phallic order.
Given the sexual configuration of the mother-child and the father-child
dyads, female entrance into the symbolic order will be, according to Lacan,
different from male entrance. Through that process woman is denied her
own subjectivity; she crosses through the mirror of the logos and assumes
her position as Other, the object by means of which man defines himself.

Independently she cannot assume and presume herself because, according to Lacan, she has no phallus and therefore can expect no access to the patronym. She enters the symbolic order as absence, lack, negativity. Thus as Sandra M. Gilbert and Susan Gubar ask, "If the Phallus is the magic wand (or want) that opens the gates of language, if the Name-of-the-Father is the password into the palace of rational discourse, what name, what wand (or want), what password can safeguard *her* rites of passage?"[43] The question is critical. But we do not learn how Buck would construct and deconstruct the meaning of autobiographies written by women, whether he would bring Lacanian assumptions about woman's place, her repressed space, to her text, thereby rendering her experience and her relationship to the language of the father in the silences of negativity.

Ultimately the theorists, like the historians, have not questioned their underlying assumptions about writing and sexual difference, about genre and gender, about the intersection between ideologies of selfhood and ideologies of gender. The poetics of autobiography, as the history of autobiography, thus remains by and large an androcentric enterprise. Despite the critical ferment brought about by feminist critiques of the academy, of disciplinary methodologies, of the canon, the majority of autobiography critics still persist in either erasing woman's story, relegating it to the margins of critical discourse, or, when they treat women's autobiographies seriously, uncritically conflating the dynamics of male and female selfhood and textuality. Too many contemporary historians and critics of autobiography remain oblivious to the naiveté and culpability of their own critical assumptions and presumptions.

Thus, in critical theory and literary history, we recognize those recurrent themes traced elsewhere in studies of women and writing: the articulation of "normative" generic definitions that in their very conceptualization preclude both aesthetic appreciation and sophisticated reading of works by women; the omission or neglect that follows from the devaluation of works by women; the impoverishment of a history of autobiography that silences women and their contribution to the genre; the facile and unexamined assumptions about gender-appropriate content, structure, style, and narrative perspective; the failure to consider gender a relevant factor in either the configuration of identity or the institution of literature itself; the unselfconscious ignorance of the relationship of ideologies of gender to ideologies of selfhood. Autobiography critics whose readings derive either from indifference to the relationship between writing and sexual difference or from conventional conceptualizations of that relationship fail to acknowledge that "the maxims that pass for the truth of human experience, and the encoding of that experience in literature, are organizations, when they are not fantasies, of the dominant culture."[44] Thus when they enter the "wild zone" of woman's *bios* (experience), her *autē* (sense of identity), her *graphia* (textuality), and her reading (interpretative strategies), they recognize some familiar codes of the languagescape—those that have been influenced by male models and by male theorizing about female models—and thereby presume to speak authoritatively about the entire zone. Yet they remain insensitive to and mystified by the dynamics of women's experience and her textuality.[45] While they know how to fit some women's autobiographies into the lines of the male tradition from some points of view, they do not know how to fit them between the lines. Nor do they know how to treat them seriously enough to conceive that women may have influenced the development of the genre on the one hand and, on the other, that they may have developed a line or tradition of their own. Applying a critical scenario and a reading sensibility informed by androcentric models of selfhood and literature, those "readers" at best offer analyses that are impressionistic, inexact, incomplete; at worst, they condemn autobiographies by women as anomalies: sometimes interesting, sometimes even skillfully written, but more often than not flawed, insignificant, idiosyncratic, irrelevant, or just plain tedious, as Delany calls the duchess of Newcastle's narrative.

Perhaps the absence of women's texts from the texts of autobiographical criticism, as well as the distorted readings or cavalier dismissals of their texts when they are included in the obligatory chapter or aside, speaks to a fundamental resistance to valuing women's experience and vision. In her introduction to a collection of essays on women's autobiographies, Domna C. Stanton asks: "How could [the absence of women's texts in discussions of autobiography] be reconciled with the age-old, pervasive decoding of all female writing as autobiographical?" She goes on to speculate that autobiographical writing may have been another one of those activities originating with women that men have "usurped and proclaimed their own by obscuring women's texts."[46] Having appropriated the idea that personal experience is a credible subject of literary attention, literary forefathers rendered the genre an androcentric contract dependent on the erasure of women's texts. Male writing about self thereby assumed a privileged place in the canon; female writing about self, a devalued position at the margins of the canon. Here once again the sexual adjective prescribes the valence of the noun. When applied to texts by men "autobiographical" signals the positively valued side of binary opposition—the self-consciously "crafted and aesthetic." When applied to texts by women, it announces the negatively valued side of opposition—the "spontaneous, natural." "It had been used," comments Stanton, "to affirm that women could not transcend, but only record, the concerns of the private self." Again and again the descriptive term "autobiographical" has been "wielded as a weapon to denigrate female texts and exclude them from the canon."[47]

That quarrel with the canon has motivated feminist literary critics whose focus of inquiry is women's autobiography to deconstruct the patriarchal hegemony of literary history, poetics, and aesthetics, and to reconstruct histories, criticism, and theories from a different perspective. They have turned their attention to considering how the autobiographer's identity as woman within the symbolic order of patriarchy affects her relationship to generic possibilities—to the autobiographical impulse, to the structuring of content, to the reading and the writing of the self, to the authority of the voice and the situating of narrative perspective, to the problematic nature of representation itself. In pursuing "the status and significance of the female signature," they have interrogated the ideologies of gender, individualism, and psychobiography.[48] One by one, individual autobiographies are being retrieved from the gaps in literary history and reread from a perspective that insists on the significance of gender in the autobiographical process and product and that challenges the naive conflation of male subjectivity and human identity. Piece by piece, there is being written a literary history of women's self-representation that explores the relationship between women's text and the development of the genre.[49] And as the individual works are read and reread, as the ones are made into many and as the pieces fit into a whole, theories of women's autobiography have begun to take shape. Going beyond the adaptation of androcentric historiography and poetics, the theories are grounded in a variety of feminocentric phenomena. The most conservative and the earliest to emerge argues that the specificity of women's autobiography comes from thematic content, determined by women's subordinate and proscribed status in patriarchal culture. Instead of adventures and vocations, of existential angst and alienation, women write about the sphere of domesticity and about the affective curve in the plot of love.[50] But the recourse to a binarism that reifies the public-private opposition eventuates in a simplistic and unsatisfactory description of textual difference. Examples that bely the opposition abound. Men write of private experiences; women, of their public activities. Moreover, as Stanton reminds us, conventions about the "private" as well as conventions about propriety in self-revelation are culturally determined.[51]

Other theories of difference have distinguished women's autobiographical writing as fragmentary and discontinuous, a narrative mode imitative of their actual experiences as daughter, wife, and mother responsive emotionally to the myriad pressures of another's needs. But there are women who have written a narrative characterized by the very linearity such theories associate with male autobiography. More critically, such theories of fragmentation and discontinuity ignore the nature of autobiographical practice. As I will suggest in chapter three, the generic contract engages the autobiographer in a doubled subjectivity—the autobiographer as protagonist of her story and the autobiographer as narrator. Through that doubled subjectivity she pursues her fictions of selfhood by fits and starts. Then there are theories that distinguish women's autobiographies by the way in which women seem to unfold their story through their relationship to a significant "other," husband, child, God. Yet those theories of difference do not effectively account for the source of woman's self-representation through relationship: Is female preoccupation with the other an essential dynamic of female psychobiography or a culturally conditioned manifestation of the ideology of gender that associates female difference with attentiveness to the other?[52] Or does all autobiographical practice proceed by means of a self/other intersubjectivity and intertextuality?

The most radical promise of difference is that articulated by the French feminists in the language of *écriture féminine*, a process by which the female body inscribes itself in the milk-white ink of women's sexual and textual desire. For such theorists, women have not yet inscribed themselves in anything other than the phallologocentric *écriture* of Western culture. Therefore, women's true autobiography has yet to be written, since women writers have, until recently, only reinscribed male writing and thereby produced a text "which either obscures women or reproduces the classic representations of women."[53] But the psychosexual essentialism of certain French feminists, with its promise of the triumph of the "unrepresentable" over the body of phallologocentric discourse, has unsettled those Anglo-American theorists who would link the mother's body and her white ink to historical phenomena as well as challenge a universalization of woman that erases contextual differences and elevates feminine silence over speech.

However feminist theorists conceptualize difference, they all recognize woman's double bind: "As long as women remain silent, they will be outside the historical process. But, if they begin to speak and write *as men do*, they will enter history subdued and alienated."[54] Thus any "arachnology," to refer to Nancy K. Miller's name for a theory of female textuality, must grapple with the formal constrictions and rhetorical presentations, the historical context and psychosexual labyrinth, the subversions and the capitulations of woman's self-writing in a patriarchal culture that "fictionalizes" her.[55] With this study of autobiography, I want to weave my own way across the critical loom, to add another thread to those of the theorists who ply the problematics of woman's self-writing and of what Virginia Woolf, in discussing the discourse of the fathers calls, "the dominance of the professor."[56] I trust I have been responsive to those who have come before and suggestive for those who will follow.

But first, I want to offer a word of caution in a gesture toward both reality and humility. I offer here no comprehensive theory of women's autobiographical writing. Complex and typologically diffuse, autobiography demands of its critics careful consideration of the working definition from which they proceed. Since all gesture and rhetoric is revealing of the subject, autobiography can be defined as any written or verbal communication. More narrowly it can be defined as written or verbal communication that takes the speaking "I" as the subject of the narrative, rendering the "I" both subject and object. From that operational vantage point, autobiography includes letters, journals, diaries, and oral histories as well as formal autobiography. But I am not writing here of autobiography in its broadest sense, or about letters, diaries, and journals or oral histories. Each of those forms urges the critic to ask different kinds of questions in addition to the common ones. I confine this exploration of the relationship of gender to genre to formal autobiography as it emerged in the West over the last five hundred years, inquiring into the textual and contextual workings of texts that were written to be published and thus addressed to that arbiter of all cultural ideologies, the public reader. Further, reluctant to work with translated texts, I have limited myself to the Anglo-American tradition.

The following chapter will clarify my conceptualization of "autobiography" as opposed to autobiographical writing. There I critique the way in which literary historians have described the cultural origins of autobiography as the generic expression of a certain idea of selfhood in the West. That history is well written and well known. But it has never been coupled with a consideration of the way in which the prevailing discourses (of church, state, economics, politics, philosophy) during the late Middle Ages and the Renaissance described and prescribed woman's selfhood, and with it her relationship to language. In fact, the discourses of the age of autobiographical origination promoted certain stories of woman's selfhood and others about man's that had a profound impact on the way women read themselves and were, in turn, read by their culture. Inevitably they determined the meaning of autobiography as a generic contract in the West.

Recognizing that the woman who chooses to write her life story must negotiate the figures of "man" and the figures of "woman" promoted by the cultural discourses that surround her, I elaborate in chapter three a theoretical framework through which to understand women's self-writing. This framework posits certain dynamics that structure women's life writing, including the way in which the autobiographer who is a woman must suspend herself between paternal and maternal narratives, those fictions of male and female selfhood that permeate her historical moment. This rhetorical woman then is product both of history and of psychosexual phenomena: Her self-representation reveals both contextual and textual forces of signification. Thus the autobiographer confronts personally her culture's stories of male and female desire, insinuating the lines of her story through the lines of the patriarchal story that has been autobiography.

TWO

Renaissance Humanism and the Misbegotten Man

A Tension of Discourses in the Emergence of Autobiography

I am a woman in the prime of life, with
certain powers
and those powers severely limited
by authorities whose faces I rarely see.

—Adrienne Rich, "I Dream I'm the Death of Orpheus"

Generally locating the origins of autobiography in the late Middle Ages and early Renaissance, literary historians look particularly at the new notion of person that catalyzed its development. I am most interested in the terms of that changing conception of person, that ideology of individualism, for those terms and the history written about them reveal certain androcentric privileges of both ages, the former age of origination and the current age of contemporary criticism. Certain assumptions about the characteristics of autobiography, about the new configuration of personhood, and about women and their relationship to history, to writing, and to identity have influenced historical interpretations of the genre and thereby underwritten canonical silences about (missed readings of) and critical biases about (misreadings of) autobiography written by women. On the way, then, to elaborating a theory of women's autobiography I would like to explore briefly the way the origins of autobiography have been recovered by synthesizing and amplifying the representations of those origins in the history of autobiography criticism. I do so because such a summary offers the opportunity to situate woman's *bios*, her *autē*, her *graphia*, and finally her reading between the lines of that story.

20

INTERPRETATIONS OF HISTORICAL ORIGINS AND THE FIGURE OF MAN

Literary historians tend to agree that the impulse toward self-representation is tied in inevitable and inextricable ways to the cultural milieu of Western civilization during the last four hundred years. Georges Gusdorf, whose seminal essay heralded a new critical preoccupation with the genre, joins others in assigning primary importance to the emergence during the sixteenth and seventeenth centuries of a "historical" consciousness governed by a sense of progress and infused with an awareness of individual differences: "The man who takes the trouble to tell of himself knows that the present differs from the past and it will not be repeated in the future; he has become more aware of differences than of similiarities; given the constant change, given the uncertainty of events and of men, he believes it a useful and valuable thing to fix his own image so that he can be certain it will not disappear like all things in this world."[1] Such cultural fascination with the unfolding or the development, the reenactment or the discovery, of an individual's unique historical identity has been attributed to myriad influences coaslescing during the fifteenth, sixteenth, and seventeenth centuries in England and on the Continent—influences theological, socioeconomic, scientific and technological, philosophical, political, and literary.

Christianity had early on introduced "a new anthropology" in the West, one that infused with potential value every destiny, from the humblest to the most exalted, because it professed the equality of all souls before God.[2] Every Christian, possessing a rational soul and carrying the *imago dei* within, could aspire to knowledge of and union with God. But this new anthropology exacted its own price in a new responsibility. The Sermon on the Mount, that central text of Christian theology, brought the inner life of intentions as well as the external life of actions under scrutiny, with the result that self-examination achieved a central role in Christian life. And yet, throughout the medieval period various ecclesiastical phenomena— papal authority, hierarchical intervention of intermediaries, hagiographical conventions, medieval doctrines about the natural depravity of human beings, and the dominance of the Scholastic synthesis, with its allegiance to classical and biblical authority—predetermined to a great extent the relationship of individuals to their God and ritualized the forms of self-examination and self-representation available to them. It required the Renaissance and the Reformation to break those bonds and to generate a new, more demanding, yet flexible concept of personal responsibility and a new, more flexible vision of human possibility that encouraged individuals to assume greater authority for their spiritual destinies and to examine themselves for the marks of grace in more personal and less ritualized modes.

Such freedom from traditional authority, however, did not undermine the universal value of the individual's quest for spiritual grace. However individualized the soul's journey might appear to be, Christians influenced by the Reformation always assumed the universality of the general direction of the soul's struggle; as a result, the most seemingly uneventful and nondescript life was of potential interest to everyone, and even the most extraordinary would manifest easily identifiable correspondences with the life of any ordinary Christian.[3] Within that theological framework, personal testimonies became beneficial to the Protestant community as alternatives to ritualized confessions; and even formalized confession, as it became ever more prominent a part of Catholic ritual after the Lateran Council of 1215, effectively reinforced a preoccupation with the truth of an individual's inner struggle.[4]

The disintegration of the feudal system, which had institutionalized a conception of personal identity as fixed within rigid social relationships, also promoted the emergence of a historical consciousness. New political agendas encouraged individuals to question the divinely sanctioned authority of monarchs and to seek a new place in the matrix of political rights and responsibilities. New economic arrangements spurred a redefinition of the relationships of individuals to the forces of production and the distribution of wealth. The great unrest and the social mobility that attended that period of disintegration, and the consequent reorientation of social, economic, and political relationships, may have generated in individuals an increased awareness of the cultural and social explanations of individual experience. Formerly defined by stable, hierarchical identities, people gradually became aware of the disjunction between where they had been and where they were, between who they had been and who they were becoming, and did so in the context of this world rather than of the world to come.[5]

Then, too, critical scientific developments emerged as the medieval synthesis of theological and scientific inquiry broke down. The heliocentric revolution of Copernicus altered the perspective from which human beings situated themselves and their efforts within the universe. The Copernican observations, supplemented by Galileo's measurements and his subsequent laws of motion, challenged among other beliefs the Scholastic distinction between the corruptible and the incorruptible realms of God's creation: The telescope revealed to the human eye the inevitability of change and thus corruptibility in the realm of heavenly bodies. That reorientation of vision had both positive and negative consequences. From one point of view, the earth achieved a kind of parity with heaven; and human beings achieved a new power, observing and then systematizing the rules of mechanics and motion that determined the nature of change. To the extent that they were successful in doing so, they overcame the seemingly arbitrary mystery of the universe and their own powerlessness before it.[6] Moreover, as the laws of nature were observed, measured, systematized, nature itself came to be understood differently. To the medieval Christian mind, nature had been suspect because it was considered to be a "Satanic" province, imperfect and corruptible; and human nature also suffered the curse of divine malediction.[7] Now for the religious, nature became a second scripture by means of which God revealed his divinity; and for the more scientifically adventurous, it became a force to be conquered through understanding and the machine. In the latter case especially, individuals could take great pleasure in the degree to which they mastered "earthly" existence. The more secularly minded could aspire to prominence in a variety of professions and pursuits in this life. The deeply religious could ponder the relationship of the individual to this second scripture and to human nature. In both cases, individuals could take a new pleasure in the life of this world rather than defer pleasure to life in the next. From another point of view, however, that new orientation of vision announced a cosmic decentering: The earth was no longer the center of the universe; the universe, no longer the conceptual whole it once was. Its silent spaces foretold of immensity beyond imagination and foretold also the collapse of comfortable ontologies, including the ontological status of human beings themselves. Thus the new science brought with it, as did the postfeudal social arrangement, insecurity, ambivalence, and anxiety.[8] Individuals, no longer able to center themselves in a permanent definition, had to struggle to understand their identity and place within new and vast cultural spaces.

Other literary historians of autobiography emphasize the impact after Bacon of the inductive method of scientific inquiry. Since the medieval mind interpreted the phenomena of this life as clear manifestations of some divine principle, in and of themselves the facts and experiences were meaningless. But with the emergence of the Baconian method of induction, the seventeenth-century mind turned its attention away from heaven toward "the data of earthly experience." Life in this world became significant as it revealed individual truth rather than illustrated universal truths beyond the individual; consequently, "the adventures of individual living, like everything else that could be observed, then became materials for a new synthesis."[9] The epistemological transformation inaugurated with Bacon's empiricism undermined the power of traditional authority as it began to privilege individual interpretation of experiential data. It also encouraged a new interest in the texture of nature, including human nature, and a new vision of the contexts of existence. In the new science as in late medieval and Renaissance painting, human beings were situated in this world in all its social, cultural, and natural variety.

Technologically, such a prosaic yet profound influence as the greater clarity of Renaissance mirrors allowed people to see more detailed reflections of themselves, sharper and more revealing, or "true," self-representations. The more exacting confrontation between human beings and their image may have promoted the "disconcerting character of the discovery of the self" and served to "bolster and strengthen the tradition of self-examination of Christian asceticism," just as the more exacting confrontation between human beings and the natural world that followed the inventions of the telescope and the microscope promoted the more careful attention to discrete details and the recognition of natural worlds beyond the realm of normal vision.[10] Further, the invention of the printing press resulted in the growth of a reading public, with its thirst for more and more books and its expectations of access to newsworthy events and stories through printed ballads and news.[11]

Philosophical and political theory also enhanced the significance of individuals and helped redefine their relationship to nature and to the social and linguistic world. The method of Descartes, grounded not in the empiricism of Bacon but in the primacy of intuition and deduction, privileged individual authority and experience at the same time that it challenged the forms, style, and methodology of ancient and later Scholastic authorities, thereby heralding "the modern assumption whereby the pursuit of truth is conceived of as a wholly individual matter, *logically independent of the tradition of past thought.*"[12] The emphasis on human reason informing Descartes's method also attended the social and political theories of such later figures as Locke and Rousseau. Those theorists of the social contract, embracing a liberal perspective, described the individual as a being born, not in the midst of a divinely or "naturally" ordered hierarchy mandating rigid relationships of dominance and subordination (as reflected in the feudal system and in medieval theology), but as a being born free, equal, and new. For them, the social contract emerged when individuals joined together to create, not natural, but conventional institutions, thus enacting the fullness of their humanity in the public realm. Such conceptions of human possibility and responsibility promoted in yet another way an "autobiographical" orientation to the world.

Finally, a variety of phenomena within the institutions of literature and language influenced the shape that the autobiographical project would take and the scope of its appeal. The social mobility and consequent unrest noted earlier seemed to promote an interest in chronicle and family history, for both forms proliferated during the late sixteenth century in England and on the Continent. Perhaps, as the political power of the great aristocratic families eroded with the emergence of a more centralized state power, representatives of those same families sought to establish for certainty's sake the ancestral record and thereby secure some basis for their tenuous and shifting social identities. Significantly, the historical perspective in those early prototypes suggests two major distinctions between Renaissance and medieval historiography, both of which were advantageous to the development of autobiography in that both led to a climate more conducive to personal histories: "first, the evolution of an improved 'sense of the past' as historians gained more insight into the cultural differences that separated contemporary Europe from the ancient world; second, the breaking of the clerical monopoly on historical writing."[13] The former distinction, the recognition of the relativity of cultural identity, encouraged greater latitude in the conceptualization of family and individual history. Moreover, it resonated with a new attitude manifest in other literary genres and in the culture as a whole. Renaissance drama, and its fascination with the playing of parts, its preoccupation with characters who step outside their normal identities, testified to the cultural phenomena "of men who are able to imagine themselves in more than one role; who stand as it were outside or above their own personalities; who are protean."[14] Travel narratives, proliferating as Renaissance merchants and explorers escaped the geographical boundaries of Europe, testified to the awakening ability of Western Europeans to imagine a variety of alternative cultures, both the known and the formerly unknown, and to define themselves through comparative and protean identities.

The latter distinction, the gradual liberation of historians from eschatologically oriented models of hagiography, increased the number of potential autobiographers; for people no longer had to measure their "corrupt" lives against the models of the saints but could lay claim to both spiritual and secular legitimacy through the authority of their own interpretations. Moreover, the secularization of thought that eventuated as the medieval synthesis and the clerical monopoly on learning broke down led to the renewed influence of classical literature. Educated individuals could look back to certain biographical conventions for models of life writing, most notably to the classical convention of *res gestae;* but the conventions did not dominate them since the ancients had no mature tradition of autobiography to command later imitators.[15] Thus the autobiographer was freer to experiment in a form more fluid and flexible than longer-lived and more traditional literary models of poetry.[16] Moreover, the breakdown of Latin's monopoly as the primary language of literature in favor of the vernacular widened even further the accessibility of the genre to include the formally uneducated as well as the educated.

Whatever contributing factors they emphasize, literary historians tend to agree that, during the sixteenth, seventeenth, and eighteenth centuries in England and on the Continent, individuals began to consider their life stories to be potentially valuable to their culture and therefore began to write about themselves with increasing regularity. And however they weight the various preconditions, historians all tend to focus on certain recurrent phenomena: the new recognition of identity as an earned cultural achievement, an arena of self-fashioning rather than an ascriptive, natural *donnée;* the corollary recognition of identity as simultaneously unique and yet dependent on social reality and cultural conventions; an increased willingness to challenge the authority of traditional modes of inquiry and to promote the hermeneutical responsibility and authority of the speaking subject; the transformation of conceptions of historiography. Together those phenomena coalesced to foster an environment in which a realignment of the human subject occurred and in which autobiography as the literary representation of that human potentiality became not only possible but also desirable. That environment became the precondition of what would eventually emerge as the ideology of individualism, that tenacious set of beliefs that fostered in the West a conception of "man" as a metaphysical entity, "a self existing independently of any particular style of expression and logically prior to all literary genres and even to language itself."[17] The human being began to hear its own voice and to desire its own form of publicity. Thus, as Elizabeth W. Bruss affirms: "First, we have selfhood, a state of being with its own metaphysical necessity; and only then autobiography, a discourse that springs from that state of being and gives it voice" precisely because, as Michael Sprinker adds, the autobiographer embraces "the concepts of subject, self, and author as independent sovereignties."[18]

I would not challenge the specificities of such an explanation of autobiographical origins. What I would challenge is the unexamined way in which that history, as it situates the emergence of the genre in a new notion of man, construes the autobiographical subject as always male and thereby ignores the interdependencies of the ideology of gender and the ideology of individualism that spawned the new discursive form. Thus delineated, autobiography and the history of autobiography became another two of those public narratives men write for each other as they lay claim to an immortal place within the phallic order. Thus delineated, both autobiography and its history represent two more stories of origins that, as they privilege patrilineal descent and androcentric discourse, erase the matrilineal trace of woman's subjectivity.[19] In response to that silencing, I would like to look once again through that plane mirror whose perfection was so important to the Renaissance and whose clarity offered the promise "of mastery of the image, of representation and self-representation" and to explore the notions of woman's nature figured in the patriarchal discourse of the age.[20] I do so because any discussion of woman's autobiography must situate her self-representational project in its cultural embeddedness. Most particularly, it must remain attentive to prevailing ideologies of woman's sexuality and textual possibilities.

THE FIGURE OF WOMAN

Christianity's "new anthropology" brought with it an unequivocal belief in the moral equality of men's and women's souls in the quest for eternal salvation; but it did not promote equality of the sexes in this world. If woman was conceived to be equal in grace, she was nonetheless inferior to man in her very nature and consequently subordinate to him in her social roles. The Scholastic synthesis of the medieval period, inherited and modified negligibly by Renaissance theologians, systematized both the prelapsarian and the postlapsarian inferiority of woman.[21] Scholastic arguments for prelapsarian subordination combined the authoritative traditions of classical philosophical discourse and biblical exegesis in articulating woman's ontological status. The Aristotelian explanation, informed by Aristotle's biological theories, maintained that woman is a less perfect being than man. Hers is a condition of essential absence: She is deprived of the active character of man in her greater passivity; she is deprived of the full realization of rational capabilities (the "essence" of human being) because her function as childbearer ties her to matter; she is deprived of heat since she partakes of the cold and damp humors; and with such deprivation of heat, she inevitably experiences the deprivation of the virtues associated with heat—courage, moral strength, and honesty among them.[22] Ultimately, a female of the species results from a deprivation of nature, a generative process not carried to its conclusion. However, since woman is necessary for the preservation of the divinely authored species, scholastics such as Aquinas refused to label her, as Aristotle had, a monstrous or unnatural creation; instead, they labeled her, as Aquinas did in his *Summa Theologica,* "misbegotten man."

For the scholastic synthesizer, Aristotle's natural hierarchy and his schema of the four causes by which everything can be identified and differentiated, meshed with the biblical account of God's creation narrated in Genesis 2–3. Adam precedes Eve, who is subsequently formed out of the matter of his side. And whereas Adam is made in the image of God, Eve is made only in the image of Adam. As a result of that divinely constituted hierarchy, Adam embodies qualities associated with the essence of human-beingness. In his creation the end of human life, rational activity, is achieved. Eve, exhibiting less of the rational faculty and existing in a comparatively imperfect body, fulfills her end, an auxiliary one, in procreation. In that way her generative function defines her essence.[23]

Eve's ontological status within the order of creation accounts for her betrayal of mankind. She has not the intellectual fullness of Adam and so, being more vulnerable, is easily persuaded by the serpent's linguistic manipulations to eat of the forbidden fruit. Afterward, her deceptive words lead Adam to betray God's commandment. Yet according to the Scholastics (and to Milton later), Adam chooses to eat of the fruit, not because he believes those words to be true, but because his affection for her leads him to choose continuing companionship in a state of transgression rather than loneliness in Eden. In one more way Adam's natural superiority over Eve is revealed. As a result, the malediction of Eve culturally embeds the appropriateness of woman's eternal subordination to man: Her postlapsarian curse is to be subject to and therefore subject of her husband's authority. And so, intellectually and morally, she remains a misbegotten man, denied the possibility of achieving full intellectual, ethical, and moral stature. Additionally, she must bear children in pain and sadness, a curse that suggests the degree to which her end signifies simultaneously her difference from yet continued identity with nature. The menstrual blood and afterbirth expelled from her body in fulfillment of her auxiliary function become pollutions within the community, as do the immoral proclivities that emanate from her sexual nature: a desire for fancy dress, ornamentation, and cosmetics.[24] Such self-adornment of the polluted flesh tries to mask but actually exposes the more significant signs of lechery and seductiveness, avarice in service to ambition, and deceptiveness, all of which derive from woman's greater involvement with the life of the senses and matter. Only her silencing by means of confinement in the private, circumscribed realm of domesticity and her exclusion from the public realm curbs the potential pollution threatening the community on the one hand and, on the other, ensures that she fulfills her natural, divinely authored destiny.

Eve is, however, not just socially silenced; she is literally silenced, as all women would be after her. The biblical tradition, interpreted first in Hebraic writings and then in the Christian writings of Paul, the church fathers, the Scholastic synthesizers, and Renaissance theologians, reaffirmed again and again the necessity of proscribing female speech. Woman was forbidden to speak during public service. Because the malediction of Eve ensured her subordination to man and her confinement in the domestic sphere, she had not the authority to do so; because the hierarchy of creation ensured her intellectual inferiority to man, she had not the wisdom to do so. Finally, she must not do so because her very presence in public might arouse man's desire.[25] Even though the patristic writers and medieval and Renaissance theologians acknowledged that woman as well as man might receive the gift of prophesy directly from God, they denied woman the right to exercise that gift in public. But the injunction against woman's speech went further: Even in the domestic space, the truly good woman would speak but little.[26]

Because that injunction against woman's legitimate claim to public discourse and the power it commands has profound ramifications for her engagement in literary self-representation, we need to look again at the

biblical myth of origins and the role of woman's speech in classical discourse. In Genesis 2, God passes on to Adam three gifts and one command.
First, he gives him the goods of Eden; and he follows with the commandment not to eat the fruit of the forbidden tree, effectively introducing the
Father's law. Second, he gives him the authority to name creation and thereby
the power to bring the natural world into existence by specifying its difference from man and his hierarchical ordination over it. Significantly, in
naming the animals, Adam recapitulates God's creation of the world
through the word in Genesis 1 (a recapitulation made possible by the inherited arrangement in which the later priestly version precedes the earlier
Yahwist version) and establishes his patrilineal inheritance. Since Adam
finds in none of the animals of creation the fulfillment of his desire, God
offers him yet a third gift: He creates woman out of Adam's side in a
striking inversion of natural childbirth. Then, empowered by the earlier
gift of naming, Adam again imitates the Father by giving woman her second birth; for although she is physically created by God, she comes into
social existence only when Adam represents her difference in the play of
language, assigning her a name that specifies her identity in relationship to
him (*ish* and *ishshah* in Hebrew). He represents not a mutually independent
being but an image of Eve reflecting his own desire. At this point Adam has
received from his Father the three forms of communication—goods, words,
and woman—that will enable transformation from the natural to the symbolic order.[27]

Like Adam, Eve too uses words; but, conveniently, she does so with a
difference. Entering into a dialogue with the serpent that imitates with an
ironic difference the implied dialogue between God and Adam in Genesis
2, she repeats the Father's law; yet because she does not recognize its significance or the serpent's subtlety, she is duped into disobeying that law and
then into telling a lie that she does not even know to be one. In understanding only the literal level of God's mandate, Eve betrays her inadequacy for
interpreting the potential difference embedded in language itself: She does
not comprehend the symbolic order with its figurative language. Responding only to the literal meaning of the serpent's speech, she believes that the
thing, apple, will give knowledge. But there is more to her use of language.
She is duped because she allows herself to express her own desires. Precisely because that use of language in service to desire is a source of disorder, Eve's entrance into the realm of public discourse eventuates in the
catastrophic expulsion of man and woman from paradise. It also eventuates
in the identification of Eve's word with the speech of the serpent: She is
double-tongued, captious, evil-speaking. In response, the Father's curse
successfully denies her the authority of her own word as the medium
through which to articulate her desire. Subject to the authority of her

husband, Eve, and after her all women, will be the object of male representation and will thereby be recuperated as the mother in the phallic order. The only signs she will bear will be the silent signs of pregnancy as both desire and womb become the media of exchange binding patriarchal culture. Ultimately, woman's sexuality must be repressed and her word silenced in order for the Father's law to survive. The threat of both is that they will disrupt the very identity and authority of man.[28]

Although classical philosophy does not equate woman's speech with her Satanic alliance, it nonetheless maintains the hierarchical distinction between the value and authority of man's speech and that of woman's speech. Though Aristotle does not comment specifically on woman's speech, he does suggest that, because woman lacks the authority and reasoning ability of a man, she cannot achieve the degree of moral and intellectual virtue that he can. And the dialogues of Plato offer an unspoken commentary on woman's speech: "The women of Plato's time" writes Jean Bethke Elshtain, "were not only excluded from politics but also debarred from participating in the process of becoming what Plato meant by a 'good' human being—a process that required a special search for truth within the all male forum for philosophic discourse, pedagogy, and intimacy that is the *mise en scène* for the Platonic dialogues."[29] This special search for truth was supported by the sophisticated invention of formal logic and dialectic and the elaborations of rhetoric, that "technologized" form of discourse, which as Walter J. Ong suggests, "developed in the past as a major expression on the rational level of the ceremonial combat which is found among males."[30] As such, its forward-moving logic of causality and its agonistic mode of argumentation become the linguistic equivalents of battlefield activity. The master of the sword and the master of the word guard the patrilineal heritage of Greek democracy and its free males. Since it lacks both the poetic and the philosophical sophistication valued by classical Athenian culture, the speech of the domestic sphere and of woman remains, as Elshtain suggests, "without meaning—unformed, chaotic, evanescent, the speech of *doxa* (mere opinion, not truth). Household speech could be neither heroic . . . nor part of the philosophic male quest for wisdom through a dialogue of a particular kind."[31] The difference of woman's speech thus secures the definition of the nature of man's speech and the nature of man as a particular kind of speaker. Her very absence from the polis, that center of public discourse, establishes man's identity.

The domestication of woman, with its consequences for woman's speech, was also empowered cosmologically by the rise to prominence of the Olympian gods as depicted in Hesiod's *Theogeny*. In that Greek myth of origins, Zeus defeats the forces of the Titans, those monstrosities spawned by the great mother goddess Gaia (earth); overcomes the chaotic, violent, and irrational forces of nature (woman, the mother); and institutes the rule of intelligence, order, and harmony that serves the transition to a socially and politically viable community.[32] That defeat was reenacted ritually in the tragedies of classical Greece. For on the body of woman the Aeschylian and Sophoclian hero gains his knowledge: on the body of Clytemnestra, of Euridice, of Antigone. Either those women are killed or they kill themselves; in either case, they are silenced.[33] Ultimately, it is not the tragic hero who is sacrificed for the good of the community; it is woman who is sacrificed so that the community, its hero and its discourse, can prevail. Even when the drama probes more deeply the complex humanity of its heroine, such as Medea or Antigone, say, it does so ambivalently, reinforcing in its imagery and its language the disruptive power of woman's sexual desire and word.

At the moment of autobiographical origination in the West, the prevailing discourse thus conjoins two traditions that serve and preserve for future generations the sacred nature of the phallic order. Woman is not configured in a radically new way with the emergence of the new conception of man. On the contrary, the new man achieves his definition insofar as woman's subjectivity and her public voice remain silenced. For our purposes, then, it is important to consider just how that erasure of woman's desire and her word was secured in the four predominant life scripts available to women of the late medieval and Renaissance periods: the nun, the queen, the wife, and the witch. To understand the relationship of woman to the emergence of autobiography, we must explore the historical forces influencing the enactments of those scripts and the discourse relating to them.

WOMAN'S BODY AND HER WORD:
FOUR LIFE SCRIPTS

The patristic writers and later the Scholastic synthesizers maintained that, in the new anthropology of Christianity, equality of men and women occurred only within the resurrected state of paradise. But even here the equality was problematic; for theologians debated among themselves the question of the sex of the resurrected soul. Augustine argued that the soul would be relieved of the necessity of active sexuality because procreation would cease in heaven; Aquinas, that desire would cease. Both asserted that the hierarchy of the resurrected state would be determined solely by the equality of intellection. But since woman's rational capacity was held to be inferior to man's, woman was by definition at a disadvantage when she entered paradise. Moreover, since intellection was considered the essence of maleness, paradise became a place void of the essence of woman. The equivalence promoted by Christian theological discourse was "an equivalence in which the woman loses that which defined her very being, the ability to bear children."[34] In paradise, that promised space of union, female difference was efficiently erased. Paradise was paradise insofar as it was a purely male space.[35]

That anthropology of paradise suggests why, within the Catholic tradition, a woman could achieve some public authority if she chose to live the celibate life of the religious. And historically, those who chose the life of the virgin, an empowering alternative to the life of subordination within marriage, played a significant role in the evolution of the early church, converting pagans, founding monastic communities, educating themselves and the young. In doing so, those women fulfilled administrative, educational, and missionary functions, all activities highly valued by the church hierarchy. Although abbesses could not administer the sacraments, they could claim jurisdiction over their members, an authority that was not insignificant when the monastery was a double one.[36] A good number of abbesses also achieved distinction as intellectual and spiritual advisers to powerful feudal families. Such virgins could speak with authority because they remained untainted by the curse of Eve and because, as daughters of aristocratic families, they could claim political and economic authority and could command the resources to pursue rigorous intellectual training. However, as the Catholic church strengthened its institutional base and moved toward a centralized and exclusively male bureaucracy under the control of the Holy Father—a political and economic reorientation of the church that gained momentum during the medieval period and that solidified during the Renaissance—the earlier power and influence of women religious, especially abbesses, was increasingly undermined. Additionally, the Gregorian revolution shifted the center of the intellectual life of the twelfth- and thirteenth-century church to the more centrally located cathedral schools and universities that denied access to women desirous of becoming religious.[37] A decentralized church preoccupied with survival, conversion, and early stabilization could easily accommodate the isolated and limited spheres of women's influence; but the consolidation of the political and economic power of the Catholic church was achieved in part by the systematic disempowerment of female religious.

The attitudes embedded in theological discourse provided ideological support for the suppression of the female religious's contribution to Christianity. Of course, most women inherited the taint of Eve, and there is a good deal of literature noted for its vilification of women. But even the virgin's choice of celibacy or the married woman's choice of chastity did not ensure her equivalence with man, for that equivalence was subverted in a variety of ways by the androcentrism inherent in theological conceptions of the virginal life. For one thing, a woman religious, like the resurrected female souls of heaven, had to repress her very essence and in an act of spiritual transvestism assume the essential nature of a man, which remained "identified with the truly human: rationality, strength, courage, steadfastness, loyalty."[38] Moreover, while the virgin might manifest the virtue of a man, she remained cloistered within the body of a woman, within, that is, the matter of her sexuality; and thus she could, no matter how virtuous, how virile, how like a man *(vir)*, arouse the lust of even the most religious men. In order to contain that potential disruption, the virgin remained cloistered. Thus her word gained authority insofar as her body erased itself from the world and insofar as she spoke like a man, imitating the church's androcentric discourse. Second, the theological justification for the denial of Holy Orders to women religious affirmed in more overt terms her sexual difference: Because Christ was male, his priest must be male, securing the patrilineal descent of the logos; because woman is in a state of subjection and thus functions as a sign exchanged by men, she cannot receive a sign of superiority of rank, nor can she pass that sign along. Third, the different rules for women religious, especially as they defined the division of labor in double monasteries, also reinforced woman's difference by emphasizing her "subordinate, inferior, and auxiliary" status.[39]

Nor did the elevation of the status of the Virgin Mary, whose cult arose in the twelfth century and continued through the Renaissance, offer much consolation to the actual virgin; for the discourse that "domesticated" Mary offered only another confirmation of woman's ineradicable difference. Although Mary represented an empowered female presence in the drama of salvation, she remained "alone of all her sex."[40] She was like no other woman, for hers was the *uterus clausus*, hers the childbirth without pain. She was the mother without the taint of sexuality and the virgin who could claim motherhood. While a virtuous religious could lay claim to the closed womb, she could never also lay claim to perpetuating patrilineal descent. Thus, while Mary's identity as virgin was compatible with the self-representation of the earthly virgin, her representation as the quintessential "mother"—nurturing, emotionally responsive, nonrational—pointed to an absence in the experience of the virtuous religious.[41] Identifying with the Virgin Mary, the female religious inevitably identified against some part of herself.

Finally, the fate of women religious during the great revival of affective piety following the Gregorian reform movement suggests the degree to which the church feared large numbers of virgins and the fine line it could draw between the virgin and the heretic. The historical record indicates that there occurred in the late medieval period a great eruption of female piety as women turned away from marriage to embrace a life of public usefulness, the *vita apostolica*. Yet that vast movement of women to the life of celibacy and chastity did not enhance the virgin's position vis-à-vis the church. Eleanor Commo McLaughlin suggests that the sheer numbers of such women overwhelmed the leaders of the newly constituted orders to such an extent that they balked at assuming responsibility for all those women who sought entrance. What emerged, she argues, was a kind of compromise: A few women were admitted and entered the appropriately cloistered life but followed a rule different from that of the men; and the "overflow" came to constitute the group known as Beguines—"semireligious laywomen who pursued a life of charity and prayer in free communities barely recognized by the Church, always on the borderline between heresy and reform."[42] In other words, unattached groups of celibate women, who were neither subordinated in marriage nor confined in the cloister, remained marginalized, anomalous, and potentially disruptive, their sexuality potentially unrepressed. Such public female activity, unauthorized by the church, threatened the social order.

The second female figure of legitimate public authority in the Renaissance was a political one: the queen. Several women who came to thrones during the Renaissance—Mary, Queen of Scots, Elizabeth I, and Catherine de Medicis—might look back to the powerful women of the feudal aristocracy as predecessors. During the early feudal period and later in some parts of Western Europe, aristocratic women could succeed to fiefs (if, that is, they agreed to marriages arranged by the lord). They could also assume the authority of proprietor of a feudal suzerain and the status of surrogate lord when a husband, son, or brother absented himself in order to lead armies in a crusade. In fact, since the feudal family functioned as the locus not only of private life but also of cultural, political, and economic activity, aristocratic women achieved the power and authority that attended such participation in the public domain. But as political and economic power gradually became centralized in the emerging nations of Western Europe—a process earlier noted in the evolution of the Catholic church—and as the aristocratic families necessarily lost the powers formerly vested in them to the authority of princes and kings whom aristocratic men had to serve in an extradomestic setting, aristocratic women lost much of their previous influence. In response to that loss of power, the aristocratic families introduced the concepts of primogeniture and the indivisibility of the patrimony to stay their further erosion. The bride right was replaced by the dowry; and in England the institution of the entail ensured that land passed only by patrilineal descent to the nearest male relative. "Everywhere," note JoAnn McNamara and Suzanne F. Wemple, "the integrity of the family's estate was maintained by the sacrifice of the economic independence of wives and the testamentary independence of widows."[43] Aristocratic women thus became disempowered in the private sphere while the public sphere shifted elsewhere.

In lieu of a male successor to the rule of nations and principalities, a woman could assume the throne. Yet the very intensity of the ideological debate about female succession and gynecocracy during the Renaissance points to the cultural discomfort attendant on female rule. The legal arguments against female succession turned on the assumption, grounded as we have seen in biblical and classical philosophical discourse, of woman's physical and intellectual inferiority. Ian Maclean finds that in the legal discussion "women's debarment from succession, office and privilege is justified by her *levitas, fragilitas, imbecillitas, infirmitas.*"[44] Those who argued in support of female succession focused on the exceptional nature of a very limited number of women: Torquato Tasso, for instance, in considering the different virtues of men and women and the way in which the female ruler negotiates the difference, concludes that by virtue of her birth the woman ruler takes on the ontological status of man and thereby assumes his moral authority.[45] As the exceptional woman becomes a representative man, her female nature is repressed; and with her transfigured voice the queen, like the nun, can authorize the laws of the land. For all that, she is a king and as a king supports and passes along the authority of man, maintaining and perpetuating the patriarchy.

Only a very few could become queens; the masses of women were or would become wives and, even more significantly, wives of a certain kind. When the family had been the locus of production as well as of reproduction, as it had been during the medieval period, the community, however misogynistic its texts may have been, valued the economic and political contributions of women. But when economic production and political power moved elsewhere, wives became increasingly disempowered politically and economically.[46] Their value became symbolic as the leisure of middle-class wives testified to the public accomplishment of husbands.

The ideology of that new kind of wifehood is forcefully revealed in the attitude of Reformation authors, in particular Martin Luther. If the Reformation initiated by Luther loosened the bonds of papal authority by proclaiming the "priesthood" of all Christians, it did not challenge the exclusivity of the male hierarchy within organized religion or the social subordination of women generally. In challenging the Gregorian "counsels of perfection" and in calling for more active participation in earthly life, however, it rejected the medieval conception of marriage as a necessary and legitimate outlet for concupiscence and affirmed the sanctity and superiority of the married state by valorizing the creativity of the womb.[47] Furthermore, Luther rejected the denigration of woman rampant in the misogynistic arguments and imagery of medieval theology and sermons. Yet it is important to note that he did so not because he considered woman equal to man; rather, he considered marriage and the procreative function of woman that expressed itself in marriage to be a positive aspect of woman's nature. Woman is, according to Luther, "weaker, carrying about in mind and body several vices. But that one good, however, covers and conceals all of them: the womb and birth."[48] In early Protestant thought, then, in contradistinction to the medieval Catholic tradition, woman could achieve her full significance not in the closing of the womb and the celibate life of the cloister but, rather, in the opening of the womb: Woman is ennobled insofar as she fulfills rather than denies her biological destiny of bearing children and nurturing her family. Only her open womb confers value on her; and its value is doubled, since it functions additionally to surround and conceal her natural viciousness. Now the married woman, not the virgin, came to play a central role in the church and in the Protestant community. And in its efforts to respond to the challenge of the Reformation, even the Catholic church recognized the value of idealizing wifehood.

Renaissance humanists recognized the value of a woman prepared to fulfill effectively her roles as wife and mother as they recognized the value of broadening the educational base of that new kind of society generally. While the educated boy would leave the familial environment to enter the rigorous training of the academy, an arena in which Latin language training became, according to Walter Ong, a male puberty rite designed to initiate the boy into the world of public discourse through a martial linguistic art, the wife- and mother-to-be would receive an informal education at home.[49] Juan Luis Vives, whose *De institutione foeminae Christianae* was most influential during the Renaissance and later, assumed the difference between men's and women's education to lie in the difference between the mastery of many words and the mastery of few, between access to cultural discourse and relative silence:

> Though the precepts for men be innumerable: women yet may be informed with few words. For men must be occupied both at home and abroad, both in their own matters and for the common weal. Therefore, it cannot be declared in few books, but in many and long, how they shall handle themselves, in so many and divers things. As for a woman, she hath no charge to see to, but her honesty and chastity. Wherefore when she is informed of that she is sufficiently appointed.[50]

Honesty and chastity point to the two loci of woman's value as a wife in patriarchal culture: In order to ensure the legitimacy of patrilineal descent, the wife must give herself sexually only to her husband, and her word that she has done so must be believable. If either her sexuality or her word is suspect, the very structure of marriage and the order that it supports are threatened.[51] Thus the fewer words woman speaks and the more carefully she chooses those words in terms of the criteria of propriety and the innocuous language of housewifery, the more effective the repression of her desire. Consequently, women were discouraged from studying rhetoric as part of their new educational program because to do so was to embrace the language of the public space rather than that of the private sphere. Once again, as Ann Rosalind Jones remarks, "the link between loose language and loose living arises from a basic association of women's bodies with their speech: a woman's accessibility to the social world beyond the household through speech was seen as intimately connected to the scandalous openness of her body."[52] Beneath the veneer of affirmation of woman's education and her value as wife lies the distrust and fear of woman's real nature: Since "a woman is a frail thing," writes Vives, "and of weak discretion, and that may lightly be deceived, which thing our first mother Eve sheweth, whom the Devil caught with a light argument," she should not be allowed to teach because in so doing she could very easily "bring others into the same error" of deception to which she herself falls readily prey.[53]

Insofar as the Renaissance wife or wife-to-be remained culturally silent, she became a model of the ideal woman, "distinguished by what she did not do, or equally important, by what men did not do to her: she was unseen, unheard, untouched, unknown—at the same time that she was obsessively observed."[54] Insofar as she became an ideal woman, she remained a kind of misbegotten man. She, too, like the queen and the nun, secured for posterity the legitimacy and the currency of patriarchal fathers. And yet she, too, like a witch, always stood as a potential threat to that order; and the realm of domesticity in which she was so securely confined stood as a potential source of tension within civilization itself. For the unrepressed sexuality always latent in her womb and in her word "exposes precisely the vulnerability of the patriarchal economy, grounded in the subjection of woman's body, will, and discourse as it is grounded in the division of land, the setting up of boundaries, and the establishment of (masculine) signs, both topographical and linguistic."[55]

In the discourse constitutive of the nun, the queen, and the wife, we recognize the repression of sexuality in either the transvestism of the soul or the silence of the mouth. In the witch, who refuses both honesty and chastity—and thus the passivity they fostered—we have the figure of all that is unrepressed and violent both sexual and verbal. Historical records indicate that the majority of witches condemned as the trials swept through Catholic and Protestant Europe during the fifteenth, sixteenth, and seventeenth centuries were women, and women of a certain kind. They were predominantly women unattached to men and therefore not in a state of appropriate subordination—the unmarried, the widow, and the religious heretic whose false doctrine was not appropriately subordinated to official church doctrine.[56] Given the ontological status of woman discussed earlier, her association with witchcraft comes as no surprise; rather, it seems inevitable. The *Malleus Maleficarum*, that central text in the ideology of witchcraft, catalogs with obvious relish the reasons for woman's particular attraction to the sabbath of the devil: her greater propensity for wickedness, her greater credulity, her "slippery" tongue, her more feeble mind and body, her willfulness, her weak memory. The authors go on to conclude: "All witchcraft comes from carnal lust, which is in women insatiable."[57] She copulates with the devil in order to satisfy "the mouth of her womb," the mouth and the womb.

Refusing to be contracted out (or past being contracted out) as a "gift" whose reproductive powers and sexual difference secure the patrilineal heritage, witches instead challenge the male procreative capacity itself with "such freezing up of the generative forces, that men are unable to perform the necessary action for begetting offspring."[58] Not only do they render men impotent, however; they also interrupt the natural course of pregnancy and mark the newborn with monstrous signs of the devil. (Interestingly, the seven deadly charges leveled against witches in the *Malleus Maleficarum* read like a manual of contraception and abortion techniques.)[59] They exercise those powers, not merely over men and women, but over all domesticated nature—the crops and livestock that are Adamic signs of male creativity and mastery. Then, too, witches stand accused of "the extermination of the faith." As they conspire in the womb of night and ally themselves with the antilogos, they refuse the discourse that supports the very structure of society.[60] In both ways they subvert patrilineal descent—of the phallus and of the logos—by literally and symbolically refusing to become the female body on which patriarchy rests. In order to preserve itself and to ensure the regeneration of body and word, the phallic order silences the witch by death. Female desire is once again mastered, male identity and authority once again preserved.

Those four life scripts establish certain relationships among female speech, female sexuality, and female goodness, among the closed mouth, the closed womb, and enclosure in house or convent.[61] Effectively, the fictions of woman's deceptive word and corrupt sexuality function as shadow stories haunting the narrative possibilities embodied in the scripts, inflecting and deflecting, informing and transforming the licit and illicit powers attributed to woman.

In the literature and the art of the period there were indeed representations of virtuous, licitly powerful women—the Beatrice of Dante, the Mary of the cathedrals and the painters, the figures of the seven liberal arts, the four cardinal virtues. Yet such female figures always appeared as larger than life, always inhabited the otherworldly space between the world of fallen man and the realm of the invisible God. Personifications and idealizations of abstract qualities, associated in their perfection with Christ, these figures were not "women": They were "the female," the beautiful yet static guide inspiring man's struggle toward God. Such representations embodied the passivity rather than the activity of woman, imagined and imaged her without a speaking voice of her own. And, whether she served as guide to earthly man or as handmaiden to the Father, she was always situated in a subordinate position vis-à-vis the male.[62] Moreover, virginity, chastity, a kind of total disembodiment were the sine qua non of her power, the context of her speech. Denied any claim to an enunciating subjectivity, such figures would serve to reinforce, as did the fictive template of the story of Eve, the erasure of real woman's desire and authoritative word.

AUTOBIOGRAPHY: ENGENDERED TEXT

The cultural currents of the Renaissance and the Reformation promoted the emergence of autobiography as a distinct expression of human possibility, promoted, that is, a new discourse and a new man. Yet the very definition of that new man reaffirms a fundamentally conservative definition of woman. She remains the mirror before which he can "assure himself *of* and . . . reassure himself *about* the very structures which define him."[63] And as Virginia Woolf reminds us: "Whatever may be their use in civilized societies, mirrors are essential to all violent and heroic action."[64] Since capturing that "violent and heroic action" has, metaphorically speaking, constituted the textual activity of autobiography, both the life script and the autobiographical inscription of woman become the mirror before which the story of man assumes its privileges.

Autobiography, or more accurately those works by men that have been associated in the aggregate with formal "autobiography," thus becomes one more of those cultural discourses that secures and textualizes patriarchal definitions of Woman as the Other through which Man discovers and enhances his own shape.[65] In privileging the autonomous or metaphysical self as the agent of its own achievement and in frequently situating that self in an adversial stance toward the world, "autobiography" promotes a conception of the human being that valorizes individual integrity and separateness and devalues personal and communal interdependency.[66] Yet, as noted earlier, that conception of selfhood is decidedly male-identified. It derives in Western patriarchy from the boy child's early relationship to the mother, as both classical and revisionist psychoanalytic theory suggests. According to American theorists such as Nancy Chodorow, such insistence and resistance grows out of the young boy's early rejection of his mother, a rejection by means of which he establishes an impermeable sense of self and enters the phallic realm of power inhabited and therefore valued by men. For

French feminists the recognition of the mother as other against which the boy defines himself is inherent in the very structure of language since entrance into the symbolic realm of signs introduces the child to the Law-of-the-Father that successfully encodes sexual differences in the hierarchies of signification, including the binary hierarchies of male-female, mind-body, activity-passivity. While the American and French feminist traditions may diverge in their description of the process, they agree that the Oedipal stage eventuates in the rejection of the female realm of biological necessity and affective relationships for phallic order and ordering. The world of domesticity is left behind for the adventures of public life and the authority of the logos. Moreover, as he rejects his mother and the realm of domesticity associated with her, the boy must also, as Chodorow argues, deny within himself the love and identification he feels for her, a denial he achieves "by repressing whatever he takes to be feminine inside himself, and, importantly, by denigrating and devaluing whatever he considers to be feminine in the outside world."[67] Through the repression of the woman within and without, the boy would repress what patriarchal culture defines as feminine: absence, silence, vulnerability, immanence, interpenetration, the non-logocentric, the unpredictable, the childish. The boy would become man. This phenomenon explains why woman from a certain point of view functions symbolically as man's unconscious.

"Autobiography," then, is ultimately an assertion of arrival and embeddedness in the phallic order. The myth of origins reenacted in the pages of the autobiographical text asserts the primacy of patrilineal descent and, with it, androcentric discourse. The father legitimizes the authority of the autobiographer as he gives name to the child; but, according to the liberal notion of selfhood that motivates autobiography, only the autobiographer can invest his name with new potentiality and then interpret it for the public. By the way, he must erase the matrilineal trace by suppressing the name of the mother and all female subjectivity unmediated by male representation. Through the repression of the woman inside and out, he would exert power over the uncontrollable and unnamed side of human experience—that which is fluid, immediate, contingent, irrational, in short, the semiotic. And yet an unspoken presence, that feminine unconscious repressed by the masculine logos, always threatens to disrupt the narrative order and to destabilize the fiction of identity the autobiographer inscribes.

Disruption of the text of male autobiography by the feminine parallels disruption of the male literary tradition by woman's text. Woman exists in her own subjectivity, however efficiently patriarchal culture has worked to suppress her. In fact, the pressure of androcentric discourse, including autobiography itself, to repress the feminine and to suppress woman's voice, betrays a fundamental fear and distrust of woman's power, which while repressed and suppressed continues to challenge the comfortable assertions of male control.[68] For she has spoken, "stealing" the genre and seeking thereby to represent herself rather than to remain a mere representation of man.[69] Women have done so because they are not only signs, serving as a medium of exchange that underwrites the phallic order, but also purveyors of signs as well, and thus purveyors (and imbibers) of all prevailing discourses.[70]

Moreover, patriarchal ideology, as any ideology, can never be entirely totalized. Pressed by its own contradictions, it fractures in heterogeneous directions. That heterogeneity explains why woman was the subject of tremendous discursive activity during the Middle Ages and the Renaissance, especially during the fourteenth and fifteenth centuries when the debate surrounding the "Querelle des femmes" intensified the competing discourses vilifying and idealizing woman. The idea of woman was in "discursive circulation" precisely because the idea of man was changing radically; since woman functions as the mirror before which man sees his own image reflected, she was necessarily held up for scrutiny.[71] During the early years of this debate, the treatises and poems such as *Le roman de la rose* (begun by Guillaume de Lorris and finished by Jean de Meun) maintained the authority of men to do the scrutinizing. Eventually, however, women spoke in response to the "Querelle." In fact, the hegemony of gender ideology during the Renaissance was ruptured and destabilized by its own internal inconsistencies. Emboldened and empowered by the new ideology of man, Christine de Pisan grasped her pen, supporting herself by writing and arguing the full humanity of woman before her sex's detractors. As Joan Kelly-Gadol notes: "Feminist theorizing arose in the fifteenth century, in intimate association with and in reaction to the new secular culture of the modern European state. It emerged as the voice of literate women who felt themselves and all women maligned and newly oppressed by that culture, but who were empowered by it at the same time to speak out in their defense."[72]

For any late medieval or Renaissance woman, especially one likely to be literate and educated, would have found herself situated within two universes of discourse—that of the newly empowered man and that of the misbegotten man. She would have been influenced simultaneously by the theological, philosophical, scientific, socioeconomic, political, and literary currents that motivated individuals to take up the pen and to write their life stories and by those forces within her culture that narrowly defined woman's appropriate identity and rendered her life script one of public silence. Suspended between these culturally constructed categories of male and female selfhood, she would have discovered a certain fluidity to the boundaries of gender. These sliding spaces of ideology and subjectivity she would have negotiated in greater or lesser degrees of conformity and resistance.

Most women of the period maintained the expected public silence. They wrote no autobiography. Some resolved it by writing "amateur" letters, diaries, and journals, writing their own stories but doing so more appropriately by confining their word to a domestic setting.[73] Some resolved it by writing biographies of their husbands, speaking obliquely, but not explicitly, about themselves and perpetuating thereby the genealogy of man. But some women, as they have done since Sappho, chose to represent their lives publicly. The very fact that women began writing autobiographies contemporary with the genre's emergence—indeed that they gave us early examples of Continental, English, and American autobiography in the life stories of St. Teresa of Avila and Madame Guyon, in *The Book of Margery Kempe*, the *Revelations* of Dame Julian of Norwich, *A True Relation* of the duchess of Newcastle, the *Life* of Anne Bradstreet—is startling, disconcerting, and infinitely interesting. Their texts, and all women's autobiographies that have followed them, testify to the reality that, despite the textual repression of woman that supports the phallic order, woman has chosen to write the story of her life, thereby wresting significance and, with it, autobiographical authority out of cultural silence. Desiring to become a generator rather than to remain merely an object of representation, she has sought to "come out of the wings, and to appear, however briefly, center stage."[74]

But she is not man coming center stage; and therein lies the crux of her matter. She does not enter from the wings so much as she enters from that space beyond the wings of the patriarchal order and its textualizations. Hers is an extremely precarious entrance, then; hers, a potentially precarious performance before an audience whom she expects to read her as woman. Her very choice to interpret her life and to reveal her experience in public signals her transgression of cultural expectations. Her very voice in its enunciations remains haunted and haunting; for the language she appropriates has been the instrument of her repression. By taking that space on the stage, then, she situates herself at the point of collision between two universes of discourse: the discourse of Man/Human and the discourse of Woman, both of which have served to engender her. The "specificity to a female retrospective," to use Nancy K. Miller's turn of phrase, lies in the negotiation of two universes informing woman's act of reading.[75] It lies in the struggle to generate the truth of her own meaning within and against a sentence that has condemned her to a kind of fictiveness.

While the struggle of the autobiographer to negotiate a doubled identification with paternal and maternal narratives affects the structure, the rhetorical strategies, and the thematic preoccupations of individual texts, in the larger cultural arena the presence of the female voice functions as a potential disruption within androcentric discourse. However compromised the autobiographer's struggle with self-representation, her very assumption of the power of public self-promotion challenges the ideals and norms of

the phallic order and represents a form of disorder, a kind of heresy exposing a transgressive female desire. Stealing words from the language, she
would know and name herself, appropriating the self-creative power patriarchal culture has historically situated in the pens of man. In doing so,
she challenges the claims of paternity—the Adamic authority of her culture
to create her out of its own body and then to name her in the fictions of
patriarchal discourse. Thus the self-representation she publicizes becomes
a "heretic narrative," as Lucy Snowe calls her story in Charlotte Brontë's
Villette.

Consequently, the contributions of women to the genre have traditionally
been perceived as forms of contamination, illegitimacies, threats to the
purity of the canon of autobiography itself; and their works, defined as
anomalous, are set aside in separate chapters, at ends of chapters. They are
silenced. Or they are lauded insofar as they imitate male models and continue thereby to enhance the image of man. Perhaps the absence of all but
two or three women from discussions of historiography and poetics reveals
some fundamental tension in the relationship between generic possibilities
and gender. Perhaps they must be erased from the great tradition of autobiography because that very erasure somehow defines it. To write them in
and to privilege them would be to undermine the very notion of artistic and
intellectual creativity in autobiography as that which is not spoken by woman. And so, to supplement this study of women's autobiography, I wish also
for someone to offer an exploration of the relationship of men to autobiography that would reread the male tradition with attention to the repression of woman and the ideology of individualism. For we need not only to
disrupt the quiet efficiencies of the prevailing canon of autobiographical
texts by insisting on situating authority in women's stories; we need also to
reread and thereby to critique the basis on which male autobiographical
authority asserts itself.[76] We need, that is, to challenge the fictions of power
and the very sources of self-knowledge privileged by "autobiography."

THREE

Woman's Story and the Engenderings of Self-Representation

> Although the oppression of women is indeed a material reality, a matter of motherhood, domestic labour, job discrimination and unequal wages, it cannot be reduced to these factors: it is also a question of sexual ideology, of the ways men and women image themselves and each other in male-dominated society, of perceptions and behaviour which range from the brutally explicit to the deeply unconscious.
>
> —Terry Eagleton, *Literary Theory*

During the past five hundred years, autobiography has assumed a central position in the personal and literary life of the West precisely because it serves as one of those generic contracts that reproduces the patrilineage and its ideologies of gender. Women who do not challenge those gender ideologies and the boundaries they place around woman's proper life script, textual inscription, and speaking voice do not write autobiography. Culturally silenced, they remain sentenced to death in the fictions of woman surrounding them. They may write autobiographically, choosing other languages of self-writing—letters, diaries, journals, biography. Even so, their stories remain private, their storytelling culturally muted, albeit persistent. But as noted earlier, there have always been women who cross the line between private and public utterance, unmasking their desire for the empowering self-interpretation of autobiography as they unmasked in their life the desire for publicity. Such women approach the autobiographical territory from their position as speakers at the margins of discourse. In so doing, they find themselves implicated in a complex posture toward the engendering of autobiographical narrative.

In the brief theoretical discussion that follows, I sketch a poetics of women's autobiography. I trust this theoretical framework will illuminate the textual and sexual imbrications of women's autobiography generally, although I claim its specificities only for texts in the Anglo-American tradition and recognize even with that caveat that there will be exceptions to my argument. Nonetheless, for me, and I would hope for you, the effort is justified insofar as it attempts to situate a congerie of phenomena in relationship to one another as it locates them in their cultural and textual embeddedness. Here, then, are the phenomena this discussion would illuminate: (1) the ways in which the autobiographer's position as woman inflects the autobiographical project and the four marks of fictiveness that characterize it—the fictions of memory, of the "I," of the imagined reader, of the story; (2) the ways in which the autobiographer establishes the discursive authority to interpret herself publicly in a patriarchal culture and androcentric genre that have written stories of woman for her, thereby fictionalizing and effectively silencing her; and (3) the relationship of that literary authority to her sexuality and its presence or absence as subject of her story. These three phenomena mark the text of her life. Yet, since I understand the "self" of autobiography not to be an a priori essence, a spontaneous and therefore "true" presence, but rather a cultural and linguistic "fiction" constituted through historical ideologies of selfhood and the processes of our storytelling, I want also to acknowledge the contextual influence of historical phenomena by accounting for communal figures of selfhood, those intertexts that shape the autobiographer's self-interpretation.[1]

The autobiographer joins together facets of remembered experience— descriptive, impressionistic, dramatic, analytic—as she constructs a narrative that promises both to capture the specificities of personal experience and to cast her self-interpretation in a timeless, idealized mold for posterity.[2] An effort of recovery and creation, an exploration into the possibility of recapturing and restating a past, autobiography simultaneously involves a realization that the adventure is informed continually by shifting considerations of the present moment. For example, the autobiographer has to rely on a trace of something from the past, a memory; yet memory is ultimately a story about, and thus a discourse on, original experience, so that recovering the past is not a hypostasizing of fixed grounds and absolute origins but, rather, an interpretation of earlier experience that can never be divorced from the filterings of subsequent experience or articulated outside the structures of language and storytelling. As a result, autobiography becomes both the process and the product of assigning meaning to a series of experiences, after they have taken place, by means of emphasis, juxtaposition, commentary, omission.[3] The play of seeking, choosing, discarding words and stories that suggest, approximate, but never recapture the past is what Elizabeth W. Bruss calls the "autobiographical act": an interpretation of life that invests the past and the "self" with coherence and meaning that may not have been evident before the act of writing itself.[4] Ultimately, the "deferred" vision is, to turn the screw and to wrench comfortable categories, a "fictive" process in that the autobiographer constantly tells "a" story rather than "the" story, and tells it "this" way rather than "that" way. The reader allows the autobiographer to create her fiction, knowing that it is, in Francis R. Hart's phrase, either "an inductive invention" or "an intentional creation" because every life contains within it multiple discourses on discourses, stories on stories.[5] Thus, the autobiographer's effort to capture the quality and to shape the development of her life is problematic to begin with. Trying to tell the story she wants to tell about herself, she is seduced into a tantalizing and yet elusive adventure that makes of her both creator and creation, writer and that which is written about. The very language she uses to name herself is simultaneously empowering and vitiating since words cannot capture the full sense of being and narratives explode in multiple directions on their own.

(This is not to say that the autobiographical contract, that complex set of intentions and expectations binding the autobiographer and the reader together, is as fluid as that which binds the fiction writer and the reader. The fictions of the autobiographer are always mediated by a historic identity with specific intentions, if not pretentions, of interpreting the meaning of her lived experience. The "unreliability" of autobiography is, as Hart so pointedly remarks, "an inescapable condition, not a rhetorical option."[6] And so, as Hart carefully qualifies, our imaginative response to autobiography is not and should not be so free as our response to fiction. In autobiography the reader recognizes the inevitability of unreliability but suppresses the recognition in a tenacious effort to expect "truth" of some kind. The nature of that truth is best understood as the struggle of a historical rather than a fictional person to come to terms with her own past, with the result that she renders in words the confrontation between the dramatic present and the narrative past, between the psychological pressures of discourse and the narrative pressures of story. Whatever "truthfulness" emerges resides, not so much in the correspondence between word and past, but in the imbrication of various autobiographical intentions into form—memoir, apology, confession.)[7]

Because the autobiographer can never capture the fullness of her subjectivity or understand the entire range of her experience, the narrative "I" becomes a fictive persona. In fact, as Louis A. Renza notes: "The autobiographer cannot help sensing his omission of facts from a life the totality or complexity of which constantly eludes him—the more so when discourse pressures him into ordering these facts."[8] Involved in a kind of masquerade, the autobiographer creates an iconic representation of continuous identity that stands for, or rather before, her subjectivity as she tells of this "I" rather than of that "I." She may even create several, sometimes competing stories about or versions of herself as her subjectivity is displaced by one or multiple textual representations. When Hart discusses the phenomenon, he uses the phrase "the paradox of continuity in discontinuity," suggesting that "effective access to a recollected self or its 'versions' begins in a discontinuity of identity or being which permits past selves to be seen as distinct realities."[9] When Renza discusses it, he suggests that a "divorce between the writing self and his textual rendition" occurs.[10] The doubling of the "self" into a narrating "I" and a narrated "I" and, further, the fracturing of the narrated "I" into multiple speaking postures mark the autobiographical process as rhetorical artifact and the authorial signature as mythography.[11]

Precisely because self-representation is discursively complex and ambiguous, a "radical disappropriation" of the actual life by the artifice of literature takes place at the scene of writing.[12] The "I," something apparently familiar, becomes something other, foreign; and the drift of the disappropriation, the shape, that is, that the autobiographer's narrative and dramatic strategies take, reveals more about the autobiographer's present experience of "self" than about her past, although, of course, it tells us something about that as well.[13] Fundamentally, it reveals the way the autobiographer situates herself and her story in relation to cultural ideologies and figures of selfhood. While the fictive patterns that could serve as plots, characters, and speaking postures for self-representation would seem limitless, such is not the case. As she examines her unique life and then attempts to constitute herself discursively as female subject, the autobiographer brings to the recollection of her past and to the reflection on her identity interpretative figures (tropes, myths, metaphors, to suggest alternative phrasings). Those figures are always cast in language and are always motivated by cultural expectations, habits, and systems of interpretation pressing on her at the scene of writing.[14] Cultural scripts of signification, the figures of verisimilitude or lifelikeness reflect privileged stories and character types that the prevailing culture, through its discourse, names as "real" and therefore "readable."[15] Paradoxically, such "idealized" and "ideologized" literary figures become "the instruments with which autobiographers make themselves unique, by creative reenactment, revision, and reversal."[16] Precisely because "every subject, every author, every self is the articulation of an intersubjectivity structured within and around the discourses available to it any moment in time," self-interpretation emerges rhetorically from the autobiographer's engagement with the fictive stories of selfhood.[17]

Fundamentally, then, the "self" that autobiography inscribes is constituted from the polyphonic voices of discourse, as Mikhail Bakhtin persuasively argues when he challenges much of Western philosophical and psychological discourse about the self. "Social man," he writes,

> is surrounded by ideological phenomena, by object-signs of various types and categories: by words in the multifarious forms of their realization (sounds, writing, and the others), by scientific statements, religious symbols and beliefs, works of art, and so on. All of these things in their totality comprise the ideological environment, which forms a solid ring around man. And man's consciousness lives and develops in this environment. Human consciousness does not come into contact with existence directly, but through the medium of the surrounding ideological world. . . . In fact, the individual consciousness can only become a consciousness by being realized in the forms of the ideological environment proper to it: in language, in conventionalized gesture, in artistic image, in myth, and so on.[18]

Through the concept of "dialogic imagination," Bakhtin displaces the essentialist ideology of individualism that makes of the "self" an atomized privacy, a unified and unique core isolable from society and "representable" in autobiography. Product of and conduit for a variety of discourses that structure ways of talking about "self," every autobiographer "is constituted as a hierarchy of languages, each language being a kind of ideology-brought-into-speech."[19] Thus the very forms and language of cultural stories of selfhood are "populated—overpopulated—with the intentions of others" in the sense that they carry in them those cultural expectations and systems of interpretation through which a culture makes palpable its effort to understand and makes durable its power to name the world, itself, and others.[20]

The meaning culture assigns to sexual difference, that is, the ideology of gender, has always constituted *a*, if not *the*, fundamental ideological system for interpreting and understanding individual identity and social dynamics.[21] The generic structures of literature and the languages of self-representation and examination constitutive of autobiography as one of them rest on and reinscribe the ideology of gender. But that ideology and the stories perpetuating it have, until fairly recently, been created from phallocentric discourses written, so to speak, by men who serve themselves, constructing woman symbolically as the mirror before which they can see themselves reflected. In fact, "woman is not just an other in the sense of something beyond [man's] ken, but an other intimately related to him as the image of what he is not, and therefore as an essential reminder of what he is."[22] In order to sustain the idea of man as that which is not woman, the mirror must remain intact; the slick, artificial surface of specularity cannot crack. Primary among the ideological intentions inherent in forms and

language, then, is the desire of culture to name and to sustain the difference of man's and woman's subjectivity and, by implication, man's and
woman's self-representational possibilities. Thus, woman has remained
culturally silenced, denied authority, most critically the authority to name
herself and her own desires. Woman has remained unrepresented and
unrepresentable.

Furthermore, the ideology of gender has reified essentialist notions of
"masculine" and "feminine" selfhood as a way of casting sexual difference
in stone: "To posit all women as necessarily feminine and all men as necessarily masculine is precisely the move that enables the patriarchal powers to
define, not femininity, but all *women* as marginal to the symbolic order and
to society."[23] Essentializing male and female difference at the same time
that they essentialize the idea of an autonomous, unitary "self," patriarchal
ideologies of gender secure the authority and priority of phallologocentric
discourse; for "it is," as Elizabeth L. Berg remarks, "the double move of
reifying a diversity of traits into a determination as masculine or feminine,
and then essentializing that determination, that holds one in the hierarchy
of the sexes."[24]

Since traditional autobiography has functioned as one of those forms and
languages that sustain sexual difference, the woman who writes autobiography is doubly estranged when she enters the autobiographical contract.
Precisely because she approaches her storytelling as one who speaks from
the margins of autobiographical discourse, thus as one who is both of the
prevailing culture and on the outskirts of it, she brings to her project a
particularly troubled relationship to her reader. Since autobiography is a
public expression, she speaks before and to "man." Attuned to the ways
women have been dressed up for public exposure, attuned also to the price
women pay for public self-disclosure, the autobiographer reveals in her
speaking posture and narrative structure her understanding of the possible
readings she will receive from a public that has the power of her reputation
in its hands. As Nancy K. Miller notes, "female autobiographers know that
they are being read as *women*."[25] They understand that a statement or a
story will receive a different ideological interpretation if attributed to a man
or to a woman. As a result, the autobiographer, at least until the twentieth
century, approaches her "fictive" reader as if "he" were the representative
of the dominant order, the arbiter of the ideology of gender and its stories
of selfhood. As arbiter, the "silent" partner in the autobiographical contract
assumes certain privileges of power. "He" does so because, as Michel
Foucault suggests, the site of confession or self-exposure dramatically reverses power's conventional dynamics: The one who remains silent and
who listens exerts power over the one who speaks.[26]

Thus the autobiographer, as she tells her story, constantly projects onto her reader engendered cultural expectations about significance in life stories, about preferred narrative orientations to self-exposure, about the bases on which literary authority can be established and public reputation maintained. Often, projecting multiple readers with multiple sets of expectations, she responds in a complex double-voicedness, a fragile heteroglossia of her own, which calls forth charged dramatic exchanges and narrative strategies. Acutely sensitive to her reader's expectations and to her own often conflicting desires, she negotiates a sometimes elegant, sometimes cramped balance of anticipated reader expectations and responsive authorial maneuvers. Particularly in the dramatic passages of her text, where she speaks directly to her reader about the process of constructing her life story, she reveals the degree of her self-consciousness about her position as a woman writing in an androcentric genre. Always, then, she is absorbed in a dialogue with her reader, that "other" through whom she is working to identify herself and to justify her decision to write about herself in a genre that is man's.

Such attentiveness to the reader exacerbates her relationship to a genre that is already characterized by an elusive fixedness. Struggling with conflicting purposes and postures, she slides from one fiction of self-representation to another as she attends to two stories, those doubled figures of selfhood in the ideology of gender. On one hand, she engages the fictions of selfhood that constitute the discourse of man and that convey by the way a vision of the fabricating power of male subjectivity. The mythologies of gender conflate human and male figures of selfhood, aligning male selfhood with culturally valued stories. Autobiography is itself one of the forms of selfhood constituting the idea of man and in turn promoting that idea. Choosing to write autobiography, therefore, she unmasks her transgressive desire for cultural and literary authority.[27] But the story of man is not exactly her story; and so her relationship to the empowering figure of male selfhood is inevitably problematic. To complicate matters further, she must also engage the fictions of selfhood that constitute the idea of woman and that specify the parameters of female subjectivity, including woman's problematic relationship to language, desire, power, and meaning.[28] Since the ideology of gender makes of woman's life script a nonstory, a silent space, a gap in patriarchal culture, the ideal woman is self-effacing rather than self-promoting, and her "natural" story shapes itself not around the public, heroic life but around the fluid, circumstantial, contingent responsiveness to others that, according to patriarchal ideology, characterizes the life of woman but not autobiography. From that point of view, woman has no "autobiographical self" in the same sense that man does. From that point of view, she has no "public" story to tell. That situating of the autobiographer in two universes of discourse accounts for the poetics of women's autobiography and grounds its difference.

And if the autobiographer is a woman of color or a working-class woman, she faces even more complex imbroglios of male-female figures: Here ideologies of race and class, sometimes even of nationality, intersect and confound those of gender. As a result, she is doubly or triply the subject of other people's representations, turned again and again in stories that reflect and promote certain forms of selfhood identified with class, race, and nationality as well as with sex. In every case, moreover, she remains marginalized in that she finds herself resident on the margins of discourse, always removed from the center of power within the culture she inhabits. Man, whether a member of the dominant culture or of an oppressed subculture maintains the authority to name "his" woman. In her doubled, perhaps tripled, marginality, then, the autobiographer negotiates sometimes four sets of stories, all nonetheless written about her rather than by her.[29] Moreover, her nonpresence, her unrepresentability, presses even more imperiously yet elusively on her; and her position as speaker before an audience becomes even more precarious.

Cultural ideologies contain paradoxes. While they threaten hegemony, they remain vulnerable to leakages, to fractures along fault lines. Patriarchal gender ideologies have not totally silenced women. While women have been relegated to "a negative position in culture," they have nonetheless resisted this *"assignment,"* as Ann Rosalind Jones suggests, by becoming "subject[s] *in* discourse" rather than remaining "subject[s] *of* discourse."[30] From their position of marginality, women have spoken. They have written public autobiography. Nonetheless, when they engage in the autobiographical project, they do so as interlopers. They become women writing a man's story; and since autobiographers who are women cannot, as Miller suggests Rousseau did, "conflat[e] in perfect conformity with the linguistic economy of the West maleness and humanity," they become involved in a dynamic dialogue with two stories, two interpretations, two rhetorical postures.[31] The autobiographer's confrontation with those "maternal" and "paternal" narratives structures the narrative and dramatic texture of her self-representation and shapes her relationship to language, image, and meaning. Manifest in women's autobiography, therefore, is a kind of double helix of the imagination that leads to a double-voiced structuring of content and rhetoric.[32] The voices of man and woman, of Adam and Eve, vie with one another, displace one another, subvert one another in the constant play of uneasy appropriation or reconciliation and daring rejection. Those tensions play themselves out differently depending on the imaginative power, artistic talent, and breadth of experience of the individual autobiographer and on her degree of self-consciousness about her place in patriarchal culture. Moreover, the struggle is particularly descriptive of autobiographies written before the twentieth century. During the twentieth century the confrontation becomes more self-reflexive, more daring, as I will suggest later.

Though I recognize that such confrontations will be unique to each text, I would like, for heuristic purposes, to explore in general outlines a variety of responses to the dilemmas inherent in the autobiographer's textual entanglements. I offer these patterns as broadly suggestive hypotheses rather than narrowly emphatic descriptions. Inevitably the texture of any particular work is richer than the generalized patterns drawn here; but they do provide useful ways of understanding the complex negotiation first of paternal and then of maternal stories that characterize women's autobiographical storytelling.

An androcentric genre, autobiography demands the public story of the public life. (Even if autobiographers concentrate on the life of the mind, they do so because they assume their public importance.) When woman chooses to leave behind cultural silence and to pursue autobiography, she chooses to enter the public arena. But she can speak with authority only insofar as she tells a story that her audience will read. Responding to the generic expectations of significance in life stories, she looks toward a narrative that will resonate with privileged cultural fictions of male selfhood. That glance is especially characteristic of the autobiographer who, having achieved a public reputation, casts her story in the culturally compelling plots, ideals of characterization, and speaking postures associated with male or "human" selfhood. In choosing to do so, she commits herself to a certain kind of "patrilineal" contract. Tracing or discovering a pattern of progressive stages, the autobiographer suggests how she has become who she is: the childhood that moved her toward some vocation, her educational and intellectual experiences, her entrance into the public arena, her successes and failures, her reflection on that achievement in later years. In so doing she reproduces the prevailing ideology of male selfhood, affirming that the individual, no matter how fiercely "he" is besieged by society around him and no matter how compromised "he" is by the struggle, can lay legitimate claim to an autonomous identity that most fully realizes "his" unique potentiality. She embraces, that is, the ideology of individualism—with its myth of presence and originary authority, reassuring her reader that women, and this woman in particular, can aspire to and achieve full "human-beingness."

In other words, this autobiographer "raises herself," as Julia Kristeva argues, "to the symbolic stature of her father."[33] Identifying with the father and his law, she opts for the scenario of public achievement that apparently structures traditional autobiography and grounds the authority to write about herself in the fit of her life to stories of the representative man. To the extent that she reinscribes the myth of origins embedded in the discourse of man, she justifies her claim to membership in the world of words, men, and public spaces, adapting and thereby reproducing the myth of paternal origins and the narratives it underwrites. As she pursues the same self-representation, she may experience the exhilarating investments, in both senses of the word, that attend the fulfillment of her desire for a public story. She assumes the adventurous posture of man.

But as she appropriates the story and the speaking posture of the repre- ③ sentative man, she silences that part of herself that identifies her as a daughter of her mother. Repressing the mother in her, she turns away from the locus of all that is domesticated and disempowered culturally and erases the trace of sexual difference and desire. Commenting on the work of Luce Irigaray and Julia Kristeva, Josette Féral suggests that woman "cannot assume this identification with the Father except by denying her difference as a woman, except by repressing the maternal within her."[34] In other words, the autobiographer who speaks like a man becomes essentially a "phallic woman," an artificial or man-made product turned in the cultural and linguistic machinery of androcentric discourse. Rejecting the realm of the mother for the realm of the father and his word, she colludes in her inscription "in the law of the same: same sexuality, same discourse, same economy, same representation, same origin" and allows for her own recuperation in the symbolic order of patriarchy.[35] To the extent that she gives her allegiance to male-defined culture and its ideology of selfhood, she gains the cultural recognition that flows to her as a person who embodies male-identified ideals; but she also perpetuates the political, social, and textual disempowerment of mothers and daughters. Accepting tacitly the fictions of woman, including the story of her cultural inferiority, accepting the fiction of man as the more valued ideal toward which to strive, she takes her place on stage, not as Eve, but as Adam, assuring man of the legitimacy of the structures and the stories he perpetuates to define himself, including autobiography itself. To write an autobiography from that speaking posture does not become tantamount to liberating woman from the fictions that bind her; indeed, it may embed her even more deeply in them since it promotes identification with the very essentialist ideology that renders woman's story a story of silence, powerlessness, self-effacement.

Hers is always a complex, ultimately precarious capitulation, open to subversive elements both without and within the text. Although her "life" reenacts the figures and supports the hierarchy of values that constitute patriarchal culture, it remains nonetheless the story of a woman. No matter how conscientiously it pays tribute to the life of man, no matter how fiercely it affirms its narrative paternity, the testimony of life and text is vulnerable to erasure from history because it is, on the one hand, an "unfeminine" story and, on the other, merely the "inferior" word of woman. Moreover, to leave womanhood behind and to speak with that kind of authority is to risk undermining the value and the privileges she can garner as an ideal woman. Potentially more damaging, however, is the threat from within. The effaced voice of her repressed sexuality and her uneasy denial of the maternal inheritance may disrupt the figure of male-identified selfhood, betraying in the narrative, dramatic, and imagistic patterns of the life an alternative and private story that qualifies and sometimes even subverts the authorized and public version of herself. That suppressed story may, in its very silence, begin to drown out the assurances of the story she thinks she tells.

Moreover, read through cultural fictions of woman's natural subordination to man, the self-assertion, self-absorption, and self-exposure manifest in the paternal narrative of the "manly" woman become equated with the cultural story of woman's "natural" narcissism. Consequently, the risks of appearing as too much the "manly" woman, that "unnatural" hybrid who defies the ideology of sexual difference, are indeed great; for in "going public," the autobiographer compromises her reputation, founded as it is on public silence. However much she may desire to pursue the paternal narrative with its promise of power, therefore, she recognizes either consciously or unconsciously that for her, as for all colonized people, the act of empowerment is both infectious and threatening. Her narrative may bring notoriety; and with notoriety can come isolation and the loss of love and acceptance in the culture that would hold her in its fictions.

In response to such imbroglios, an autobiographer may shift the grounds of self-representation and respond to cultural expectations about appropriate female speech and behavior. Now she weaves the story of woman into her text, simultaneously maintaining allegiance to the maternal origin by reassuring her reader and herself that she is really an ideal woman who embodies the characteristics and enacts the roles assigned her in the fictions of patriarchal culture. When cultural fictions equate responsiveness to others and identity derived from relationship with feminine "goodness" and "virtue," then self-effacement, passivity, and "culturally conditioned timidity about self-dramatization" become enshrined as the ideal qualities of the eternal feminine.[36] The self-effacing speaking posture characterizing such ideal womanhood, like the womb of Martin Luther's wife, conceals all faults, including the fault of ambition inherent in the presumption of writing her story at all. Yet if she conforms totally to that ideal script, she remains bound (her book, her "self") always in her relationships to men (and their progeny) and defined always in relationship to a life cycle tied to biological phenomena and the social uses to which those phenomena are put: birth, menarche, maidenhood, marriage, childbirth, menopause, widowhood. Thus her life story is like every other female life story: In the end the protagonists are indistinguishable and always replaceable—a reality of which Margaret Cavendish is only too aware when she asserts at the conclusion of her autobiography that she writes to distinguish herself from her husband's other wives. And so, if she pursues a self-representation structured in the fictions of goodness and self-effacement, she remains silenced, literally as she gives the world a book it will not bother to read and symbolically as she reenacts woman's role as the mediator of man's life, a passive sign to be passed around in patriarchal fictions. Literally, she can write no formal autobiography.

Sometimes, however, phallogocentric discourse has permitted women powerful life scripts, such as those of the queen and the female religious. As a result, the autobiographer may commit herself to a certain kind of matrilineal contract, tracing her story through a series of powerful foremothers. But those foremothers are powerful precisely because their life stories have been blessed and sanctified by male authorities, so that the autobiographer's authority derives, not from the foremother, but from the fathers who permit her her powerful script. Male voices, reaffirming the ideology of female subordination to male authority, haunt her text. Moreover, those forefathers sanctioned a certain kind of story about female power. As noted in chapter two, figures like the nun and the queen were women who left behind that which was identified as female and who entered a "manly" or spiritual contract by sacrificing the female body and desire for the word of man. Any autobiographer who follows their model reveals her desire for an empowered life story but rests her claims to sanctity and power on assurances to the reader that she has successfully escaped the drag of the body, the contaminations of female sexuality. To the extent that she establishes her chastity within the text, to the extent that she reaffirms through the text, as well as in the text, her subordination to all fathers, she is allowed the voice of authority.

In all the speaking postures examined thus far, the authority to speak as both "representative" man and "representative" woman derives from the erasure of female sexuality; for the male identified fiction commands the repression of the mother, and the "good woman" fiction commands the suppression of female eroticism, though not, of course, self-effacing love and devotion. In fact, whether she leaves womanhood behind for the figure of androcentric selfhood or embraces the figure of the ideal woman, the autobiographer acknowledges, sometimes explicitly, more often implicitly, an uneasiness with her own body and with the sexual desire associated with it. Moreover, woman's goodness is always marked by her narrative and dramatic orientation to sexual desire. Thus, as she writes, she both asserts her authority to engage in self-interpretation and attempts to protect herself from the cultural fictions of female passion and contaminated sexual desire.[37] Given the cultural alliance of woman's speech with the forces of unleashed sexuality in Western discourse, given the exacting expectations of female goodness such association enjoins, the woman who would write autobiography must uphold her reputation for female goodness or risk her immortal reputation.

The textual entanglements I have sketched here for heuristic purposes tend to characterize autobiographies written by women up to the twentieth century and certain subcategories of autobiography that continue to appear. In her negotiation of maternal and paternal narratives, the autobiographer does not engage consciously the prevailing ideology of gender or challenge the authority of autobiography as a generic contract. With the twentieth century and the ambiguities and confusions of modernism, however, alternative autobiographical possibilities for women emerge as alternative relationships of woman to the autobiographical narrative of man arise. The autobiographer begins to grapple self-consciously with her identity as a woman in patriarchal culture and with her problematic relationship to engendered figures of selfhood.

Instead of interpreting herself unself-consciously through those narratives of both man and woman privileged by patriarchal discourse, she grapples with the ideology of gender that has pressed on her, sifting her experience through the sieve of fictions naming woman and her sexual difference. She begins by seeking to understand her problematic relationship to the language and the narratives she has been taught to speak; for she must come to grips with the power of phallogocentric discourse to erase the female subject by confining her to its fictions, thereby delimiting her access to words themselves. Perhaps, as Elaine Showalter and other Anglo-American critics suggest, the autobiographer recognizes that she has not enjoyed full access to the realm of the symbolic: She may find that she "ha[s] been denied the full resources of language and ha[s] been forced into silence, euphemism or circumlocution" when she has sought to present her version of female subjectivity.[38] Therefore, she may seek to appropriate the language of the patriarchs, commanding the full resources that language makes available to man, resisting "silence, euphemism, or circumlocution" in pursuit of equal access to the public space.

But the autobiographer may also pursue an alternative scenario of linguistic destiny, depending on her political and philosophical stance toward her place as woman in patriarchy. If she does so, something more begins to take place as the autobiographer explores her access to the language of self-representation. She begins to realize that woman remains "unrepresentable" because autobiography as a formal, public contract requires her unrepresentability, because it makes no space for female desire and "self"-hood. What Christiane Olivier says of language characterizes as well literary contracts: "Sexism in language [may be] the result of man's fear of using the same words as women, his fear of finding himself in the same place as the mother."[39] Generic androcentrism recapitulates that tendency in sexist language. Formal autobiography remains the place where man stakes out his claim to sexual difference and ordination. It marks his refusal to remain "in the same place as the mother."

Thus, as Carolyn G. Burke notes in her discussion of French feminism's central interest in woman's relationship to the symbolic, "when a woman writes or speaks herself into existence, she is forced to speak in something like a foreign tongue, a language with which she may be personally uncomfortable."[40] The discomfort derives from her cultural ventriloquism, a gesture of impersonation that requires the autobiographer to speak like a man; for, speaking like a man, she may be unable to recognize the lineaments of her experience in the language and fictions that surround and inform her text. Furthermore, she may encounter her own complicity in reproducing the very cultural stories that have engendered her as they have repressed the maternal trace.

And so the autobiographer may choose to confront self-reflexively the process of her own autobiographical storytelling as opposed to the autobiographical storytelling she has inherited from the patriarchs. To this task she brings "muted" ideologies generated and promoted by women in response to the prevailing ideologies of the dominant group. "Functions of the dispossession of women, as well as of women's natural resources in the face of this dispossession," such alternative ideologies acknowledge the realities of her experience as both particular and universal woman as well as infuse with value the stories and the storytelling of woman.[41] Instead of using the same "sentence" as man uses, she experiments with another sentence.

In search of the new sentence, she traces her origins to and through, rather than against, the mother whose presence has been repressed in order for the symbolic contract to emerge. Through the marginalized space inhabited by actual mothers and daughters, she pursues the source of the patriarchy's reproduction of woman as a means to discovering some new truth about her sexuality. Since "patriarchal discourse situates woman *outside* representation" as "absence, negativity, the dark continent, or at best a lesser man," initially she encounters the confusions of woman's self-"unrepresentability."[42] For she tries to tell stories that have not been told before, ones that have remained unspoken within the ideological framework of the dominant discourse. In response she tries to discover a language appropriate to her own story. To this end, she may, as Sandra M. Gilbert and Susan Gubar propose, think back through her mother to discover "woman's command of language as against language's command of woman."[43] Rejecting the old "tongue" of the father and all patriarchs who have sentenced her to death, she may, as Margaret Homans suggests, remember and then reinvest with her own meaning a maternal language through which to probe a legitimate gynocentric self-representation.[44] Through that language she may celebrate a different relationship to psychosexual development, one that Nancy Chodorow characterizes as more attentive to personal interconnectedness between self and world.[45]

For French as well as some Anglo-American theorists, that alternative tongue and alternative psychosexual development would embrace what Kristeva calls the pre-Oedipal rhythms of the semiotic.[46] Harking back to a phase before the symbolic logic of binary opposition insists on male privilege and superiority, the language of feminine desire—the écriture féminine of Hélène Cixous, the womanspeak of Luce Irigaray, the jouissance of Kristeva—finds its voice in alliance with the mother and her milk, her body, her rhythmic and nonsensical language. Now the subject position from which woman speaks may be, like the voice of the mother, outside time, plural, fluid, bisexual, de-centered, nonlogocentric. Having returned to her origins in the mother and the silent and silenced "culture" she shares with all women, the autobiographer manifests a different relationship to story-telling as a woman. However problematic French theories may become as they lapse into another kind of essentialism, one that reifies a female destiny outside time and history, they nonetheless attempt to disrupt the complacent superiorities of patriarchy's gender ideology. Promoting an alternative, woman-centered and woman-defined discourse associated with the imaginary and the subversive of the phallic logic of the symbolic, they join with theories of Anglo-American feminists to "proclaim woman as the source of life, power and energy."[47]

The autobiographer also confronts another possibility for autobiographical practice. Coming to terms with the uses and abuses of a father's language that twists and turns her in the fictions of biologic essentialism or of a mother's writing that implicates her in another kind of essentialism, the autobiographer may struggle to liberate herself from the ideology of traditional autobiography and to liberate autobiography from the ideology of essentialist selfhood through which it has historically been constituted.[48] Now she may demystify for herself and her reader the powerful voices of all those autobiographical fathers who have passed on the genre and its life expectancies by challenging the very bases on which the ideology of sexual difference rests. Speaking from her position at the margins, she resists participation in the fictions at the center of culture, including the fictions of man and of woman. Or, if she does not reject them, she self-reflexively appropriates bits and pieces of those fictions for her own purposes. Embracing the polyphonic possibilities of selfhood, she wrenches the autobiographical contract in ways more responsive to an experience and a de-

sire detached from the reigning ideologies of masculine and feminine. She
thereby destabilizes notions of male and female difference, rendering gender ideology an elusive thing by conjoining dichotomies.

Ultimately she may transform herself and cultural stories generally by
shifting generic boundaries so that there is neither margin nor center. For
as she experiments with alternative languages of self and storytelling, she
testifies to the collapse of the myth of presence with its conviction of a
unitary self. Having untied her relationship to the conventions of the autobiographical contract from the idea of an atomized, individualistic, central
self, she de-centers all centerers and effectively subverts the patriarchal
order itself. Now an avatar of a new "Eve," a woman released from the
sacred sentence of all fathers, the autobiographer refuses to obey the pro-
hibitions of the father's culture with its narratives of sexual difference,
including autobiography. She seeks instead to pursue her own desires, to
shatter the portrait of herself she sees hanging in the textual frames of
patriarchy, and to create the conscious and the unconscious of her sex by
claiming the legitimacy and authority of another subjectivity. With that new
subjectivity may come a new system of values, a new kind of language and
narrative form, perhaps even a new discourse, an alternative to the prevailing ideology of gender.

Interested as I am in the ways autobiographers negotiate the imperatives of
"paternal" and "maternal" fictions, I want now to turn to individual lives, to
listen to individual voices. Throughout the ensuing discussions you will
note the imprint of these patterns I have sketched out. I do not want them
to become procrustean figures overdetermining critical readings of particular works. They are critical fictions about autobiography. Yet they help to
locate the autobiographer's relationship to the empowering and silencing
narratives of her culture. To the extent they are suggestive rather than
prescriptive, they enrich the readings that follow.

The readings proceed chronologically because I want to convey the range
of women's autobiography from its first voluble outpourings to its most
recent self-reflexive meditations on women and autobiographical storytelling. Indeed, the past six centuries are rich with the stories women across
Europe and later in America left behind as they entrusted their lives to the
future. There are many autobiographies from which to choose. I have
chosen five that I particularly like. The first was written in the fifteenth
century; the last, barely ten years ago. They were all written in English. I
harbor no pretentions to inclusiveness or exhaustiveness since this is no
history of women's autobiographies. Other historians and critics will give us
more inclusive, more exhaustive surveys. I want here to focus closely on a
small number of texts in order to explore the way in which cultural fictions

of male and female selfhood thread their way through the self-writing of women, how the struggle to find an autobiographical voice emerges in the play of reader expectations and narrative demands. For my own purposes I want to tease out the process of engendered representations at different cultural moments in the English tradition. This approach allows me to talk about stories of female mystics in the fifteenth century, stories of criminality in the eighteenth century, stories of evolutionary selfhood in the nine-teenth. By ranging over five centuries I hope to pay tribute to the variety and resiliency of women's autobiography.

Because of its historical location as the first extant woman's autobiogra-phy written in English, because it offers an early manifestation of woman's sacred self-writing, I begin this set of readings with *The Book of Margery Kempe*, written in 1436. During the fourteenth and fifteenth centuries, as I noted in chapter two, female religious broke out of the cloister and wan-dered over the face of Europe. Unattached to male orders, unattached to husbands, these women traversed the public spaces and assumed public voices, leaving behind them the marks of female religiosity. But their anom-alous position and unconventional independence threatened social rela-tions and tested the boundaries of heresy. Margery Kempe, a medieval mystic from a burgher family in England's southern coastal town of Lynn, left behind a most remarkable story of one such woman's life. Through her *Book* Kempe sought to convince her reader and her church that her name belonged in the genealogy of great female mystics, perhaps even in the genealogy of saints. She looked back on powerful foremothers for a legiti-mate and authoritative life script: Maternal narratives thus helped her structure generally her self-representation. But she remained a strange figure, a mystic who had married and had borne fourteen children. As a result, the presentation of herself as a truly chaste woman became both urgent and difficult. Moreover, she was dependent on the mediation of men throughout her life of piety and her autobiographical project: They listened, and they judged. Kempe's narrative thus becomes for me a fas-cinating work, full of life and energy and travail as it captures the quality of medieval Christian life, the mobile atmosphere of pilgrimages, the pres-sures of orthodoxy, the smell of the burning stake against which the heretic was pressed in her heresy. But the real drama of her narrative is played out in her relationship to the stories of her mystic foremothers and to the male mediators on whom she depends in telling her story.

Writing two centuries after Kempe, Margaret Cavendish, duchess of Newcastle, left to posterity one of the earliest secular autobiographies writ-ten in English. Unconcerned about charting her relationship to God, Cav-endish instead amassed details about herself that she put together in *A True Relation of My Birth, Breeding, and Life*. In her lifetime Cavendish achieved a certain reputation as an author, a certain notoriety as an eccentric woman; later, as Virginia Woolf noted, "the crazy Duchess became a bogey to frighten clever girls with."[49] It is evident throughout her story that, for her, authorship functioned as a public activity for women analogous to the warfare that distinguished men. While she hungered for the public arena in which she could pursue her obvious ambition, however, she also maintained sometimes conservative views of woman's proper behavior and identity. Thus her "life" is riddled and sometimes stifled by a profound ambivalence about her desire for public recognition and her desire for appropriate feminine selfhood. Her mother, an ideal figure of self-effacement, loomed large in her imagination; but so did the story of her father's heroism (and the heroism of male relatives generally). As we read her autobiography we cannot help but be moved by the tension she sustains between two competing self-representations, the story of maternal self-effacement and the story of paternal self-assertion.

Both Margery Kempe and Margaret Cavendish cling in their texts to the story of female selfhood privileged by their culture. Eccentric they are. Ambitious they are. Certainly that ambition and the restlessness they feel about the limitations their culture imposes on their ambition permeate their lives and "lives." In a variety of ways, their desire for self-display qualifies their profession of ideal womanhood. Nonetheless, they both attend carefully to the story of woman expected of them. In the next two autobiographies I discuss, one a secular and the other a "sacred" story, paternal narratives predominate.

During the eighteenth century women had access to a legitimate career: Through acting, they could achieve public recognition for their talents. One of the women who walked across the stage was Charlotte Charke, the unconventional daughter of Colley Cibber, poet laureate and famous dramatist of the century. From her early youth Charke created herself through impersonations. As a child she assumed the clothes and posture of her father to parade through town. Later, after losing both husband's and father's affections, she supported herself by impersonating a man. Playing the male on stage and off, Charke led the life of a cross-dressed quixote. At the moment she writes her life story, she seeks one more means of financial income and also seeks rapprochement with her father. But her stance as the sentimental heroine truly repentant for her past life cannot mask the powerful stance of the transgressive woman who would play the male rogue. Moreover, her actual and rhetorical cross-dressing unmasks for the reader a fundamental self-denial or confusion, an ambivalence of identity in a woman who cannot place herself comfortably in conventional ideologies of gender.

One hundred years later, Harriet Martineau, the respected philosopher and writer of the mid-nineteenth century, wrote her voluminous life history, a simultaneously secular and "sacred" autobiography that traces for the reader a story of the development of a mind. In this female *Bildungsroman*, Martineau tells the evolutionary story of a woman who emerges from the theological darkness of childhood, through the metaphysical vagaries of adolescence and young adulthood, into the progressive and philosophical positivism of maturity. Rejecting the figures of Christian autobiography because such stories did not provide a space for female selfhood, this philosopher of political economy and proponent of freedom adapts the more radical Comptian paradigm of self-development. In a language evoking the prophetic vision of the Bible, Martineau heralds a new time and a new person, a time when woman can live life "as if she were a man." Presenting herself as the virgin philosopher (similar to the virgin queen, the nun), Martineau justifies her unrepresentative female life and her representative male life by carefully constructing her identity as a certain kind of woman. Particularly interesting in this autobiography, then, is the way Martineau accounts for female selfhood in a story about woman's "paternal" selfhood. Ultimately disturbing, however, is the way in which the male generic contract forces the life and vitality out of the autobiography.

All four of these autobiographers desired the power, authority, and voice of man. None of them accepted the silenced life demanded of most women in their times. They had energy, intelligence, courage, and not a little "madness" about them. And the energy, intelligence, and courage come through their texts. But so do the confusion, the crampedness, the compromises, the ambivalences—that is, the damages to woman of seeking to appropriate the story of man in a culture that would condemn her to its sentence. They are products of the margin who desire access to the father country. As such they offer fascinating and complex examples of the problematics of negotiation of maternal and paternal narratives. All four women reveal how problematic becomes the autobiographer's engagements with the ideological voices of female difference and with the generic contract of autobiography that is forcefully androcentric.

The twentieth-century autobiographer takes the problematic and makes it the matter and the medium of her text; but I will say more of this later when I turn to Maxine Hong Kingston's *Woman Warrior*. For now, let me look back five hundred years and listen to the voice of that eccentric and resourceful mystic, Margery Kempe.

II

Readings

FOUR

The Book of Margery Kempe

This Creature's Unsealed Life

> "Ah, Lord, maidens dance now merrily in
> Heaven. Shall not I do so? For, because I
> am no maiden, lack of maidenhood is to
> me now great sorrow; methinketh I would
> I had been slain when I was taken from the
> font-stone, so that I should never have
> displeased Thee, and then shouldst Thou,
> blessed Lord, have had my maidenhood
> without end."
>
> —*The Book of Margery Kempe*

Margery Kempe's spiritual autobiography originates not in the stillness of
the medieval virgin's cloistered cell but in the loud pains of parturition. In
opening her *Book* with a description of the birth of her first child, Kempe
announces her contaminated relationship to the spiritual life, for, with her
child, she bears/bares the ineradicable mark of physical corruption: The
moment of childbirth refers backward to an earlier moment when, her
womb pierced and unsealed, she is irreversibly severed from the wholeness
and integrity of the virgin's state.

Kempe, who would through her narrative make her claim on posterity by
legitimizing her idiosyncratic and suspect holy vocation, casts the contaminated moment in an eschatological framework. Childbearing she presents
as a moment of total disorientation, vulnerability, and sinfulness, a time that
brings her to the brink of physical and spiritual death. In her exhaustion,
she writes, "she despaired of her life, weening she might not live"; but more
significantly, she despairs that, having relied on her own unorthodox form
of penance rather than on the church's authorized form, she may die before
formally confessing a sin from her past.[1] For that heretical practice she
blames the devil, who seduces her into the paths of heresy with his assurances and his tauntings. To regain the grounds of spiritual orthodoxy,

she calls for a priest, seeking to free herself of the unnamed guilt and to secure her salvation.[2] But the confession, unlike the child, is aborted. As she nears naming her sin, the priest, visibly impatient, effectively silences her. Deprived of the ritual through which a male authority with the power and the privilege of judging might cleanse her of and liberate her from the silences that bind, Kempe "went out of her mind and was wonderously vexed and laboured with spirits" for over half a year.[3] In complex ways, sexuality, death, male authority, and the constriction of woman's word become entangled in the opening scene of Kempe's narrative.

Her foul sexuality expressed, her desire to tell her story repressed, Kempe has not the power inherent in virginity and orthodoxy to resist the devil.[4] Giving herself up entirely to him, she loses control of her rational faculties and descends into the madness of slanderous speech and violent physicality. In hysterical and heretical utterances she turns language against God and all those forces representing His authorized vision as she rails against marriage, community, church: "She slandered her husband, her friends, and her own self. She said many a wicked word, and many a cruel word; she knew no virtue nor goodness; she desired all wickedness; like as the spirits tempted her to say and do, so she said and did" (24). Kempe's diabolical possession manifests itself not only in verbal heresies but also in physical excesses directed self-destructively at herself:

> She would have destroyed herself many a time at their stirrings and have been damned with them in Hell, and in witness thereof, she bit her own hand so violently, that the mark was seen all her life after.
>
> And also she rived the skin on her body against her heart with her nails spitefully, for she had no other instruments, and worse she would have done, but that she was bound and kept with strength day and night so that she might not have her will. (24)

Representing herself as a true daughter of Eve, Kempe gives us a woman in thrall to the devil's seductions: sexual, faithless, violent, and destructively verbal.

At that nadir of spiritual depravity, a second birthing scene emerges. Whereas the first birthing brings the consuming flames of hell and damnation, the second promises the lights and sounds of salvation. Whereas the first involves a natural birth, the second, like Eve's nativity scene in Genesis 2, reverses the natural order as man gives birth to woman. The two birthing scenes thus play female motherhood and its corruption off against male "motherhood" and its wonders. For into the midst of Kempe's madness, Christ the nurturing mother enters: "Our Merciful Lord Jesus Christ, ever to be trusted, worshipped be His Name, never forsaking His servant in time of need, appeared to His creature who had forsaken Him, in the likeness of a man, most seemly, most beauteous and most amiable that ever might be seen with man's eye, clad in a mantle of purple silk, sitting upon her bedside, looking upon her with so blessed a face that she was strengthened in all her spirit" (25).[5] After relieving her of these madnesses, Christ motions her toward a spiritual rebirth, promising her a new life and a new relationship to her body and to language. Where the devil before him had sanctioned an unorthodox discourse and seduced her into the ways of the "evil woman," Christ offers her another discourse by which to give voice to her desire and through which to achieve cultural authority and power as "good woman": the discourse of the religious ecstatic. With that promise, her spiritual journey and her *Book* commence.

Kempe stumbles, of course, and her narrative goes on to trace her temptation, a second illumination, and the long, complex journey toward union with God and spiritual legitimacy as a chosen vessel bearing His word.[6] In its broad, impressionistic outlines, the structure of the *Book* and the self-representation it promotes conform to the normative life of the medieval mystic (or Christian pilgrim) whose story was common cultural property in the late fourteenth and early fifteenth centuries. While Kempe may have been illiterate, as her use of an amanuensis testifies, she gives evidence in her text that she was thoroughly steeped in that story. She had an illiterate's familiarity with Holy Writ (which she repeats to the astonishment of her clerical audiences), with the *Incendium Amoris*, the *Stimulus Amoris*, Walter Hilton's *Scale of Perfection*, and the *Revelations* of St. Birgitta of Sweden. She had a layperson's familiarity with stories of saints' lives (which probably served as lively sources of conversation during the long hours of pilgrimage).[7] As a devout layperson who attended church often and who traveled extensively, she would have listened to sermons and biblical readings as well as to the prayers and meditations composed by the clergy for laypersons, all of which would have reinforced certain characteristics of the truly devout Christian, and more particularly of the truly devout female religious, mystic, and saint. As any autobiographer, then, Kempe could not come to her life story with a "new" pair of retrospective eyes. She came to her narrative influenced by prevailing and cherished "fictions" about woman's mystical life. The *Book*'s very legibility (for herself, her amanuensis, and her projected reader) derived from its resonance with biographical and hagiographical representations of female mystics.

The tradition of affective piety through which Kempe shapes her identity and her text followed the Gregorian reform movement and coalesced throughout the twelfth, thirteenth, and fourteenth centuries around such figures as Anselm of Canterbury, Ailred of Rievaulx, Bernard of Clairveau,

Francis of Assisi, and Bonaventure. Whatever their individual contributions to its theological explanations, all these figures privileged meditation on the humanity of Jesus and the details of his life on this earth, especially the events of the Passion. Such preoccupation with Christ's humanity (as opposed to His Godhead) moved the soul and led the Christian to imitate His poverty, chastity, humility, and good works. Thus the tradition promoted spiritual transfiguration, union with God through intense and dramatic communings, and active engagement in good works intended to save the sinful.[8]

The mysticism spawned by that tradition appealed to large numbers of women for a variety of reasons. In mysticism, with its intensely personal, emotional, and direct experience of Christ, women could find possibilities for spiritual selfhood otherwise denied them in a church that, with the Gregorian reforms, denied women access to formal education and therefore access to the arena of intellectual debate and exegesis. Second, the *vita apostolica* may have appealed to women because it offered a life of spiritual activity to uncloistered laypersons. Third, with the rise of affective piety, female figures of immense power emerged from relative obscurity to introduce a female presence and a potential locus of identification in a formerly male preserve. As Christ's humanity became the focus of medieval piety, the Virgin Mary and Mary Magdalen became central figures in the quotidian drama of His life and Passion. Both Marys were associated with weeping, its expressive sympathy and its cleansing promise. Mary Magdalen, the "fallen" woman who achieved sainthood, offered the promise of salvation to the sinner. The Virgin Mary provided a "feminine" force that mediated the harshnesses of the demanding and judgmental Father. Perhaps the elevation of Mary and her "feminine" qualities functioned to legitimate certain aspects of woman's nature in an otherwise misogynistic Christianity. Or perhaps the mystery of Mary's virgin birth may have offered women the promise of legitimate female attachment to the central mysteries of Christianity.[9]

An impressive number of women emerged as influential figures during the rise and prominence of affective piety. They created for the age stories (some based on fact, some based on legend) of extraordinary women who persevered, suffered, and triumphed in their spiritual destinies. Thus Kempe could look to a pantheon of famous women mystics and saints whose lives would have provided plentiful opportunities for identification, appropriation, revision. Generally, those women provided two alternative scenarios for selfhood: (1) primarily English stories of confinement within the cloister or the cell of the withdrawn woman; and (2) primarily Continental stories of worldly mobility of the unenclosed religious (many of whom were Beguines).[10]

The former scenario was particularly strong in the England of Margery Kempe. The country and the culture had produced few female saints in comparison to the Continent and almost no female spiritual leaders who functioned outside the cloister. Moreover, its literature privileged the enclosed and silent life of woman, betraying by the way unrelieved misogynistic assumptions. For instance, the *Ancrene Riwle*, written by an unknown priest—most probably a secular one—in the early thirteenth century and addressed to three sisters who were anchoresses under his spiritual guidance, offers an authoritative discussion of the internal and external phenomena marking female piety. For the author of the *Riwle*, the imperative enclosure of woman derives from her ultimate responsibility for any lust she arouses in man. She can escape the guilt insofar as she remains shielded from the outside world (and from men's eyes) and pursues a holy life of humility, hard work, prayer, and particularly silence. Even more openly contemptuous, the *Hali Meidenhad*, in its effort to call young girls to the life of the virgin, levels against the state of matrimony the full force of its contumely and musters on behalf of the virgin state the full promise of salvation: "Break not thou that seal that sealeth you together!" the author warns.[11]

For early church fathers and medieval theologians, the difference between the married state (through which woman experienced sexuality and procreation) and the virgin state was the difference between the realm of mortality and corruptibility and that of infinite incorruptibility.[12] This distinction between the immutable and the corruptible applied to the discourse on virginity of both males and females; but the equality manifest in the conceptualization of the virginal life was complicated by the mind-body dualism deeply rooted in Western thought. Such dualism analogized and then conflated the body-mind antithesis with the female-male antithesis: "Since the carnal realm was regarded as female," suggests Rosemary Radford Reuther (and other feminist theologians), "the female virgin must undertake a double repression, not only of her bodily feelings (necessary for the male ascetic as well), but of her female 'nature' as well. The woman virgin is said to have transcended her female nature and to have been 'transformed into a male.' By contrast, asceticism is said to restore the male to his natural 'spiritual virility.'"[13] The profession of virginity—the espousal of the nun to Christ—and retirement to the cloister enabled the medieval woman to transcend the malediction of Eve: The closed womb, the closed mouth, and enclosure ensured woman spiritual legitimacy and authority within the paternal legacy of the medieval church. In the womb-like space made for her by the Father, the fathers (patristic writers), and the priestly fathers who advised her, she could escape the contamination of the maternal origin and, with the integrity of her material body intact, silence the threat of her womb and her words.

Economic and political phenomena reinforced the cultural embrace of that ideology. Because the church required a significant dowry of an entering woman in order to support her during the long years of enclosure, she almost invariably came from the ranks of the aristocracy, that class commanding economic, political, and discursive privileges. Both church and aristocracy benefited from the arrangements of enclosure. For one, nunneries provided a legitimate place for unattached daughters of the aristocracy; and population estimates suggest that throughout the medieval period there was a significant excess of females that would require such a haven. Moreover, the nunnery provided a place to locate female children for whom parents, in their desire to maintain the integrity of the estate by retaining wealth in the hands of male heirs, did not want to arrange marriages. They needed only to provide a less generous dowry. In its turn the church benefited from the literal currency of the required dowry, the political currency of aristocratic alliances, and the symbolic currency of aristocratic prestige.[14] Within the context of that intricate web of mutual benefits, the virgin daughter of the aristocracy "profited." From within the enclosure she could assume a role of public (both spiritual and practical) significance and thereby gain a life and a voice of some discursive power and authority; and she could be assured of a quiet haven safe from the tyranny of a forced alliance.[15]

As the opening scene of her *Book* so vividly reveals, however, Kempe could not join the company of female virgins. Married, mother of fourteen children, she bore with them the ineradicable marks of her fallen nature. Nor could she claim membership in the aristocracy, for she was undeniably middle class, albeit from an influential burgher family. Consequently Kempe had to look toward another paradigm of female piety, one that had emerged during the fourteenth century and coalesced around stories of female mysticism coming from the Continent rather than from England.[16] St. Birgitta of Sweden, Bl. Dorothea of Montau, Blessed Angela of Foligno, and Mary of Oignies—these names and the tradition embodied in them were passed along not only through popular tales and oral histories such as those surrounding Blessed Angela and Mary of Oignies but through texts written by and about these women: the *Revelations* of St. Birgitta, *The Orcherd of Syon* (a translation of the *Dialogue* of St. Catherine of Sienna), the *Book of Spiritual Grace* by Mechtild of Hackborn, and various lives, but most particularly the *Vita Latina* of Bl. Dorothea of Montau.

At least five characteristics of the lives of those foremothers would have resonated in Kempe's imagination with the texture of her own experiences (or to put it another way, would have resonated with her early experience and provided a template through which to structure her life, certainly as she narrated it, perhaps even as she lived it). Most prominantly, the majority of those women were not virgins. Though they lived chaste lives once they embraced the spiritual life, they had been married and had borne children. The fact that they had found a space of sanctity despite the opened womb testified to the possibility that woman could transcend the drag of the body and the limitations of a life lived as wife and mother in subordination to earthly man. Second, despite their past, those foremothers all experienced the mystical visions and spiritual communings characteristic of affective piety in the late medieval period. Third, those women led lives of active involvement in the world, traveling on pilgrimages that took them as far as Jerusalem, founding religious orders, advising popes and courts. (Interestingly, such worldly mobility seemed to promote their role as critics of worldliness). Furthermore, those women functioned as "counselors" to clergy and laypeople alike; and their prayers mediated between fallen people and their Christ. Thus, while they did not preach per se, they did through their word bring salvation to others. Finally, several of them left to posterity narratives of their religious experiences.

Kempe's "life" forms itself around and binds itself through the collective stories of those mystic foremothers. Through specific allusions to the names in this maternal genealogy and through striking parallels between her story and those of her foremothers, Kempe locates her strange and apparently unconventional life firmly in the conventions of Continental mysticism that emerged from hagiographical and autobiographical materials.[17] Those ideal women, whose lives speak in her text on her behalf, aid her in locating herself squarely in a genealogy that confers legitimacy on her claims to true sanctity and holiness.

As a married woman Kempe can only secure her genealogical place among those mystic foremothers, and the hagiographical discourse immortalizing them, by establishing her identity in life and her representation in text as an impeccably chaste woman. The moment that marks the origin of Kempe's narrative thus locates the origin of her struggle as a sexually contaminated woman who has sacrificed the integrity of her body to the fruits of lust. In this context, her postpartum madness reveals a logical subtext. Through physical excesses she enacts a ritual of self-punishment that suggests her understanding, however unconscious, that her body is the source of cultural insignificance. Motherhood, tying her to Eve's curse, threatens to imprison her in cultural fictions limiting female possibilities for selfhood. To rive her skin and bite herself is to try to scratch out and eat away the source of "bededness" and to set the agenda of her spiritual quest. Trapped between the sheets of both the marriage bed and the discourse allying chastity with spiritual authority, Kempe can claim no life beyond marriage and no cultural story unless she convinces her reader that she successfully "silenced" an already expressed sexuality.

In the early part of her narrative, she rushes in disjoined chronology to tell the story of her escape from the "marriage debt," an escape that demands her victory over external and internal landscapes of temptation. On the one hand, Kempe describes how she falls victim to her own sinfulness. After her initial illumination, she lapses into her old ways. She dresses in costly and ostentatious clothes, donning what she considers to be the symbolic vestments of her true social status. She attempts to make her own independent fortune first in brewing and then in milling, revealing a desire for worldly power and recognition. Most tellingly, "the snare of lechery" is visited upon her "when she believed that all fleshly lust had wholly been quenched in her" (34). Throughout, Kempe represents herself as a kind of Christian everyman, or more precisely, a cultural "everywoman." Consumed by vanity, greed, lubricity, she is an avatar of fallen womanhood and Eve's true heiress.

On the other hand, she also represents herself as an unwilling victim, who, motivated by an appropriate disgust with sexual desire, struggles to secure sovereignty over her own body from forces external to herself—her husband, social institutions, the law.[18] For instance, the second moment of illumination comes when, lying beside her husband one evening, she hears "a sound of melody so sweet and delectable, that she thought she had been in Paradise" (30). With the holy sounds come tears of mystical devotion—both a medium for cleansing and a new kind of public voicing—and her fierce renunciation of sexuality and the marriage bed: "And after this time she had never desired to commune fleshly with her husband, for the debt of matrimony was so abominable to her that she would rather, she thought, have eaten or drunk the ooze and the muck in the gutter than consent to any fleshly communing, save only for obedience" (30–31). But her husband, who continues in thrall to sexual passion, will not comply. "He would have his will," she writes:

> And she obeyed, with great weeping and sorrowing that she might not live chaste. And oftentimes this creature counselled her husband to live chaste, and said that they often, she knew well, had displeased God by their inordinate love, and the great delectation they each had in using the other, and now it was good that they should, by their common will and consent of them both, punish and chastise themselves willfully by abstaining from the lust of their bodies. Her husband said it was good to do so, but he might not yet. He would when God willed. And so he used her as he had done before. He would not spare her. And ever she prayed to God that she might live chaste. (31)

Kempe unifies the potentially contradictory representations of herself as both innocent victim and culpable victimizer by assigning her life's architecture to the divine will. It is Christ who visits her with temptations to lechery in order to humble and humiliate her. It is Christ who provides her with a strategy for gaining sexual autonomy from a lecherous husband. (Because she has followed Christ's directive to fast on Fridays, she is able to drive a clever bargain with her husband: She will eat and drink with him if he will leave her body alone.)

By the eleventh chapter, Kempe asserts her successful release from the marriage debt and her consequent achievement of chastity. There is, however, an irresolvable tension inherent in this "chastity" story that effectively unmasks it as a kind of fiction: Kempe *seems* to achieve chastity early in her spiritual life, when, in actuality, she compresses into a short narrative space a struggle that goes on for a good twenty years—or half the timespan of her narrative—until such time as her husband agrees to live separately from her.[19] She tries to suppress that other story by erasing the signs of her contaminated history from the text. Of her children, only her oldest son takes a place in her story, and that in the short second book: Saving him from damnation, she testifies to her function as religious intermediary. No other children are present in her story. Her husband too is oddly present and absent. While he is an important figure in the early pages of her narrative, she never gives him a name: She thereby erases his specificity. Then, between the early parts of the narrative, where he is her nemesis, and the later part, where he is her burden, he disappears. When she re-introduces him as incontinent and infantile in his old age, she makes of him a kind of last-born infant and renders him no husband at all. Paradoxically he is simultaneously absent and present as husband since all sexuality has ceased. She once again serves his body, but now she serves him as a martyr of Christ rather than as a wife.

But since she cannot be true to her experience and entirely "fictionalize" the past, remnants of the other story of continued sexual activity crack the surface of her narrative. What is particularly interesting, however, is not that the other story resists erasure but that Kempe so effectively neutralizes it as a source of disruption, presenting herself as chaste in face of the evidence that she has not been. For instance, disjoining chronological moments, she juxtaposes events that occur later in her life with those that take place earlier: "On a day, long before this time, while this creature was bearing children and was newly delivered of a child" (67). While such prefatory remarks seem to call attention to the reality of her unchaste life, the narrative discontinuity actually confuses chronology and thereby sustains the illusion that most of Kempe's religious life took place after she achieved chastity. In embedding the story of her "contaminated" life in the story of her "chaste" life, she absorbs the time of shame into the time of true piety. At other times she surrounds evidence of the contaminated story with the signature of Christ, absorbing the sins of conjugality into the spiritual conjugality she establishes with Christ. In imagery redolent of the church's account of Christ's conception, she describes how He serves as an annunciatory angel informing her of her pregnancy (67). She admits that she feels her pregnancy with "great pain and great dis-ease" but that Christ assured her that He wanted her to bear more "fruit" for Him. In that way she transforms a forbidden act into an act of obedient service commanding "reward and merit" (82). Or she construes her motherhood as an occasion for Christ to reveal His infinite compassion and love and His special affection for her as His chosen one:

> "Yea, daughter, trow thou right well that I love wives also, and specially those wives who would live chaste if they might have their will, and do their business to please Me as thou dost; for, though the state of maidenhood be more perfect and more holy than the state of widowhood, and the state of widowhood more perfect than the state of wedlock, yet, daughter, I love thee as well as any maiden in the world." (82)

And throughout she describes how Christ charges her again and again to wear white so that she "shalt be arrayed after [His] will" in the symbolic and very public vestments of purity.

Kempe also wraps a story of self-punishment around the story of sexual repression, thereby reinforcing her disregard for material and bodily well-being. She tells how, after her conversion, she wears a hair shirt under her girdle, concealing it so effectively that even her husband is unaware of its existence; she fasts conscientiously; she wakes at two or three in the morning in order to spend hours in prayer; later she desires to kiss lepers as a sign both of her affection for and identification with the diseased and the discarded and of her cavalier attitude toward her health. Through such behavior the material body is sacrificed in a kind of martyrdom, and Kempe can transcend the "faults of female nature."[20] Moreover, she continually describes how she suffers hardships as an outcast: She is abused, harrassed, threatened with burning at the stake. She travels with little money, remaining dependent for sustenance on the kindness of strangers. Neighbors and strangers, at home and abroad, turn on her so that, as Christ tells her early on, she is "eaten and knawed by the people of the world as any rat knaweth stockfish" (348). In such gustatory imagery, Kempe emphasizes the physical punishment and vulnerability inherent in her precarious vocation and represents herself as a true martyr for Christ.

Luce Irigaray argues that such elaborate and debasing marks of martyrdom characterize female mysticism during the medieval period. Intimately tied to woman's identity as misbegotten man, a creature allied with matter, they betray her corruption as they signal the locus of her purification:

How could "God" reveal himself in all his magnificence and waste his substance on/in so weak and vile a creature as woman? She has so often been humiliated, and every particle in her being seems but decay and infection. *Waste, refuse, matter.* Thus she will abase herself over and again in order to experience this love that claimed to be hers, and pass again through those imaginings that forbid her to respond. She takes on the most slavish tasks, affects the most shameful and degrading behavior so as to force the disdain that is felt toward her, that she feels toward herself. And perhaps, at the bottom of the pit, she finds her purity again. In this way, the blood, the sores, the pus that others clean away and she absorbs will wash her clean of all stain. She is pure at last because she has pushed to extremes the repetition of this abjection, this revulsion, this horror to which she has been condemned, to which, mimetically, she had condemned herself. She is chaste because she has faced the worst perversions, has prostituted herself to the most disgusting acts, the most filthy and excessive whims.[21]

Acts of martyrdom provide Kempe with yet more evidence of her true chastity.

Finally, Kempe displaces the story of earthly (and corrupt) love with the story of spiritual love and, as she does so, displaces the figure of herself as a fallen daughter of Eve with the figure of herself as ideal Christian woman. Her silence about physical motherhood prepares the way for her story of spiritual motherhood. Imitating Christ and His symbolic motherhood, she presents herself loving, nurturing, chastising, caring for humanity itself as well as bearing, like the Virgin Mary did, the word of God.[22] She describes how, developing her spiritual relationship to Christ, she embraces all "conventional" female roles. To support those claims, she brings Christ's justificatory assurances into her text in such scenes as the espousal scene where she literally joins him in marriage: He says to her that she will live with Him forever as "'My dearworthy darling, as My blessed spouse, and as My holy wife'" (366). Those roles, the very roles Kempe seeks to convince her reader she has escaped in her earthly existence, are now sanctioned by Christ and invested with the spirit, cleansed, purified, blessed.

Maintaining her identity as an ideal, rather than a marked, woman, Kempe catapults herself into the public arena where she claims authority and legitimacy for her voice. Hers is the record of a very public, rather than reclusive, piety. If in the originating incident of her narrative Kempe recalls that traumatic moment when she could not speak the words she would, the narrative itself is an outburst of words through which she tells of a life spent wailing, weeping, critiquing, prophesying, interpreting, "conversing in Scripture," and reproducing the communications of the Lord—all characteristic modes of public utterance in the life of a medieval mystic. Throughout her *Book*, then, Kempe amasses the details and re-creates the dramas encircling three kinds of speech—mystical visions and communings, weepings, and cultural criticism, including prophesy. As she does so, she justifies before her reader the quality of her spiritual life and reveals the dynamics of power inherent in such speech.

Despite the cultural disempowerment and insignificance attendant on her illiteracy, class status, and sex, Kempe can claim cultural authority for her word precisely because Christ has singled her out as His friend. She presents herself, then, as the beloved of a Christ who converses with her daily through visions and intimate communings. The unexceptional quality and the notable quantity of those exchanges create a narrative world thickened with the routine intimacy, familiarity, and regularity of their spiritual relationship. The laywoman describes again and again how she received the word of God on a daily basis, in the most ordinary of circumstances. Her rarer extended communings with Christ and elaborate visions of holy events complement the impact of the more routine conversations. (See chapters 5, 14, 22, 35, 36, 64, 65, 66, 77, 85, 86, 87, 88.) In these mystical scenes, she presents a Christ who becomes her advocate and defender as she recreates the words He speaks in justification of her behavior. For instance, in chapter 88 He supports her spending time saying beads; in chapter 84 He assures her He knows she would serve Him in many ways; in chapters 74 and 77 He justifies her weeping; in chapter 66 He sanctions her eating flesh; throughout He praises her again and again for her steadfastness, love, and service to Him. In such scenes Kempe's own voice is effaced as she immerses her reader in Christ's voice, thus introducing into her worldly text the sacred word of the God who speaks on her behalf. Furthermore, the communings and revelations that make of her a purveyor of God's Word provide her with access to the sacred stories of her culture. In repeating her visions before her questioners, her confessors, and ultimately her reader, she effectively appropriates biblical stories, investing them with her own interpretations and rewriting them through her own life. For instance, in chapters 79–81 she recreates the scenes of Christ's Passion and places herself within them. In that way Kempe becomes doubly voiced and holy: She is both an actor in and interpreter of the sacred drama. As actor and creator, she joins her voice to the voices central to the mysteries of Christianity (to Christ's, the Virgin Mary's, the Saints').

Kempe describes the onslaught of tears as part of a second conversion experience: Lying in bed, she hears the beautiful melody of heaven and weeps for her own sinfulness. From this point on, weeping, and later wailing and moaning, become a central component of her special calling. Certainly, the efficacy of tears and the sanctity of weeping gained a cherished place in medieval religion. In the ideology of mysticism, tears became a sign

that the individual had been moved by the great sorrow of Christ's human
suffering, the suffering of general humanity, and the sinner's own culpability. Simultaneously, as water, tears symbolized renewable and recoverable
cleansing, the perpetual promise of rebirth.[23] Thus Kempe's voice wept in
consonance with the prominent voices of medieval mysticism, especially the
female voices: with Mary Magdalen, the patron saint of weepers; with the
Virgin Mary, who in her role as *Mater Dolorosa* gave added significance to
tears and their cleansing power; and with the more contemporary Mary of
Oignies, whose story Kempe alludes to in asserting the legitimacy of her
own outpourings.[24] Effectively, weeping identified Kempe with those ideal
figures of spiritual motherhood in a church that denigrated and vilified real
mothers.

Early in her narrative, directly after chapter 11, where she seems to have
established her chastity and thus her right to speak, Kempe describes the
first manifestation of yet another kind of voice she assumes, that of the
prophet. On one of her travels, a monk asks if he will be saved. After
weeping for him, Kempe asks Christ for guidance:

> "My dearworthy daughter, say in the name of Jesus that he hath sinned in
> lechery, in despair, and in worldly goods keeping."
> "Ah! Gracious Lord, this is hard for me to say. He will do me much shame, if
> I tell him a lie."
> "Dread thee not, but speak boldly in My name, for they are not lies." (51–52)

Kempe locates the basis for her prophetic powers in Christ's authorization
of her "bold" speech; and she continues throughout the narrative to emphasize her public role as counselor, chastiser, and prophet. Approached by
laypeople who desire information about their own and loved ones' salvation, she responds with news from heaven and homilies about the true
Christian life. Approached by worried townspeople, she prophesies the
coming of natural disasters and suggests means of averting certain destruc-
tion. Despite the possibility that she will be labeled a heretic for her presumptions, she embraces the responsibility for speaking directly to monks
and canons, bishops and archbishops about their shortcomings, chastising
them to redirect their lives away from sinfulness and hypocrisy to the true
worship of the Lord. So long as the doctrine informing her prophetic
speech remained orthodox, the church could not deny Kempe her role,
sanctioned as it was by Christ, by the texts of Christianity, and by the
example of her mystic foremothers.

Locating herself continuously in those modes and moments of public
speech, Kempe presents herself as a prominent voice in her culture. But
the *Book* simultaneously reveals the fragility and the marginality of her

public position as it chronicles the increasing vulnerability of her apparently ubiquitous voice: The more she emerges as a public figure, the more she invites censure, even charges of heresy; and the more she invites censure, the more she must justify her words and behavior. Kempe describes the conscientious pilgrimages, short and long, undertaken to test her interpretations and her words against the orthodox interpretations of the church hierarchy. Her visions must be repeated to church authorities for verification. The weeping and wailing must be defended against charges of affectation and fraud. The social criticism often involves her in controversies with unsympathetic church officials. Moreover, as she re-creates those exchanges with church officials, she captures prevailing patriarchal attitudes toward woman and the illegitimacy of her word. One old monk wishes she were "enclosed in a house of stone, so that, there, no man should speak with thee" (54). Another asks her whether she is inspired by Christ or by the devil since she talks of Holy Writ "and that hast thou not of thyself" (54). The archbishop commands that she leave his diocese immediately, adding, "'Thou shalt swear that thou wilt neither teach nor challenge the people in my diocese'" (188–89). And the people who watch her being carried away to prison advise: "'Damsel, forsake this life that thou hast, and go spin and card, as other women do, and suffer not so much shame and so much woe'" (194).

Kempe does not consciously address the fear of woman's speech and its potential subversiveness implicit in such comments. But the theme of woman's disruptive word makes itself felt in her narrative, even in its originating scene. The very loss of reason that comes on with the birth of her first child allows Kempe to engage in a wild and rebellious ritual of verbal abuse directed against all those forces—husband, friends, church, God, even herself—that have colluded in confining her possibilities for selfhood to the rigid script of marriage and the corruption of the birthing bed. Conjoining woman's evil destructiveness and woman's speech, Kempe thus figures her opening story in such a way as to reaffirm patriarchal attitudes and to justify cultural strictures limiting woman's access to language. Re-creating herself as a faithless daughter of Eve, she remains faithful to the prevailing ideology of gender by mirroring her culture's fiction of the "bad" woman. Elsewhere, she reveals the potential disruptiveness of woman's voice even as it serves the most holy (as opposed to diabolical) intentions. For instance, as she re-creates her confrontation with the White Friar, who will not let her worship while he preaches, she elaborates a drama of two kinds of word: Kempe's inarticulate, irrational weeping drowns out the articulate language of an authoritative church official. Kempe, as the less powerful of the two figures, is subsequently banned from church attendance; priests are forbidden to commune with her or read Scripture to her;

and some in the community would run her out of town. Everyone, in other words, would keep her still.

But Kempe cannot be silenced, as the very writing of her *Book* attests. In the proem she alludes to the ostensibly didactic motivation for dictating the *Book:* she would offer her "life" as an exemplum intended to help "sinful wretches . . . have a great solace and comfort to themselves and understand the high and unspeakable mercy of our Sovereign Saviour Christ Jesus, Whose Name be worshipped and magnified without end" (345). His love, her life attests, can make of even the meanest sinner a being of special calling. Yet her life has not been unambiguously exemplary: It has been in many ways suspect because lived on the margins of convention. Thus Kempe writes her story not only to edify Christians by "example and instruction"; she desires also to justify her life as holy woman and to silence the voices of critics and skeptics who eagerly accuse her of heresy, hypocrisy, and madness. To the extent that she succeeds in this defense, she stakes her claim to an eternal place among her mystic foremothers, especially those who like Birgitta earned sainthood. As exemplum, defense, and record of holiness, then, the *Book* becomes Kempe's final word for posterity.

Within the text Kempe justifies not only the life she lived but also the writing of the *Book* itself, tracing the origins of her *Book* to the voices of male authorities. During her peregrinations she meets some "worshipful clerks" who "averred . . . that this creature was inspired with the Holy Ghost and bade her that she should have written down and make a book of her feelings and revelations. Some proffered to write her feelings with their own hands, and she would not consent in any way, for she was commanded in her soul that she should not write so soon" (346). She waits twenty years until such time as Christ Himself "commanded her and charged her that she should get written her feelings and revelations and the form of her living, that His goodness might be known to all the world" (346). Kempe effectively locates the motivation for storytelling in Christ and His divine purposes. Moreover, she makes of Him a supportive partner. At devotions one evening she is distracted from saying beads by her preoccupation with the *Book*. " 'Dread thee not, daughter,' " she recalls Christ saying to her,

"as many beads as thou wouldst say, I accept them as though thou saidest them, and thy study that thou studiest to have written by the grace I have shewed to thee, pleaseth Me right much, and he that writeth also. For, though ye were in the church and wept both together as well as ever thou didst, yet would ye not please Me more than ye do with your writing, for, daughter, by this book, many a man shall be turned to Me and believe there-in." (368)

In the chapter following, Kempe describes how "Our Lord Jesus Christ with His Glorious Mother and many saints also came into her soul and thanked her, saying that they were well pleased with the writing of this book" (298). All heaven watches her progress.

Kempe also invests the story of her storytelling with the miraculous signature of the Lord, surrounding it with strange and mystical events. When she is instructed to begin her narrative, no one helps her until a mysterious, unnamed Englishman living in "Dewchland" suddenly appears and passes some time with her.[25] When the man dies suddenly, leaving the book unfinished, Kempe takes it to a friendly priest who cannot understand or transcribe the illegible script. Convinced by her enemies not to help her, he does not make a second attempt to read the script until four years have passed, at which time his eyesight fails him. Suddenly, with renewed faith in her project, his eyesight returns.[26] Other mystical signs attend her project. Moments of dictation are accompanied by fever and frenzy. If she is ill she becomes well as soon as she commences writing. She hears holy melodies as she dictates; and at other times she is moved to tears. At one point "there came a flame of fire about her breast, full hot and delectable" (298).

The association of her "life" story with divine mystery seems to be a strategic necessity for Kempe, who as an illiterate laywoman must literally and symbolically place her life in the hands of men. The voices that haunt her text from beginning to end—inside its pages and outside—are the voices of male church authorities, suspicious of anomalous female desire, power, and words. Again and again Kempe describes how she travels to see anchorites, priests, monks, bishops, archbishops, in order to test the orthodoxy of her visions and the consonance of her life with the conventional story of affective piety and female mysticism. In fact, the rather stable story of spiritual conversion is syncopated by the constant mobility, the unending quest to gain exoneration, blessing, and support and to avert condemnation and burning. The more idiosyncratic her life becomes, and the more disturbing its resonances with Lollardy, the more she becomes dependent on the beneficence of male mediators to save her from the stake. Just as her life remains in the hands of male authorities, so too does her "life" remain in the hands of a male amanuensis. Without the two men, but particularly without the second, her life will be condemned to silence.

Her profound vulnerability manifests itself in the tensions between Kempe and her amanuensis. Chapter 24 opens with an acknowledgment of the tenuousness of Kempe's position vis-à-vis her scribe:

> The priest who wrote this book, to prove this creature's feelings many and divers times asked her questions, and information of things that were to come,

unknown and uncertain at that time to any creature as to what would be the outcome, praying her, though she was loath and unwilling to do such things, to pray to God therefore, and ascertain, when Our Lord would visit her with devotion, what would be the outcome, and truly, without any feigning, tell him how she felt, or else he would not gladly write the book. (88)

In fact, the scribe blackmails Kempe: She must prove her powers of prophesy or he will not continue her "life." "Compelled somewhat for fear that he would not otherwise have followed her intent to write this book," Kempe "performs" for him, but then reveals that even with her compliance "he would not always give credence to her words" (88). (Interestingly, the priest's obstinacy provides Kempe the occasion to narrate two stories about her prophetic powers, reaffirming her gift for her reader but also for the scribe who takes down her words.)

The scribe also questions the legitimacy of her tears. Thus in chapter 62 she describes how, after he is moved by the preaching friar to spurn her, Christ guides him to the story of Mary of Oignies and then "visited the priest, when at Mass, with such grace and such devotion when he would read the Holy Gospel, that he wept wonderfully, so that he wetted his vestment and the ornaments of the altar, and might not measure his weeping and his sobbing, it was so abundant; nor might he restrain it, or well stand therewith at the Altar" (230). Because he is so moved, the amanuensis regains confidence in Kempe's weeping. Nonetheless, Kempe recognizes how tenuously she holds the allegiance of the scribe whose position is itself tenuous vis-à-vis his superiors.

Ultimately, Kempe remains vulnerable to the scribe's literary skill:

> The priest who wrote this treatise, through stirring of a worshipful clerk, a bachelor of divinity, had seen and read the matter before written much more seriously and expressly than it is written in this treatise, for here is but a little of the effect thereof, for he had not right clear mind of the said matter when he wrote this treatise, and therefore he wrote the less thereof. (231)

Both Kempe and her amanuensis allude here to the textual tradition associated with the efficacy of mystical tears: the story of Mary of Oignies, the *Prick of Love* by St. Bonaventure, the *Incendio Amoris*, and the story of Elizabeth of Hungary. But at the same time that she places her text in that sacred genealogy, thus enhancing its authenticity and seriousness, she apologizes for its inadequacy: She is dependent on a scribe who "had not right clear mind" and could not give the *Book* the power she would have desired.

The fragility of the amanuensis's support—his hesitation for "cowardice" to undertake and then to sustain the task of transcription, his testing of her prophetic powers, his movement toward and away from her, his lack of

attentiveness to his literary effort—reveals his inner turmoil about the legitimacy of her story and his participation in it. A controversial figure, Kempe
involves her supporters in her controversies and thus renders them vulnerable to the theological and political imbroglio of the medieval church.[27] Yet
both Kempe and the amanuensis are able to surround his fluctuations and
skepticisms with the interventions of Christ. Both of them, thereby, justify
for each other and for the reader this "life." Interestingly, the dynamic
played out in this drama of narrative creation recapitulates the story in the
originating scene of the *Book*. There Kempe calls for a priest to hear her
confession; but, because he is uninterested, impatient, and generally unwilling to respond sympathetically to her experience, she does not speak.
Unable to confess, she goes mad. At the scene of writing she is once again
entangled in that dependency: The scribe hesitates. Kempe cannot be entirely sure he will allow her to get her words out. Like her earlier confession,
her "life" may remain silenced.

Kempe's *Book* provides a final retelling of her story, one designed to win
definitive male approval and promotion. By securing the continued collab-
oration of the priest who transcribes her "life," she would ensure the legitimacy of a life passed through the hands and pens of an official confessor.
By maintaining through that "life" her allegiance to male roles and prerogatives, thus to male authority, divine and priestly, she would ensure her
place in the genealogy of stories revered by her culture. With that sanction
she can, like her mystic foremothers, leave to posterity an "authoritative"
life and text, one that might, just might, be passed on by the patriarchal
church hierarchy and provide the basis for later sainthood and canonization ceremonies.

Kempe was a middle-class woman who could not rest content with the
"silenced" identity that attended her reproductive activities and her spousal
role.[28] She desired to achieve public significance as ideal woman and thus to
win a public role and a public voice. Though Kempe nowhere explicitly
acknowledges her desire for sainthood, she does give her reader an illiterate's version of a saint's life: her purpose inspirational and instructive; her
experiences filled with the miraculous and the extraordinary; her life quintessentially humble; her "martrydom" gladly assumed for the greater glory
of God. Moreover, the references to St. Birgitta scattered throughout the
text suggest that the life and story of Birgitta somehow drive her own self-
representation. Kempe was born the year Birgitta died. She was resident in
Rome at the time of the consecration of Birgitta's canonization (1413–
1415). She was familiar with "Bride's book" and its stories of Birgitta's
marriage and motherhood, her visions, her outspoken criticism of the
court, her constant pilgrimages, her service to the poor, her indifference to

money, her prophesies, and her writing of her own book. Kempe begins her own narrative at the same chronological moment as Birgitta begins hers; and she continues to weave throughout her narrative all the motifs that characterize Birgitta's piety. Yet she goes beyond structural and thematic resonances to comment specifically on her status vis-à-vis Birgitta. She tells the vicar of St. Stephen's that she knows of no book, Bride's book among them, "that spoke so highly of the love of God" as her own communings with God. In chapter 20, as she recalls seeing the host flickering and the chalice moving during communion, she describes how Christ tells her: "'Thou shalt no more see It in this manner; therefore thank God that thou hast seen. My daughter, Bride, saw Me never in this wise'" (80). Immediately after this passage, Kempe recalls Christ's assurance to her that "'right as I spoke to Saint Bride, right so I speak to thee, daughter, and I tell thee truly that it is true, every word that is written in Bride's book, and by thee it shall be known for very truth'" (80). Kempe presents Christ as sanctioning both her own and Birgitta's visions, thus elevating herself to the level of the aristocratic, literate saint. By joining her own story to the story of Birgitta, Kempe allies herself with one of her culture's most ideal "ideal" married women.

Yet, despite her efforts to construct her life and "life" around the ideal of the married mystic, a worldliness that surprises and fascinates permeates her narrative. We feel it in the sheer uncloistered restlessness that makes shambles of chronology. The narrative discontinuities speak of the jumbled rush of experience as it must have been lived and certainly as it is recollected. It speaks too of the endless mobility of Kempe's life that carries her over the countryside of England and on the great pilgrimage routes of Europe and the Middle East. The episodic energy and the restless, self-absorbing verbosity give to the text a vitality that belies and compromises the representation of herself as an ideal, sexually repressed woman. The descriptive language resonates with earthiness and physical specificity and reveals a preoccupation with the details of her contemporary world. Moreover, the erotic language of mysticism that she draws on, characteristic of the language of medieval piety, keeps subverting, unintentionally, her assurances of her renunciation of sexuality.

And always there is the voice of Kempe's narrative, intimate, close to the surface of the text, self-effusive rather than self-effacing. Always in the foreground, never in the background, she seems to use the occasion of narrative (as she used it in life) to talk about the subject of most interest to her—her own special importance. She re-creates scenes, dialogues, events with an eye to presenting herself as a major protagonist in Christ's divine plan, who would spread her own word as well as God's throughout all Christianity. Because of all that unbounded aspiration and uncloistered

imagination, the reader never quite believes in her self-denial. In the opening scene of her *Book*, Kempe describes her descent into madness and her
diabolic invective against all those forces supporting the patriarchal order. I
suggested that her witchlike collusion with the devil functioned both to
support the patriarchal order and to disrupt it. Vividly, starkly Kempe's
originating experience dramatizes the price woman pays for her society's
repression of female desire—and the price society pays. There is in the
whole *Book* that same doubled ambivalence. Certainly, Kempe's story testifies to her allegiance to patriarchal authority and authorities (Christ and
His appointed mediators on earth). But there is something elusive and
destabilizing about her *Book*. Somehow her story, no matter how concerned
it is with orthodoxy and with imitating the church's fiction of an ideal
woman, speaks of the unbounded possibilities of female storytelling.

Kempe's very life challenged and unsettled domestic, social, and ecclesiastical conventions. As a voice speaking from the margins of the official
hierarchy and its discourse, then, hers was simultaneously more powerful
and less powerful than those official voices. And her text both imitated
conventions of official life stories, accepting the ideological requirement of
female purity and subordination to man, and somehow escaped them by
wrenching the autobiographical form to serve the purposes of her own
desire for power and authority. It is no wonder that, after her lifetime, her
story was silenced in centuries of absence. It might have remained so had it
not been discovered by Hope Emily Allen in 1934 in the archives of the
Butler-Bowden family. Ironically, her culture as it confronted anomalous
female desire erased it from history, almost.

FIVE

The Ragged Rout of Self

Margaret Cavendish's True Relation *and the Heroics of Self-Disclosure*

> When the rumour spread that the crazy
> Duchess was coming up from Welbeck to
> pay her respects at Court, people crowded
> the streets to look at her, and the curiosity
> of Mr. Pepys twice brought him to wait in
> the Park to see her pass. But the pressure
> of the crowd about her coach was too
> great. He could only catch a glimpse of her
> in her silver coach with her footmen all in
> velvet, a velvet cap on her head, and her
> hair about her ears. He could only see for
> a moment between the white curtains the
> face of "a very comely woman," and on she
> drove through the crowd of staring
> Cockneys, all pressing to catch a glimpse of
> that romantic lady, who stands, in the
> picture at Welbeck, with large melancholy
> eyes, and something fastidious and
> fantastic in her bearing, touching a table
> with the tips of long pointed fingers, in the
> calm assurance of immortal fame.
>
> —Virginia Woolf, *The Common Reader*

Margery Kempe tested for her culture the boundaries between madness and divinest sense, to paraphrase an Emily Dickinson poem. A mother of fourteen children who wore white to symbolize her chastity, an illiterate middle-class woman who conversed with holy men about Scripture, a worldly adventurer who spread herself on the floor of her neighborhood church to weep and wail at the suffering of Christ made her presence felt and her voice resonate throughout the medieval world, if not throughout the centuries to follow. Domesticating Christ, Kempe facilitated her own empowerment in the larger arena of public debate. Two hundred years later Margaret Cavendish also tested the boundaries of madness for her culture. Mad Madge, as her contemporaries sometimes called her, was no extroverted woman like Kempe. Painfully shy and retiring, she nonetheless acknowledged the same desire for public significance as Kempe did. She, too, sought empowerment within the public arena of heroism; and like Kempe she achieved both public praise and notoriety. With more self-consciousness and less volubility, Cavendish was another "eccentric" woman who went about shaping her life and her life story for posterity.

Critics of seventeenth-century autobiography, when they have discussed Cavendish's autobiography, *A True Relation of My Birth, Breeding, and Life,* have remarked on the surprising and unprecedented self-scrutiny evident in her work. Paul Delany states that "it would be giving the Duchess more than her due to describe her as a penetrating self-analyst, but in her ingen-uous way she does reveal much more about her personality than most autobiographers of her time"; and he goes so far as to trace her auto-biographical lineage to Rousseau: "The line of development is unbroken from her work to a modern, subjective autobiography like Rousseau's—his kind of preoccupation with his own singularity is already implicit in the Duchess's *Relation*."[1] Suggesting that the duchess's narrative "adumbrates, if it does not achieve, a scientific emphasis," Wayne Shumaker concludes that it is "full of psychological significance—more so, perhaps, for the modern than for the seventeenth-century reader—and, whatever the motivating purpose, can properly be regarded as a study of character in a broadly sketched environmental setting."[2] Recently, Cynthia S. Pomerleau contends that autobiographies by women in the century, Cavendish's included, "seem more modern, more subjective, more given to self-scrutiny, more like what we have come to know as autobiography" than those works by men that have been conflated with the autobiographical tradition of the seventeenth century.[3] All three, motivated by different critical scenarios, identify in Cavendish's narrative, even if they do not stop to explore it, a protomodern preoccupation with the self qua self that promotes a thickness of self-repre-sentation distinguishing her autobiography from others of the period.

"That romantic lady," as Virginia Woolf describes her, would have rev-eled in such recognition of her "true" distinction, though not perhaps at its failure until recently to command serious attention.[4] She was born Mar-garet Lucas about 1624 at St. John's in Essex, the youngest of eight chil-dren. Her father, a landed gentleman, died when she was two, after which she was raised in an apparently sheltered, even idyllic environment by her mother and older siblings. With the advent of the Civil War, the circum-stances of the young woman's life altered dramatically. Two of her brothers died as a result of the fighting. Family property was confiscated. Then she

left home to serve, from 1643 to 1645, as maid of honor to Queen Henri-
etta-Maria. In 1645, she accompanied the queen into exile in Paris, where
she met and married William Cavendish, then marquis, but later duke, of
Newcastle. They spent seventeen years in exile in Paris, Rotterdam, and
Antwerp, during which time Cavendish turned to writing as a "profession."
During the fifteen years between 1653 and 1668, she wrote and published
fourteen works: five scientific treatises, five collections of poetry and fantasies, two collections of essays and letters, and two collections of plays, as
well as a biography of her husband and an autobiography. With the Resto-
ration she and her husband returned to England and retired from court to
live on their country estate at Welbeck, where she died in 1674. Before her
death Cavendish became a controversial figure, as the passage from Woolf
so sympathetically suggests. She wrote. She wore theatrical costumes. She
promoted the importance of a chaste life. She thereby gained a reputation
for madness. And yet she received the adulation of some prominent writers
and scholars of the period.[5]

Cavendish wrote her autobiography at the relatively young age of thirty-
two; she thus looked back, not on a long life, but on a short span covering
childhood, young adulthood, early marriage, and the beginning of a "career." She had, in fact, only just begun to write and had not yet achieved
public recognition of her talents. But she had married well; and the duke
was himself a celebrity. Earlier she had written a biography of her husband,
an occasion to idealize him and to defend him against detractors. Her
decision to write her own story suggests that Cavendish also wanted to
immortalize herself and to defend herself against her own detractors.

Men and women writing autobiographies in the seventeenth century—
Cavendish particularly—would have grappled with complex problems of
self-representation in a fragmented tradition. They would have struggled
with the contours of individual experience, personal intentions, the formal
options, and the expectations of their readers, influenced by a cultural
ambiance that encouraged exploration of all kinds, including self-explora-
tion, but offered few clearly defined models, in part because many of the
autobiographies written during the period remained unpublished for several hundred years.[6] There were, however, two generalized conventions
that provided provisional topographical opportunities: the narrative of religious conversion tracing its roots to Augustine's *Confessions* and the secular
res gestae tracing its roots back to the classical period.[7] Yet in both nascent
conventions the figures of selfhood would have complicated the autobiographical project for a woman. Religious autobiographers tended to be
members of formal church hierarchies who perceived the significance of
their lives to derive from their status as members of the "militant elite" or
"spiritual aristocracy."[8] While the Protestant sects that emerged from the

Reformation validated woman's authority to read her life for the signs of God's grace, except for the Quakers, they continued to deny her access to public roles and responsibilities. Excluded from the ministry because of patriarchal notions about her "natural" subordination to the authority of her husband and her suspect relationship to language, a woman could not claim membership in the church hierarchy and could not, therefore, claim her life's significance to derive from that kind of activity. Nor did the conventions of secular autobiography offer unequivocal guidance, for they depended in the seventeenth century on the premise that the sum of public acts constituted an individual's "life."[9] In other words, formal "autobiography" remained clearly androcentric.

When Cavendish initiated her autobiographical project, neither sacred nor secular figures promised to conform comfortably to the experience of her life. Whatever her relations to and ideas about the other world, they remained outside the purview of her narrative, which she grounds exclusively in the world of people, education, individual characteristics, not in the exploration of divine providence and personal salvation. Moreover, since her only relationship to public events came from her ascribed status as the daughter of Master Lucas and the wife of the duke of Newcastle, she could not write in the tradition of *res gestae* unless she wrote about the men who had given her her names. (She did so, of course, when she wrote the biography of her husband, to which her own autobiography was appended soon after its first publication. But she originally separated her autobiography from his biography, in 1656 publishing her "life" in a folio entitled *Natures Pictures drawn by Fancies Pencil to the Life*.)

As did other educated and predominantly aristocratic women who wrote secular autobiography during the century, Cavendish turned to her private experience for the matter of her narrative. Pomerleau argues that "for women, and not for men, the domestic choices were, partly by default, a medium for self-expression; and as men began gropingly to write about their public lives, so, amazingly, did a few women write about their private lives." She goes on to contend that "the idea that oneself, one's feelings, one's spouse and domestic relations were properly and innately worth writing about was essentially a female idea, however tentatively conceived at the time."[10] For that reason, Donald A. Stauffer finds women's autobiographies of the period "more personal, informal, and life-like" since the women are "engrossed in the more enthralling problems of their own lives."[11] Moreover, educated women writing their lives approached autobiography with a different orientation toward rhetoric and writing than educated men did. Denied the classical training offered to young men, a training built on imitation and repetition of classical models, elaborated through the structure of argumentation and agonistic combat, articulated in the voice of "objectivity," women often wrote in a style and with a rhetorical voice more fluid and familiar.[12]

Evidence suggests, however, that other women did not presume, as Cavendish did, to garner for themselves significance beyond that attached to conventional figures of women's selfhood, so that they shunned formal autobiography, never writing expressly about themselves for the public. Some, such as Lucy Hutchinson, based their claim to significance on their domestic roles as mothers and as companions to men of public stature, whose biographies they wrote. For instance, Hutchinson abandoned her autobiographical project after describing her parentage and early years, and turned instead to the biography of her husband in a release of great and skillful verbosity as if her own life story ended after adolescence when marriage subsumed her identity in her husband's.[13] Ann Lady Fanshawe wrote specifically for her son's edification and assumed an appropriately self-abnegating stance as she focused on her husband's career.[14] In both purpose and design these texts served to enhance the image of man. Others may have written of their own, rather than their husbands', exploits in the larger social and political arena, but they limited the audience for their work to family members as Anne Lady Halkett did.[15] Consequently, such works by women fell well within cultural expectations governing women's relationship to self-writing and reaffirmed an ideology of autobiography as a male preserve.

Cavendish, having dutifully written the biography of her husband and having had no children whom she could edify, journeyed well beyond those other autobiographers by publicizing her life. She usurped the authority to write her own story for the world, authoring her autobiography as she authored scientific treatises and works of poetry, philosophy, utopian fantasy, drama, biography. She recognized, however, that her readers would read her as "woman," inflecting their response to her narrative with patriarchal expectations of woman's identity, condemning her "unfeminine" desire to use her intelligence and ambition in pursuit of public acclaim. For, as Hilda Smith suggests, Cavendish "understood, better than any of her sisters, the multifaceted nature of women's oppression. She noted their poor education, exclusion from public institutions, political subordination within the home, physiological dictates of childbirth, and society's pervasive vision of women as incompetent, irresponsible, unintelligent, and irrational."[16] A self-consciousness about her identity and status as a woman therefore dominated her works and prompted her critique of the ideology of gender. Yet, as Smith also notes, her critique, while extensive and even radical, was not without its contradictions: "She often suggested that society's perception was correct; women had made few contributions to past civilization, not because they were ill educated but because they had less ability than men."[17] Such contradictions worry the autobiography itself. Influenced by the discourse on man and its empowering narratives, Cavendish wanted to become not merely an ascriptive footnote in the course of history but a person of acknowledged achievements and historical distinction whose eminently "readable" life would gain her "fame in after ages."[18] Yet as she pursued this vision she threatened herself with still another kind of exile, not from the court, not from England, but from that larger domain of "womanhood" with its privileged stories of selfhood. Moreover, she was herself a product of that discourse and so, as she grew accustomed to seeing herself reflected in "the looking-glass of the male-authored text," internalized the narrative of feminine goodness, a silent plot of modesty, naivité, virtue, dependency, innocence, and self-concealment.[19] The anxiety occasioned by such doubling of narrative purpose manifests itself in the fundamental ambiguity at the heart of Cavendish's self-representation.[20] Indeed, there are in *A True Relation* two competing self-representations: that of the woman who fulfills the patriarchal imperatives of female selfhood and who defends the integrity of her innocence; and that of the woman who demands from the world recognition of her own independent achievements. The tension that drives Cavendish's narrative and that leads to the unprecedented self-scrutiny noted by critics of her work, is the tension generated as Cavendish struggles to reconcile, if in the end she only fails to do so, her desire to maintain the silence of the ideal woman and her desire to give voice to her own unconventional and heroic narrative.

Cavendish begins her story with a brief biography of her father, revealing the degree to which she located her identity in his status and character: "My father was a gentleman," she writes, "which Title is grounded and given by Merit, not by princes."[21] Probably because he was dead before Cavendish turned three, she invests the slim biography with such mythic resonances. He represents the ideal hero who "did not esteem Titles, unless they were gained by Heroick Actions." But he represents also the hero robbed of heroic possibilities. The critical moment around which the lost possibility coalesces is the scene of the duel her father fought when a young man. A sign of masculine bravery and integrity, the duel reveals her father's allegiance to the "Laws of Honour." And yet the times are not conducive to that particular expression of heroism: Because of political complications, her father is exiled from England by Queen Elizabeth. When he finally returns after Elizabeth's death, "there was no Employments for heroick Spirits" since the times of "wise" King James remain peaceful. In the end, her father never gains a "title" and never, as a result, gains a historically prominent lineage or a heroic story such a title would command. The story she tells of her father is one of exile and frustrated desire.

In its themes of heroism and of exile, this paternal biography resonates with the daughter's desire for story and her own sense of confusion and frustration about self-representation. In many ways Cavendish is her father's daughter. Like her father before her, she would leave behind the legitimate trace of her "Heroick Actions," those "manly" accomplishments that would ensure her "fame in after ages." Like him, she suffers from frustrated desire, as political, social, and cultural circumstances deny her access to the realm of public activity and significance that lie outside the womb. Like him, she suffers "exile" for her attentiveness to that andro-centric code of honor. And just as her father's life is lived out in a heroic eventlessness that silences his claims to titles, so too Cavendish's life of inactivity threatens to silence her claim to a cultural story of her own. Thus, as she begins her narrative, Cavendish confronts the cultural silence of the very life she would represent.

In this context it is interesting to consider the relationship of Cavendish's autobiography to the biography she wrote of her husband. Since her husband had been a central (and controversial) leader of the Royalist forces and a companion to the king, his life provided the material and the occasion for Cavendish to engage in heroic storytelling. (Unlike her father, her husband gained esteem and public titles from his heroic feats during fiercely troubled times.) Cavendish organized her story in four parts. The first two parts tell of her husband's participation in the Civil War; but more than that, they offer a partisan's defense of the hero's actions as a way of answering his critics and enhancing his reputation. Thus she presents him as the hero-warrior devoted to his sovereign, abused by the mediocre people around him; and her story appropriates conventional features of the classical *res gestae*. In the third part she turns to a description of his character, humor, disposition, birth, breeding, and education, in an apparent attempt to flesh out the details of the inner, the personal, life of the hero. The fourth part introduces the voice of the hero himself as she assembles a collection of his own writings and commentaries. Ultimately, Cavendish creates in the story of her husband an ideal figure who enacts "the heroic ethic of the masculine world."[22]

While Cavendish desires to place heroic action in the plot of her own life, she can in fact replicate only the third part of the biography's structure in her story, the personal rather than the public story. Thus she amasses rather disjointed descriptions of her birth, education, family, disposition, and humor, and winds them around a slim chronological narrative of her personal development from childhood to young adulthood. Yet Cavendish does introduce brief narratives of male heroism into her story as she digresses with adulatory descriptions of the characters and adventures of father, brothers, brother-in-law, and husband. Of her brothers she affirms that "they loved Virtue, endeavoured Merit, practic'd Justice, and spoke Truth; they were constantly loyal, and truly Valiant" (272). Of her brother-in-law: "He was nobly generous, wisely valiant, naturally civill, honestly kind, truly loving, Virtuously temperate" (286). Of her husband: "my Lord is a person whose Humour is neither extravagantly merry, nor unnecessarily sad, his Mind is above his Fortune, as his Generosity is above his purse, his Courage above danger, his Justice above bribes, his Friendship above self-interest, his Truth too firm for falsehood," and on and on (296). Such passages clearly evince not only Cavendish's desire to defend her family but also her obvious admiration of quintessentially male-identified values and qualities of character. They also provide a parallel story of masculine activity alongside her own story of public silence.

Such "male" stories seem to add value, authority, and legitimacy to Cavendish's "life" by a process of association. She enhances her own figure and status as a result of the ideal figures of such male relatives. Yet ironically, such privileging of male biography and ideals of personality in the story effectively subverts a central quality of character she would claim for herself: Like her father, who refuses to buy the status of nobility and who would only earn it through significant heroic action, Cavendish seeks to earn her recognition and fame through significant public action and merit of her own, not to purchase it ascriptively through the heroic feats of men. By incorporating those "masculine" stories so fully into her own, she partially undermines her effort to follow in her father's footsteps. Moreover, she turns her woman's autobiography into a biography of men.

The attentiveness to males—to father, brothers, husband—testifies simultaneously to a very "feminine" orientation to storytelling and to the world in that it pays homage to the superior value and virtue of male-identified activities. Such an orientation becomes particularly critical for Cavendish since, as certain passages in the text reveal, she is acutely aware of the reputation she is gaining as an "unwomanly," even a somewhat "mad," woman. She alludes to rumors and "false reports," projecting throughout her text a public and a reader critical of her desire for public display of her person (in the ostentatious clothes she wears), of her word (in the court appeals she makes, in the books she writes), and of her ambition. Responding to the pressure of those cultural voices, Cavendish struggles to defend her identity as an ideal woman, thereby assuring her reader that she has followed, not in her father's, but in her mother's footsteps. And so, interweaving throughout the digressive narratives of male relatives (and the idealization of the masculine ethic) is the story of her "maternal" inheritance with its idealization of true womanhood—the story, as Mary C. Mason suggests, "of an emerging young woman."[23]

If her father as exemplar of masculine integrity sits at the threshold of her autobiography, her mother, the exemplar of the true feminine, inhabits the center of her story—literally and figuratively. The daughter represents her mother as the embodiment of perfect beauty: "She was of a grave Behaviour, and had such a Magestic Grandeur, as it were continually hung about her, that it would strike a kind of awe to the beholders, and command respect from the rudest" (282). She is also the "affectionate Mother, breeding her children with a most industrious care, and tender love, and having eight children, three sons and five daughters, there was not anyone crooked or any ways deformed, neither were they dwarfish, or of a Giant-like stature, but every ways proportionable" (283). And finally, she is the model wife and widow, who

> never forgot my Father so as to marry again; indeed, he remain'd so lively in her memory, and her grief was so lasting, as she never mention'd his name, though she spoke often of him, but love and grief caused tears to flow, and tender sighs to rise, mourning in sad complaints; she made her house her Cloyster, inclosing her self, as it were therein, for she seldom went abroad, unless to Church. (282)

Read in tandem these descriptive passages pay empassioned tribute to a remarkable woman, an ideal of timeless beauty and devotion, an image of female perfection that is cloistered, quiescent, eternal.

Throughout *A True Relation*, Cavendish tenaciously insists that she has imitated the maternal model of the ideal feminine and that she has achieved the sanctity and aristocratic gentility of inner life on which the imitation depends. She does so by characterizing herself as "the sheltered innocent" who lives "the cloistered life," drawing repeatedly on the language and imagery of both figures to sustain that narrative identity. For instance, as Cavendish nostalgically represents it, her childhood was lived out in an idyllic, protected, totally innocent world. Here mother and older siblings created for her a conventual environment closed off from the public realm where males acted heroically; and in that enclosed space the child and young woman was bred "according to . . . the Nature of my Sex . . . Virtuously, Modestly, Civilly, Honourably, and on honest principles" (268). Her education included "singing, dancing, playing on musick, reading, writing, working, and the like" (271). Yet intellectual accomplishment and independence of mind were discouraged to such an extent that she can write of her sisters that they "did seldom make Visits, nor never went abroad with Strangers in their Company, but onely themselves in a Flock together agreeing so well, that there seemed but one Minde amongst them" (276–77).

Describing her entrance as a young woman into the world of the court,

Cavendish identifies herself as the sheltered innocent leaving the virtuous life of the cloister to confront a "fallen" world where cunning, sophistication, intrigue, debauchery proclaim the reign of evil. Deprived of the guidance of her siblings, she was "like one that had no Foundation to stand, or Guide to direct me, which made me afraid, lest I should wander with Ignorance out of the waies of Honour, so that I knew not how to behave myself" (278). As a result, she "durst neither look up with my eyes, nor speak, nor be any way sociable, insomuch as I was thought a Natural Fool" (278). Thus, although she might have gained an education, she clings to innocence, maintaining that "being dull, fearfull, and bashfull, I neither heeded what was said or practic'd, but just what belonged to my loyal duty, and my own honest reputation; and, indeed, I was so afraid to dishonour my Friends and Family by my indiscreet actions, that I rather chose to be accounted a Fool, then to be thought rude or wanton" (279). When she describes her later attempt to petition the English courts for access to her husband's lands (which had been confiscated during his exile), she again characterizes herself as "unpracticed," "unlearned," "ignorant," "not knowing." And when she analyzes her bashfulness (292–93) and her way of living (300), she emphasizes again and again her isolation from the fallen multitude and her "aversion to such kinds of people." For Cavendish, the representation of herself as foolish, uncomfortable, ignorant, fearful, bashful, and speechless in public testifies to her superior virtue, the basis on which her true merit as model woman rests.

Cavendish also establishes that her virtue derives from her chaste relationship to men and to sexual passion. During her childhood, she tells her reader, her mother "never suffered the vulgar Servingmen to be in the Nursery among the Nurse Maids, lest their rude love-making might do unseemly actions, or speak unhandsome words in the presence of her children, knowing that youth is apt to take infection by ill examples, having not the reason of distinguishing good from bad" (270–71). She describes herself as a young woman who "did dread Marriage, and shunn'd mens companies as much as [she] could" (280). And she maintains that she "never was infected [with amorous love], it is a Disease, or a Passion, or both, I only know by relation, not by experience" (280). These passages taken together reveal her vision of sexuality as a form of "infection" and of men's company as conducive to another kind of dis-ease. Adding chastity to the catalog of goodness, Cavendish reveals, by the way, the degree to which the life story of the ideal woman demands the repression of sexual desire. In fact, in her relationship to the duke, she represents herself as totally without desire, as a kind of clean slate waiting to be written on: "My Lord the Marquis of Newcastle did approve of those bashful fears which many condemn'd, and would choose such a Wife as he might bring to his own humours, and not such an one as was wedded to self-conceit, or one that had been temper'd to the humours of another, for which he wooed me for his Wife" (280). Here she joins the imagery of sexual purity, religious devotion, and self-efface-ment when describing her vision of marriage, recapitulating the metaphor of the cloistered life (associated with her mother) with obvious rhetorical flamboyance: "though I desire to appear to the best advantage, whilest I live in the view of the public World, yet I could most willingly exclude myself, so as Never to see the face of any creature, but my Lord, as long as I live, inclosing myself like an Anchoret, wearing a Frize gown, tied with a cord about my waste" (309).

The powerful appeal of feminine "silence" for Cavendish may have de-rived in part from her profound experience of displacement during exile from England and her desire to reclaim her rightful place in the order of English society. Thus a preoccupation with traditional patterns of social arrangements, and with the sexual arrangements at the center of them, characterizes her autobiography as it does much of secular autobiography of the late Renaissance. As Delany notes, "secular autobiographers were often unusually concerned with their social status, either because it had changed significantly for better or worse, or because they had perceived a shift in the relative standing of the class to which they gave allegiance."[24] The very identity of Cavendish's family had altered dramatically, irrevoca-bly: Two of her brothers had perished as a result of the Civil Wars; her mother had been stripped of her lands and assets; her husband had been exiled. In such a context Cavendish seems to cling to the old, the estab-lished, the fundamental patterns of sexual relationships that root her per-sonal identity. Pomerleau, writing of women's autobiographies in the cen-tury, suggests that "the old patterns may actually have provided an element of serenity and stability in a world where the sanctity of these patterns could no longer be taken for granted."[25] A proud supporter of the authority of the monarch and a critic of the democratic impulses of the opposition (and of democracy generally, evidenced by her aristocratic scorn of the fallen multitude), Cavendish maintained, despite her acute recognition of the oppression of women, despite her often strong condemnations of the in-stitution of marriage, a commitment to the authority of the familial pa-triarch as well as to that of the royal one.[26]

Cavendish's insistence before the reader on identifying discomfort with virtue, bashfulness with merit, childlike fear with ideal feminine purity and ignorance testifies to the intensity of her desire to imitate the self-abnegat-ing model of ideal womanhood represented by her mother and thereby to secure the love and acceptance of the world. Yet her rhetoric in key pas-sages betrays another vision of that model of womanhood. If we return to the central passages describing her mother and read them once again, we see that the language evokes, however subtly, images of feminine enclosure and physical and psychological entombment. Of her mother, Cavendish writes that

> her beauty was beyond the ruin of time, for she had a well favoured loveliness in her face, a pleasing sweetness in her countenance, and a well-temper'd complexion, as neither too red nor too pale, even to her dying hour, although in years, and by her dying, one might think death was enamoured with her, for he imbraced her in a sleep, and so gently, as if he were afraid to hurt her. (283)

Cavendish obviously wants to testify to her mother's perfection and mystical power. Yet in doing so she testifies to much more. Forever devoted to a dead husband, willingly cloistered in her womb-like convent, marvelously preserved from the physical ravages of time, and caressed easily by death, this mother is also the figure of frozen stillness, a necromantic presence whose real power derives from the hold her memory has on the daughter. Paradoxically, the daughter subverts the grasp of this mother, whose image commands obedient imitation, by betraying in the very language of entombment a fundamental dissatisfaction with the ideal. For to be cloistered in such an ideal, however well preserved and comfortable it may be, is to be dead to independent expression, knowledge, and heroic possibilities. Ultimately, that ideal of self-representation is unmasked as a "fiction," compellingly prescriptive yet untruthful and invalid. While Cavendish would duplicate her mother's story, her language reveals the desire for a duplicitous transgression of its lines.

The language of the text subverts the representation of her mother as ideal woman in yet another way. Cavendish acknowledges that, however much her mother might have emphasized "being" and deemphasized "doing" in her educational scheme, she embraced a socially acceptable practical role foisted upon her by widowhood: "though she would often complain that her family was too great for her weak Management, and often prest my Brother to take it upon him, yet I observe she took a pleasure, and some little pride, in the governing thereof: she was very skilful in Leases, and setting of lands, and Court-keeping, ordering of Stewards, and the like affairs" (285). In this telling description, Cavendish notes the deference and self-abnegation of her mother's public mask and the private sense of satisfaction and power concealed by that mask. In other words, she identifies the fictional nature of her mother's public persona: Before her, her mother, too, masked her pleasure in power.[27] In this characterization, therefore, Cavendish captures her own dilemma—how to maintain the virtuous woman's silence and simultaneously pursue public power. Moreover, she reveals her strategy for negotiating the dilemma—the fabrication of a self-effacing mask. But in doing so she calls into question the very truthfulness of her representation of herself as the virtuous, silent woman.

Of course, the first evidence of a self-asserting protagonist is the auto-biography itself. The title announces the very desire for public acknowledg-ment Cavendish tries unsuccessfully to mute; for once she commits herself to the autobiographical project, she dissociates herself from the figure of the self-abnegating woman. By writing she authorizes her own story: She speaks publicly. Then the opening of the narrative, discussed earlier, re-veals her strong identification with the father and the heroic values of the world of men. Male heroics are denied her, however; thus she takes up the pen, a choice that seems natural to her as the preface to one of her other works suggests: "That my ambition of extraordinary Fame, is restless, and not ordinary, I cannot deny: and since all Heroick Actions, Publick Employ-ments, as well Civill as Military, and Eloquent Pleadings, are deni'd my Sex in this Age, I may be excused for writing so much."[28] While she does not turn her autobiography into a conscious exploration of her development as an artist, she does provide, if only unconsciously, a thin strand of a story tracing her emerging authorship.

The figure of an empowered and ambitious self becomes visible in such passages as the one in which she describes her early fascination with dress: "I never took delight in closets, or cabinets of toys, but in the variety of fine clothes, and such toys as onely were to adorn my person" (302). She thus grounds in early childhood her preoccupation with fashioning herself in her own representations, albeit in a conventional script of women's lives:

> My serious study could not be much, by reason I took great delight in attiring, fine dressing, and fashions, especially such fashions as I did invent myself, not taking that pleasure in such fashions as was invented by others: also I did dislike any should follow my Fashions, for I always took delight in a singularity, even in accoutrements of habit. (303–304)

Unique, "loud" clothes break the silence and the anonymity at the core of feminine goodness, publicly distinguishing her from all other girls by giv-ing original lines to her body. Through such fashioning, the young woman gives form to her fantasies of creative selfhood, and the autobiographer, recalling such moments, unmasks her desire for "making up" in both senses of the phrase: making up stories about herself and making herself up for public exposure.[29]

Suzanne Juhasz, in an essay on contemporary autobiographies by wom-en, alludes to the dynamic relationship of literary women to the realm of fantasy, suggesting that "because there is usually a profound discrepancy between the options that society offers to women and the potential that they find within themselves, women frequently have complex inner lives, worlds of fantasy."[30] Cavendish's autobiography reveals that fantasy became a means she early developed to mediate between the cultural imperative of self-annihilating silence and more heroic possibilities of selfhood. Shy, contemplative, yet ambitious—as she tells her reader a number of times—in fantasy and later in writing Cavendish can become the empowering author of her own story and fashion herself as a protagonist of heroic proportions, thereby wresting greatness and distinction from insignificance. Unable to grasp the sword or to ride a horse into battle as her husband (and male relatives) can, she can grasp the pen and ride words across pages. And she can create in her writing women of heroism who take on all the roles of men, including fighting, ruling, discovering, as they do in such works as *Bell in Campo* and *The Description of a New World*. Thus writing, with its promise of regenerative, capacious, galvanizing selfhood, not the "Lord" of her text, represents life itself to Cavendish, since it enables her to exercise her reason and imagination, and to body forth her originality by shaping interpretations.[31] (In fact, the marquis, at least as he is represented in the autobiography, performs a function much like the woman "in some corner" of Freud's male daydreams.[32] He becomes a kind of male muse who acknowledges, who seems even to inspire, her writing.) What Stephen Jay Greenblatt claims for the prominent literary men of the Renaissance applies as well to Cavendish: "the Renaissance figures we have considered understand that in our culture to abandon self-fashioning is to abandon the craving for freedom, and to let go of one's stubborn hold upon selfhood, even selfhood conceived as a fiction, is to die."[33]

Cavendish's language and imagery suggest the degree to which she imagined writing as a female equivalent to male warfare, a heroic arena in which women might gain access to distinction through merit. In describing her method of writing and her handwriting, she appropriates a trope from the dominant discourse, noting that

> when some of those thoughts are sent out in words, they give the rest more liberty to place themselves in a more methodicall order, marching more regularly with my pen, on the ground of white paper, but my letters seem rather as a ragged rout, than a well armed body, for the brain being quicker in creating than the hand in writing, or the memory in retaining, many fancies are lost, by reason they ofttimes outrun the pen; where I, to keep speed in the Race, write so fast as I stay not so long as to write my letters plain. (298)

Yet this language also reveals the degree to which she felt ambiguous about the presumption inherent in such an analogy. Having established the analogy, Cavendish associates herself with the routed and defeated rather than with the heroic and victorious. Hers is a battle lost, at least in terms of the orderliness of her ideas and her handwriting, which by the end of this passage is what her "writing" has been reduced to. Or more precisely, she is really an interloper on the field of battle as the distinction she draws between her husband's writing and her own attests. While the marquis "recreates himself with his pen, writing what his Wit dictates to him," she "pass[es] [her] time rather with scribbling than writing, with words than wit" (297). This disclaimer recapitulates the earlier rhetoric of ignorance and reaffirms—at the moment she would reveal her desire for significant action and accomplishment—her continued allegiance to the conventions of ideal female gentility, in particular the modesty that forbids the assertion of female authority and authorship.

Elsewhere Cavendish takes pains to distinguish herself from other, less virtuous women who speak publicly in their own behalf as "Pleaders, Attornies, Petitioners, and the like, running about with their several Causes" (290). Such women

> doth nothing but justle for the Preheminence of words, I mean not for speaking well, but speaking much, as they do for the preheminence of place, words rushing against words, thwarting and crossing each other, and pulling with reproaches, striving to throw each other down with disgrace, thinking to advance themselves thereby." (290)

Again Cavendish appropriates the combat trope, but with an intriguing difference. Here she would accuse other women of unfeminine activity and self-asserting public display, and so doing reaffirm her own modesty in public. But ironically, while she means to mark the difference between herself and other women who use language publicly, the imagery in the passage identifies her with them. Like them, she would through writing enter the world of male combat and seek distinction on the field of battle. Like them, she seeks preeminence. That confusion in her recourse to the combat trope betrays the confusion at the heart of her project and betrays the "fictionality" of both self-asserting and self-effacing representations.

The problematic nature of Cavendish's public exposure is represented both literally and figuratively in her relationship to her carriage. Twice in the narrative she alludes to the pleasure she feels in riding about and reveals her motives for such public exposure: "because I would not bury myself quite from the sight of the world, I go sometimes abroad, seldome to visit, but only in my Coach about the Town" (300). Reality beyond the cloister must be engaged in order for her to enlarge the experiential bases of her fantasies and to feed her vanities: "I am so vain, if it be a vanity, as to endeavor to be worship't, rather than not to be regarded" (309). Like the hero who rides through the streets in his triumphal chariot, Cavendish would be worshipped by the populace. Yet the "fallen" public, that awesome, often truculent, intractable, vulgar reality, threatens to shatter the fantasy of purity and distinction. Thus, for an "ideal" woman cloistered within the protective walls of bashfulness but desiring an audience larger than her Lord to validate her true originality, the carriage becomes the vehicle that promises both assertive self-display and the requisite self-concealment emblematic of an inner goodness so critical to the chaste, virtuous woman. If the public is allowed to see but not to touch, Cavendish is allowed to be seen but not to be touched by the fallen multitude.

The autobiography is itself a metaphorical carriage, a vehicle that parades the body of Cavendish's life before the public, allowing her to escape the confinement of silence. But that secular gesture of self-display threatens to take her on a transgressive ride beyond the conventional path of woman's selfhood. The final passage of Cavendish's autobiography captures the central dilemma in its poignant self-reflexiveness. In the first clause she acknowledges a prominent motif embedded in the ideology of gender: Women manifest a natural tendency to vanity, and vanity in woman is evil. Thus the public display of the woman who would write autobiography marks her as a true daughter of Eve. The scene of autobiography is no place for woman. Just as she earlier acknowledges public censorship of her sartorial fashioning, Cavendish here recognizes the inevitability of public censorship of her literary self-fashioning, of the very autobiography she has just written. In response, she assumes a defensive posture, strategically citing authoritative precedents: "but I hope my readers will not think me vain for writing my life, since there have been many that have done the like, as Cesar, Ovid, and many more, both men and women, and I know no reason I may not do it as well as they" (309). In a gesture of petulance, she would bring the authority of Caesar and Ovid to bear on her enterprise. Perhaps she identifies with the betrayal of the former and the exile of the latter, since as a Royalist she is living through just such betrayal and exile. Certainly, she identifies her autobiographical authority with the literary authority of the man of public action and the poet. But, as Patricia Meyer Spacks notes, the models to whom she refers are male—her reference to female precedents notwithstanding—and their deeds a matter of public significance.[34] She can cite no female models of significance, no tradition of women's autobiography. Moreover, the text betrays Cavendish's own ambivalence about such comparisons. The very next clause speaks to the lack of public significance in women's lives and by implication in their narratives: "but I verily believe some censuring Readers will scornfully say, why hath this Lady write her own Life? since none cares to know whose daughter she was, or whose wife she is, or how she was bred, or what fortunes she had, or how she lived, or what humour or disposition she was of?" (310). The catalog of content, a summation of her own autobiographical material, betrays the absence of heroic action and public deeds, the conventional subject matter of formal autobiography.

Her defensive posture intensifies: "I anser that it is true, that 'tis to no purpose to the Reader, but it is to the Authoress, because I write it for my own sake, not theirs" (310). While she declares that the reader's expectations are insignificant to her, the pose remains more rhetorical than convincing. For the next and final passage reveals powerfully the fundamental motivation of the effort:

> Neither did I intend this piece for to delight, but to divulge; not to please the fancy, but to tell the truth, lest after-ages should mistake, in not knowing I was daughter to one Master Lucas of St. Johns, near Colchester, in Essex, second wife to the Lord Marquis of Newcastle; for my Lord having had two Wives, I might easily have been mistaken, especially if I should dye and my Lord Marry again. (310)

These closing words of her text testify eloquently to her desperate need to be "read" accurately by those readers who will, if they so choose, distinguish her for posterity from her husband's other wives. Ultimately, then, the issue is one of identity versus anonymity. Cavendish is writing for her very life. Ironically, however, only her identity as daughter and wife will differentiate her from her husband's other wives. So for all her effort to follow her father's example and to maintain the value of merit as the source of "fame in after ages," Cavendish can rely only on her ascriptive status as wife and daughter to place her historically. In that light it is interesting to note again that originally the autobiography appeared by itself in her collection of her writings, *Natures Pictures drawn by Fancies Pencil to the Life;* only later was it appended to the second edition of the biography of her husband, a kind of historical footnote. Thus her story becomes a satellite revolving around the body of man's story. Paradoxically, while she authors his life, his life, in fact, authors and authorizes hers.

Cavendish could not tell her autobiographical story the way her culture had come to expect it to be told. She could not discover in her life the plot for *res gestae* or for spiritual quest. Somehow, she had to make the private story suffice instead of the public one. Decked out in those "odd" autobiographical clothes, she insisted on being regarded, if only by a public bent on laughing at her. However flawed, however entangled as it inevitably was in the very patriarchal plots that mocked her attempts at self-fashioning, her autobiographical carriage ride is in its own way as frustratedly heroic as her father's youthful duel. Like her father, she was doomed to "die" in the realm of feminine silence and the repetitive anonymity that characterized women's narrative possibilities in the seventeenth century or to become an exile from the autobiographical conventions of her culture. Engaged as she is in that effort, she cannot help but be more self-revealing than contemporary autobiographers who inscribed their self-representations in the more "impersonal" conventions of *res gestae* or spiritual awakening or in the narratives of domestic drama that provided the autobiographer more comfortable, because more clearly delimiting, narrative personae. Cavendish can give neither us nor herself those comfortable masks. She gives us, instead, a woman struggling uncomfortably with an androcentric genre.

In its narrative chaos the prose surface of Cavendish's *True Relation* reveals the desperate pleasure the very act of writing must have offered her. Suppressed energy and vitality permeate the text and its constant transformations. Sentences start in one direction, shift, scatter, reconvene, then go off suddenly elsewhere. That may be, as some critics remark, the sign of her undisciplined mind, the mind of a woman denied the intellectual training reserved exclusively for men. As such it reveals the price she paid for being a woman. But it also reveals the fierce desire for power at the heart of Cavendish's personal struggle for "fame in after ages." And so, out of all the mutability and the mobility, the interpenetration of story lines, the proliferation of digressive details, Cavendish constitutes both her "character" and her "life," representing herself as a woman of desire and of potentially unbounded imagination. For all her confusions and ambivalences, for all her protestations of cloistered selfhood, she evinces that unenclosed originality she so admired.

SIX

A Narrative of the Life of Mrs. Charlotte Charke

The Transgressive Daughter and the Masquerade of Self-Representation

"This tragic story, or this comic jest,
May make you laugh, or cry—as you like best."

—Prologue to "The What d'Ye Call It,"
A Narrative of the Life of Mrs. Charlotte Charke

Margaret Cavendish set upon the "open road" to announce to the world her desire for "fame in after ages." Yet she carefully sheltered herself within the carriage-like enclosure of proper feminine gentility. As a result, the fundamental ambivalence she felt about her desire for a transgressive female heroism permeates the story she tells about herself. Charlotte Charke, also a famous, or rather notorious, daughter and wife, evinced little ambivalence when she launched her own independent career almost one hundred years after Cavendish began writing. In an age when acting was the legitimate secular profession open to women, Charke strutted across the stage invigorated by the theatrical possibilities of self-dramatization. Unlike Cavendish, she embraced the transgressive life of the open road with a kind of male bravado. Yet to the extent that she did so, she lost the affection of her father and fell into a life of destitution. It is a story of transgression, prodigality, and vagabondage that Charke tells as she attempts to regain her father's love. Of course, stories of the road and the rogue fascinated the eighteenth century generally, more so than they did the less politically and socially stable seventeenth century. Nonetheless, this particular story of female vagabondage startles the reader even now.

The autobiographer prefaces *A Narrative of the Life of Mrs. Charlotte Charke* with an epistolary dedication entitled "The Author to Herself." Denounc-

102

ing the excesses of flattery common to dedications, she parodies her dedicatee's eminence: "I hope I shall escape that Odium so justly thrown on poetical Petitioners, notwithstanding my Attempt to illustrate those WONDERFUL QUALIFICATIONS by which you have so EMINENTLY DISTINGUISH'D YOURSELF, and gives you a just Claim to the title of a NONPAREIL OF THE AGE."[1] In fact, she replaces excess flattery with excess mockery: Her dedicatee's distinction as a woman without peers lies in such "virtues" as "thoughtless Ease," a misguided "Fortitude of Mind," an "exquisite Taste in Building . . . magnificent airy Castles," "an indolent Sweetness of . . . Temper." She is indeed peerless, but as an "Oddity of Fame," a "curiosity," rather than as a serious eminence. Nonetheless, Charke appeals to her for assistance: "If, by your Approbation, the World may be persuaded into a tolerable Opinion of my Labours, I shall, for the Novelty-sake, venture for once to call you FRIEND,—a Name, I own, I never *as yet have known you by*" (vii–viii). Expressing hope that her patron will be struck with "reproach" so that the two of them "may ripen our Acquaintance into a perfect Knowledge of each other, that may establish a lasting and social Friendship between us," she suggests that such a rapprochement now seems both desirable and possible since "your two Friends, PRUDENCE and REFLECTION . . . have lately ventur'd to pay you a Visit; for which I heartily congratulate you, as nothing can possibly be more joyous to the Heart than the Return of absent Friends, after a long and painful Peregrination" (ix). Charke's dedicatee is, of course, herself, a self-reflexive phenomenon that makes of the dedication a particularly complex introduction. Maintaining the critical distance of cavalier self-mockery, the autobiographer creates of herself a quixotic figure, a kind of perpetual naif, who, destitute of common sense, blunders along in life. In this "unflattering" portrait she becomes overimaginative, indolent, careless, unrealistically optimistic, imprudent, unreflective. And yet, with this prefatory gesture, the autobiographer also announces at the outset a flair for dramatic posturing, an energetic preoccupation with theatrical entertainment and self-fabrication that enhances the reader's pleasure.

The "entertaining" self-parody, the dramatic bravado, and the rebellious speaking posture betray, on the one hand, the depth of Charke's isolation from community. The fact that she dedicates her autobiography to herself reveals the extent of her dissociation from respectable society: She recognizes no one of social standing as worthy of her attentions and, by implication, reveals her understanding that she may not be worthy of theirs.[2] And the self-parody speaks to her recognition that for the reader she is a truly eccentric character, one who lives outside the conventional norms of that middle-class society into which she was born. Mirroring in her self-mockery the moral stance of the community from which she has been banished,

Charke would affirm her identification with it. Through such affirmation she unmasks a sentimental longing for psychological rapprochement with and physical return to that community. On the other hand, the self-mockery and dramatic bravado betray the fragile exuberance, defiance, and pride of the outcast: There is relish in the role of the quixote. As Patricia Meyer Spacks suggests, "the dedication of her book to herself, defiantly asserting her self-sufficiency, conveys her determination to celebrate herself if no one else will celebrate her."[3] Thus, while Charke eschews flattery, she effectively enhances the portrait of herself as eccentric rebel and, additionally, piques her reader's curiosity with the promise of unusual revelations.

Two desires and two narrative intentions therefore emerge in Charke's opening dedication. Eager to reveal her strange story, Charke seems to flaunt her waywardnesses before the reader, relishing even the self-deprecation. A true actress, she entertains her audience by playing the "role" of a quixotic, even roguish protagonist, a prodigal who strays from the family, defying convention to lead the transgressive life of the female vagabond. Such "role" playing is doubly entertaining: The narrative of a quixote always challenges cultural norms and teases conventional pieties; and the story of the female transgressive titillates even further the reader's desire for scandal. Moreover, the drama of ironic self-deprecation subverts the sense of self-importance and self-aggrandizement inherent in the autobiographical project. But entangled in those quixotic entertainments lies the story of the prodigal who desires to return "home." Through this story, Charke presents herself as the sentimental heroine, a woman who accepts and reflects the values of the community, including its expectations of appropriate female behavior. The doubled identification of Charke as sentimental penitent and female rogue both informs and unhinges the narrative and drama of her autobiography.

Born into a comfortable middle-class family at the beginning of the eighteenth century, Charlotte Cibber was the youngest child of a famous father. After receiving a generous education, especially for a girl, she married too quickly a man who exploited her for his ambition's sake: The daughter of the famous actor and author, she was an attractive match for an aspiring musician. The marriage failed, forcing Charlotte, now Charke, to support herself and her child. She began what seemed to be a promising career on the stage, following in her father's and brother's footsteps. After alienating herself from family and friends, however, she spent the rest of her life on the margins of society, pursuing a variety of "careers," as puppeteer, grocer, sausage maker, waiter, and finally as strolling player. Imprisoned several times for debts, she lived continually on the verge of disaster. Eventually, she tried to support herself by writing novels and the autobiography through which she sought her father's absolution for her prodigal life.

Attentiveness to the father was particularly critical for a woman of the eighteenth century, as Spacks emphasizes in her analysis of four autobiographies, Charke's among them: "Women did not expect their husbands' continued love. Emotional investments in fathers, made earlier and enduring longer, paid off more dependably, although sometimes stormily."[4] The father provided protection. Under his roof and under his authority, the daughter could be sure of survival. Writing expressly to overcome the profound estrangement from her father, therefore, Charke becomes one of those "women identifying themselves as daughters," joining others who "declared their dependency, their need, and their sense of where that need might be gratified, asserting their identities to inhere in their roles rather than their deeds."[5] Alluding explicitly to the stormy nature of her relationship with Colley Cibber in the opening pages of the autobiography proper, Charke confesses that

> since my Maturity, I lost that Blessing: Which, if strongest Compunction, and uninterrupted Hours of Anguish, blended with Self-conviction and filial Love, can move his Heart to Pity and Forgiveness, I shall, with Pride and unutterable Transport, throw myself at his Feet, to implore the only Benefit I desire or expect, his BLESSING, and his PARDON. (14)

Unable to speak directly with her father, who refuses to acknowledge her claims on his love, Charke turns to print as the medium through which to achieve reconciliation and to affect a reprieve from her reputation as undutiful daughter: "I hope, ere this small Treatise is finish'd, to have it in my Power to inform my Readers, my painful Separation from my once tender Father will be more than amply repaid, by a happy Interview" (15). The fact that her story is serialized over a period of eight weeks significantly enhances the very real drama of the "life."[6] Both she and her readers await the outcome of her petition for absolution, await, that is, the father's word.

To regain her reputation as the dutiful daughter and to return metaphorically to the home of the father (and all patriarchal fathers), Charke must duplicate for her culture its privileged story of female selfhood. As she writes her story and awaits the father's word, therefore, she appropriates the speaking posture and story of the sentimental heroine, that dependent, vulnerable, and victimized woman struggling to do the morally right thing, struggling to please the father. When, in the early installments, her father's word is imminent, she assumes a particularly generous stance, playing the devoted daughter through the language of true filiality. In dramatic commentary and descriptive passages, she presents her father as a tender, affectionate parent whose "paternal Love omitted nothing that could improve any natural Talents Heaven had been pleased to endow me with" (16). She lavishes praise on him as she acknowledges the breadth of his parental love:

> My Obligations to him in my bringing up are of so extensive a Nature, I can never sufficiently acknowledge 'em; for, notwithstanding 'tis every Parent's Duty to breed their Children with every Advantage their Fortunes will admit of, yet, in this Case, I must confess myself most transcendently indebted, having received even a Superfluity of tender Regard of that Kind. (25)

If she is at all critical, as she is in discussing his role in her marriage to Mr. Charke, she mutes the criticism, delicately referring to his indulgence and tenderness as possible sources of her difficulties, only conceding that "out of pure Pity, [he] tenderly consented to a conjugal Union" between his daughter and Mr. Charke (51).

Coupled with the presentation of her father as loving and generous is her presentation of herself as "a sincere and hearty Penitent," an undeserving daugher who acknowledges the "Oddity of [her] youthful Disposition" (51) and who apologizes for her pursuit of an independent career. Throughout, she plays the prodigal humbled by her errancy: "I have too much Reason to know, that the Madness of my Follies have generally very severely recoil'd upon myself, but in nothing so much as in the shocking and heart-wounding Grief for my Father's Displeasure, which I shall not impudently dare deny having justly incurr'd" (23–24). Labeling her childhood escapades "strange, mad Pranks," she "beg[s] Pardon for not having put [her education] to a more grateful and generous Use, both for HIS HONOUR and MY OWN CREDIT" (25). Not only does she confess sins of filiality; she also apologizes for sins of friendship, asking pardon from those whom she has wronged in the past with former meannesses. Moreover, she promises a conversion to orthodox filiality: "I shall lay it down as a Maxim for the remaining Part of Life, to make the utmost amends by PRUDENT CONDUCT, for the MISCARRIAGES OF THE FORMER; so that, should I fail in my Hopes, I may not draw any farther Imputation on myself" (25).

While she admits that the loss of her father's affection comes "partly through my own Indiscretion," however, she qualifies her culpability by assigning greater blame to others. Imitating other sentimental heroines, she plays the destitute and deserted victim of a vicious, corrupt world, a "conventional" woman, passive and vulnerable.[7] She may have dabbled in rebelliousness; but ultimately her errancies were exploited by others who would separate her from her father: "I dare confidently affirm, MUCH PAINS has been taken to AGGRAVATE MY FAULTS, and STRENGTHEN his Anger; and, in that Case, I am certain my Enemies have not always too strictly adher'd to TRUTH, but MEANLY had recourse to FALSE-

HOOD to perpetrate the Ruin of a hapless Wretch, whose real Errors were sufficient, without the Addition of MALICIOUS SLANDERS" (24). A stepmother and a sister, jealous of her place in her father's heart, intervene maliciously between father and daughter. A husband's "loose and unkind Behaviour," exploding any illusions of an acceptable marriage, "made me extravagant and wild in my Imagination" (53). "The cruel Censure of false and evil Tongues" further exacerbates her alienation from her father. Thieving strangers take her goods and her money.

Charke sanctifies the role of victimized heroine by infusing it with the virtues of Christian piety, especially charity and forgiveness. Acknowledging obligations she owes to others who have helped her, she repays their charitable deeds with "printed" thank-you's: " 'Tis certain, there never was known a more unfortunate Devil than I have been; but I have, in the Height of all my Sorrows, happily found a numerous Quantity of Friends, whose Commiseration shall be taken Notice of with the utmost Gratitude, before I close this Narrative" (84). Specifically she mentions her sister and the actor Garrick, both of whom she showers with appreciation. She presents herself as maintaining her commitments to others, despite her continuing destitution. Affirming the importance of sibling loyalty, she pleads for charity for a sister as destitute as she. She even goes so far as to advertise in a later installment her sister's new restaurant, hoping thereby to help her succeed financially (146). Finally, she plays the charitable Christian by forgiving those who have wronged her. Of her husband, she writes: "But peace to his *Manes!* and, I hope Heaven has forgiven him, as I do from my Soul; and wish, for both our sakes, he had been Master of more Discretion, I had then possibly been possessed of more Prudence" (79). By playing the generous Christian to the hilt, she establishes her spiritual superiority over those malicious (but comfortably positioned) people who have directed neither charity nor forgiveness toward her.

Finally, Charke plays the sentimental heroine by assuming the posture of a moralist who seeks common ground with her audience of ladies and gentlemen. Conscientiously, she maintains the decency and morality of her narrative itself, announcing in the opening paragraphs:

> I must beg Leave to inform those Ladies and Gentlemen, whose Tenderness and Compassion may excite 'em to make this little Brat of my Brain the Companion of an idle Hour, that I have paid all due Regard to Decency wherever I have introduc'd the Passion of Love; and have only suffer'd it to take its Course in its proper and necessary Time, without fulsomely inflaming the Minds of my young Readers, or shamefully offending those of riper Years; a Fault I have often condemn'd, when I was myself but a Girl, in some Female Poets. I shall not descant on their Imprudence, only wish that their Works had been less confined to that Theme, which too often led 'em into Errors, Reason and Modesty equally forbid. (12)

Taking a high moral tone, she purposively dissociates herself from earlier women writers by denouncing their excessive preoccupation with passion and the theme of love. By doing so, she allies herself with those cultural critics during the mid-eighteenth century fiercely concerned about the very questionable morality of the literature of love, including the new novel. Such critics decried the impact that stories of romance and love would surely have on the minds and hearts of the young ladies who read them. Poetry, romance, and novels of love, they argued, were potentially as seductive of the affections and the morals, even the bodies, of women as was any nefarious man. Or, rather, imaginative seductions prepared the way for actual ones.[8] Echoing those sentiments, Charke disengages herself from the potentially subversive element of common narrative, from its immoral and indecent themes, as she asserts her text's decency, reasonableness, modesty, prudence.

And she maintains that posture toward her narrative throughout. After describing some of her early escapades, she comments: "Were I to insert one quarter Part of the strange, mad Pranks I play'd, even in Infancy, I might venture to affirm, I could swell my Account of 'em to a Folio, and perhaps my whimsical Head may compile such a Work; but I own I should be loth, upon Reflection, to publish it, lest the Contagion should spread itself, and make other young Folks as ridiculous and mischievous as myself" (23). Not only does she present her narrative itself as moral; she also, within the content of her tale, embeds moral directives. She discusses the importance of adding experience of the world to sedentary education. Telling the story of her "fortunate Escape" from a vile deception, she presents a maxim to "set others on their Guard, who may be liable to an Accident of the same Kind" (197). She describes her plan to support an impoverished sister, not "with any Regard to myself, but with the pleasing Hope of being the happy Example to others, from whom she may have an equal Claim, both from NATURE AND GRATITUDE" (68).

Affirming at once her repentence and her childlike innocence of numerous charges of errant rebelliousness, Charke devotes much of her time in the first installments of the autobiography to establishing her identity as the sentimental heroine victimized by parental dotage, family intrigue, marital exploitation and infidelity, communal viciousness, and unkind fortune. Before her reader and her father, she plays the devoted daughter who embodies the virtues of Christianity, its devotion, charity, morality, its magnanimity and forgiveness. Beyond that, she defends herself against charges that she was "a giddy, indiscreet Wife" and presents herself, in some of the most lavishly sentimental passages, as a devoted mother who tries to protect her own daughter from unwarranted suffering in the midst of poverty and humiliation. Right-minded but wrongly treated, she is "woman," more victim than agent, unjustly thrown into a cruel, inhuman world. Moreover, she speaks as sentimental heroine in a voice that is neither ironic nor self-mocking as is the voice of the transgressive Charke, but one that is dramatically sentimental, emotionally intense, lavishly devotional, humbly self-effacing. As she shares the panoply of values, visions, and voices dear to eighteenth-century sensibility and thus dear to her reader (and father), Charke seeks to exonerate her transgressive life by affirming her true membership in the class from which she herself as prodigal daughter has strayed. To the extent that she appears humbled by her errancy, blameless before the malice of others, and a true woman of her class, she vindicates herself and commands her father to reconsider his rejection of her.

As noted earlier, however, Charke's proleptic dedication hints at *two* narrative possibilities, a doubled story of doubled desires. On the one hand, it tells the modest story of the Father's daughter, the sentimental penitent who would resume her place of dependency and subordination. On the other, it tells the titillating tale of the outcast, the daughter who would vigorously, even violently, defy the Father as a "son." If, through the former role she embraces conventional forms of female selfhood and tells a woman's story in the voice of the didacticist and penitent, through the latter role she defies the conventional forms of female selfhood in eighteenth-century society: She becomes the woman who adventures in the world as a man and who speaks in the jaunty, self-mocking voice of the rebel. While the sentimental heroine's story takes place in the dramatic passages where Charke addresses her reader and, through her reader, her father, the rogue's story consumes the narrative portion of the autobiography. Therefore, entangled in the story of the penitent is a competing story, the sensational, the transgressive, the exotic story of the rogue and her progress.

In the opening pages Charke identifies herself as "one who has used her utmost endeavours to entertain" the reader with a dramatically compelling "adventure" story. Even as she makes claims for the universality of her experience—"I have, I think, taken Care to make 'em so interesting, that every Person who reads my Volume may bear a Part in some Circumstance or other in the Perusal, as there is nothing inserted but what may daily happen to every Mortal breathing"—she promises "to give some Account of my UNACCOUNTABLE LIFE" (13). In fact, the irony of the preceding disclaimer is acute: After reading her narrative the reader can hardly identify with much that has happened to her. And she herself acknowledges that her readers "will own, when they know my History, if Oddity can plead my Right to Surprise and Astonishment, I may positively claim a Title to be shewn among the Wonders of Ages past, and those to come" (13). Thus she reveals an understanding that the idiosyncratic and transgressive, that is, the "criminal" nature of her experience as a female nonpareil who lives outside the bounds of convention and propriety, will "please" and "satisfy" her reader. In doing so, it will foster sales of her "life."

As soon as she begins to tell her story, Charke re-creates the transgressive lines of her life. She describes how, at the age of four, she donned her brother's waistcoat and her father's hat and wig and walked up and down a ditch waving to everyone who came along. "But, behold," she continues, "the Oddity of my Appearance soon assembled a Croud about me; which yielded me no small Joy, as I conceived their Risibility on this Occasion to be Marks of Approbation, and walked myself into a Fever, in the happy Thought of being taken for the 'Squire" (19). The next year she mounted a small foal and rode through town followed by a procession of common people, to the great amusement and shame of her father. She describes how as an adolescent she became preoccupied with hunting and shooting, contemptuously rejecting the activities more appropriate for young girls. She assumes the role of doctor, impersonating a healer as she dispenses weird concoctions to the country people surrounding her family's home. Next she acts the part of the gardener, then stableman, then assumes the role of her mother's protector as she "saves" her from the supposed threats of the displaced stableman. Her mother, she remembers, "communicated her Fears to me, who most heroically promised to protect her Life, at the utmost Hazard of my own" (44). That occasion offered her "an Opportunity of raising my Reputation as a courageous Person, which I was extream fond of being deemed" (44–45). Moreover, she notes that she received during those years "a liberal [education], and such indeed as might have been sufficient for a Son instead of a Daughter" (17), and further that she failed in learning the fundamentals of home economy, the conventional "curriculum" for girls, "in which needful Accomplishment, I have before hinted, my Mind was entirely uncultivated" (30).

The picture Charke provides of her childhood and early adolescence suggests the degree to which the young girl desired to be the central figure in an "adventure" played out in the wider world and the degree to which that world was open only to men. Dressed as her father, she enjoys the brief belief that she is taken for him, a figure of prominence in the child's and the community's eyes. She yearns for and enjoys the adulation that the crowd accords to male heroes (herself in the ditch, on the horse, before the intruder in her home). She recognizes and enjoys the power inherent in male skills (the control of the gun) and roles (the doctor's healing, the stableman's protection). As a young girl, Charke desired to be the "son" by "dressing" in her father's clothes and by following in his footsteps. As a son she could effectively play a public role, protecting her mother, ministering to her neighbors, guarding property. The older autobiographer labels the childhood preoccupation with impersonation "my former Madness"; but the label is more rhetorical and revelatory than convincing. Those "madnesses" unmask her early desire for public significance (and attention), for activity, adventure, meaning. They suggest also that for a woman male impersonation, with its clothes, its strutting posture, its mobility, provides access to the world of movement and meaning and promises the powers and privileges, the self-enhancements and presentments that accrue to male selfhood and autobiography. She calls them madnesses for her reader's, but most particularly for her father's, sake, in order to neutralize the transgressive desire inherent in such cross-dressing. But they are unqualifiedly the fantastic entertainments and empowerments of a female child who, desiring to press more meaning out of life than she sees in the lives of women around her, including the mother whom she erases from the text, defies conventional expectations of a young girl's proper education, disposition, values, and sense of identity.[9] Beyond that, her pranks reveal, not so subtly, the young Charke's desire to displace the father, to challenge his authority and to escape her dependence on him. They are gestures of independence and personal authority, the gestures of a son rather than of a daughter.

After reconstructing her childhood self as the girl who would be boy, it is not surprising that Charke does not go on to trace the "conventional" story of a woman's actual and autobiographical life in the eighteenth century: youth spent in preparation for marriage, young adulthood spent in pursuit of the proper marriage partner, life after marriage spent fulfilling the roles of wife and mother, and a narrative "life" devoted to cataloging the accomplishments of husbands and edifying the youth of sons. This plot would more closely mirror the plot enacted by that sentimental heroine she plays in the dramatic scenes of her autobiography. When she describes her marriage, she does so sparely: Mr. Charke quickly vanishes and dies. In fact, the event that serves as the happy conclusion of so much eighteenth-century fiction brings with it the disillusionment and economic insecurity that force Charke to venture into the world as a female vagabond. Instead of providing the stabilizing plot for Charke's female life, marriage catapults her into the destabilized plot of roguish adventures.

As Charke chronicles the "unnatural" life of a female vagabond who moves through a startling variety of worldly adventures and careers in search of economic and psychological independence, she establishes resonances with the picaresque tale. Although Charke does not tell of a life lived as a literal criminal—she does not steal, murder, violate the law—she does narrate the life of a "criminal" woman, a prodigal daughter who travels through the world entangled in a "rogue's progress" of adventures, misfortunes, betrayals, deceits. As the female prodigal, she presents herself as restlessly defiant of conventions and norms, careless of reputation, alienated from her middle-class family, reduced by poverty to make a living among the homeless and the destitute, implicated in deceits and deceptions. In that world of homelessness and mutability, impermanence and vagabondage, Charke becomes a comic rogue, an endlessly self-fabricating figure who enacts multiple roles calling for multiple identities.[10]

But Charke goes further, introducing into her story an even more subversive duplicity; for what was playacting for the child becomes critical deception for the woman. She describes how, during the long years of peregrination, she dons male clothing and male identities in order to "venture into the World." Playing "the well-bred Gentleman" Mr. Brown, she becomes "the unhappy Object of Love in a young Lady, whose Fortune was beyond all earthly Power to deprive her of, had it been possible for me to have been, what she designed me, nothing less than her Husband" (106–107).[11] For a short period she becomes a "gentleman's Gentleman." She works as a waiter in a restaurant until the woman who owns it falls in love with her. Then she goes on her nine-year adventure as a "male" strolling player, even describing the experience in the male imagery of war: "I think going a Strolling is engaging in a little, dirty Kind of War, in which I have been obliged to fight so many Battles, I have resolutely determined to throw down my Commission" (187). Sometime during this period she is put in jail where, dressed as a man, she spends the night singing the songs of Macheath from *The Beggar's Opera* (215). Charke's narrative tells the story of a girl who would play the boy, a woman who would play the man, an actress who would play male roles, a sexual transgressor. In fact, the deceit of gender is the fundamental deceit around which her life turns. Presenting herself as a prodigal "son," she entertains her reader with an illicit tale of roguish cross-dressing as Mr. Brown moves through the world with energy, duplicity, and aggressiveness.

Terry Castle cautions that it is frustratingly difficult to establish an etiology of cross-dressing in earlier centuries.[12] Certainly, Charke never self-reflexively accounts for the psychological motivation behind her continued cross-dressing or the advantages of such duplicity. Any evidence of an etiology remains implicit in the childhood pranks she catalogs. The tendency to dress as a man and to play a man's role seems always to have been part of her life and imagination. And the language with which she reconstructs those earlier scenes suggests that for her the father's, rather than the mother's, world offers possibilities for self-expression. "Symbolically embracing otherness," Charke puts on the identity of a man in order to move more easily through her world, in order to escape the limitations and the vulnerabilities of female identity and life scripts.[13] On the psychological level, her cross-dressing speaks to female desire for authority, adventure, power, and mobility, the accoutrements of male selfhood. It speaks also to

female desire for freedom from the physical and psychological vulnerabilities of female dependency. Male impersonation promises empowerment.

Most important, on the narrative level the story of the cross-dressed
rogue allows Charke to write an autobiography. In providing the reader
with an interesting, even titillating story of rebellious duplicity and filial
errancy, it allows her to tell a story that will be read by her culture. But
beyond its pleasurable quality, the story of female rogue mirrors the culture's idea of "male" life scripts. Responding personally in life and narratively in text to the generic expectations of significance in life stories,
Charke finds a story that resonates with privileged cultural fictions. There is
adventure, mobility, action, self-assertion. There is a public career. There is
the challenge to the father, with the subsequent life of economic independence. Finally, there is the suppression of the mother and the realm of the
feminine that characterizes male autobiography. Assuming the adventurous masquerade of man, Charke reinscribes the myth of origins constitutive of the story of man and claims her place in the world of men, words,
and public spaces.

In the very writing of the autobiography, Charke engages in a carnivalesque
drama of impersonation, linking the process of writing autobiography with
the dynamics of selfhood captured in the remembered moments of her life.
As noted earlier, the scenes of childhood Charke includes in the early pages
of her autobiography center on her impersonations, her preoccupation
with acting as someone else, with assuming the postures and the lines of
others. On one level, the scenes become the "substantive content of the
remembered experience"; but on another, such moments speak to "a special
order of experience in the life itself that for the autobiographer is insepara-
bly linked to the discovery and invention of identity."[14] Assuming other
people's identities, roles, lines, living the plots of fictive heroes and heroines, Charke creates herself through recourse to the lives and lines of others. In that way her embrace of "impersonation" becomes, to use Olney's
phrase, a kind of "metaphor of self."[15] Moreover, if impersonation becomes
early on the characteristic way of creating her identity before the public, it
becomes also the characteristic way she presents her autobiographical self
to the world. Through writing her life story, Charke continues the process
of acting out before an audience, and "repeat[s] the psychological rhythms
of identity formation" that reach far back into childhood.[16]

The product of a cultural scavanger, Charke's autobiography is the narrative of an imposter who masquerades in a variety of roles, plots, and characters, establishing throughout her autobiography resonances with fictional
and dramatic heroines and heroes. She speaks through a cacophony of lines

from plays, poems, and novels, borrowing the language of literature to shape her narrative in the patterns of maternal and paternal stories of selfhood. In her endlessly fictive imagination, Charke patches together the thematic motifs and the rhetorical tones of social satire, low comedy, high tragedy, sentimental fiction, picaresque adventure, and criminal biography. Charke assumes all rhetorical postures, takes on all characters, plays all scenes for the dramatic possibilities inherent in them. Her autobiographical narrative imitates those theatrical productions she describes in the text: Lines, characters, speeches, and events from a variety of disparate plays and stories are woven into one polyglot presentation.

The prevalence as well as the ambivalence and confusion of this polyglot, this storytelling selfhood—which suspends Charke between the imperatives of maternal and paternal narratives—is dramatized powerfully in the central scene of the autobiography, the moment when Charke describes how her father has returned her letter of supplication unopened. Precipitating "a full Account of, I think, one of the most tragical Occurrences of my Life, which but last Week happened to me" (117), her father, "forgetful of that TENDER NAME, and the GENTLE TIES OF NATURE, returned [the letter she sent him] in a Blank" (117). Responding to his silence, Charke assumes a variety of figurative stances. She becomes the ill-served prodigal who is not "joyfully received by the offended Father." She becomes the convicted criminal on the verge of death:

> Nay, MERCY has even extended itself at the Place of Execution, to notorious Malefactors; but as I have not been guilty of those Enormities incidental to the foremention'd Characters, permit me, gentle Reader, to demand what I have done so hateful! so very grievous to his Soul! so much beyond the Reach of Pardon! that nothing but MY LIFE COULD MAKE ATONEMENT? which I can bring Witness was a Hazard I was immediately thrown into. (121)

She becomes Cordelia, the inherently virtuous and loving daughter, wronged by a malign Goneril "who neither does, or ever will, pay the least Regard to any Part of the Family, but herself," cast away by a misguided old father who becomes a kind of fool (122). Finally, she reaches for the moral superiority of the Christian saint by claiming her own act of forgiveness and thereby her greater Christian charity. Metamorphosing from role to role, figure to figure, Charke plays the dramatic scene to her audience with resourcefulness as well as with desperation.

The scene of painful metamorphosis functions as a scene of betrayal. Yet it is not Charke's father who has betrayed her most profoundly. Literature, storytelling itself, has betrayed her. Grasping at autobiographical "roles," she becomes their victim because the very metamorphosis from female role to male role calls attention to the fictive quality of Charke's narrative postures and because neither maternal nor paternal narratives serve her.

Certainly, the maternal story of the sentimental penitent, the story of vulnerable, dependent, and victimized woman, does not, cannot work for her. If she is a Cordelia, that epitome of dutiful daughter betrayed by a malign Goneril, she is a Cordelia whose father never realizes her virtue, never calls her back home to his heart. Or, rather, she is no true Cordelia, precisely because the narrative posture is transparent as imposture. If she is a Clarissa, struggling to maintain her purity and integrity in the face of familial betrayal, she is a Clarissa who does not "die" to preserve her virginity. Nor is she a Pamela, the serving girl whose true spirit wins her a title. Instead of climbing up the economic ladder through the preservation of her virginity, Charke has descended the economic ladder after sacrificing hers. Nor is she the true Christian saint, willing to suffer and to forgive her tormentors. The female roles cannot serve her because they do not fit the reality of her circumstances or the texture of her disposition. For, while she attempts to maintain the "dramatic" penitential stance of the victimized heroine who, finding herself unjustly alienated from family and social class, struggles mightily to remain true to conventional Christian values, this woman seems to relish more her role as good-natured transgressive "picaro." She becomes more rogue than penitent, romping through the world in search of adventure, however desperate that romp may be. She also romps through her narrative more as male impersonator than as sentimental heroine.

Donning the narrative clothes of the prodigal, she parades herself through town as a "manly" narrator. The "manliness" of the narrative style lies in Charke's anarchic energy, evidenced in the aggressiveness with which she tells her story and engages her reader (and her father) in her autobiographical challenge. It derives also from the loose, episodic chronology, the explosive bursts of events, characterizations, pronouncements. And the speaking posture of that "manly" narrator is jaunty, cavalier, brash, brusk, infused with the comic bravado of the self-styled rogue who remains immune to cuts and criticism, who creates herself self-expansively and self-mockingly. Willing to entertain her reader even at her own expense, Charke seems recklessly careless of her reputation: "I am certain, there is no one in the World MORE FIT THAN MYSELF TO BE LAUGHED AT. I confess myself an odd Mortal, and believe I need no Force of Argument, beyond what has already said, to bring the whole Globe terrestrial into that Opinion" (86). Mocking her own efforts to achieve meaning and public significance in her life, she nonetheless maintains the energy and power of the narrative transgressor. For one twentieth-century critic, "Charlotte Charke remains the same strolling player, careless, wild, irresponsible even in her quotations"; and "the effect produced by her narrative is one of undirected power, thunderous and murky, masculine."[17] Although that critic does not necessarily admire the reckless masculinity of Charke's narrative, he testifies to its active power.

The aggressiveness of Charke's narrative style disrupts and subverts the penitential anguish of the letter scene. Playing the transgressive and roguish "son," she prefaces the histrionic lamentation of the misunderstood and abused penitent with a defiant gesture of rebellion. Exacting a kind of vengeance on the father she would woo, Charke introduces into the text two anecdotal stories she labels as apocryphal. She describes how rumor has it that, dressed as a highwayman, she

> stopp'd [his] Chariot, presented a Pistol to his Breast, and used such Terms as I am ashamed to insert; threaten'd to blow his Brains out that Moment if he did not deliver. . . . Upbraiding him for his Cruelty in abandoning me to those Distresses he knew I underwent, when he had it so amply in his Power to relieve me: That since he would not use that Power, I would force him to a Compliance, and was directly going to discharge upon him; but his Tears prevented me, and, asking my Pardon for his ill Usage of me, gave me his Purse with threescore Guineas, and a Promise to restore me to his Family and Love; on which I thank'd him, and rode off. (114)

Categorically denying having accosted her father in that way, Charke effectually "accosts" him in recounting the rumor. As a "fictive" rogue she gives the scene to the deep-seated anger at her dependency on her father and at his abandonment of her and thereby reveals her desire for vengeance. Beyond that, she creates a father emasculated, even "feminized." Pitiful, helpless, humiliated, unheroic, he is reduced to tears of contrition. Finally, in this fantasy the daughter-"son" assumes the power of life and death over the father, reversing the dynamics of power in their real-life relationship. Charke may protest against the viciousness of the rumor, but, as she incorporates that story within her story, she enacts a fantasy of filial defiance. The second story has to do with her response when her father runs into his fishmongering daughter: Rumor has it she slaps him in the face with a fish. Again, the introduction of the rumor, if only to deny its facticity, unmasks Charke's anger and resentment at the unnatural refusal of her father to accept his prodigal daughter's repentence. In both rumors she makes of her famous father a Colley Cibber victimized by female violence, reduced to humiliating and unmanly postures. In both stories she makes of herself a Charlotte empowered to strike back, to inflict a wound on the enemy, a hero vigilant before the forces of oppression. Ironically, while Charke desires rapprochement with the father and his world, she exacts a kind of vengeance.

The "masculine" defiance captured in the apocryphal gestures characterizes the rhetorical posture of Charke's narrative after her letter has been returned unopened. She does not cower before the rejection of her father. Having vented her distress at his rejection, she subdues the stance of penitent and continues her narrative with renewed energy and intensity. What others might be reticent to reveal, Charke, with her flair for theatrical self-presentation, reveals with a kind of abandon, apparently reveling in telling her reader about her trials and tribulations. Claiming that she tells only the truth of her experience, she focuses unabashedly on her vagabondage and destitution, re-creating vivid scenes of pathos, describing constant destitution, humiliating nights in jail, flights from bailiffs and creditors, recourse to begging at the doors of rich friends. The narrative becomes a chaotic, luxuriating romp of life lived on the margins. In the midst of her narrative she even presents her plans for future enterprises, revealing a kind of "chronic" optimism underlying her errant rebelliousness. And she lashes out more directly at father, siblings, and strangers who have betrayed her. Specifically, she continues to undermine her father's authority by questioning his generosity and by making of him a kind of unnatural father. He may be famous and well respected; but, her story reveals, there is a black, "unnatural" side to the famous and revered poet laureate. Moreover, this undutiful daughter gives the reader the story of a famous father and daughter that enhances their pleasure in the scandals of the well known. The spectacle of Colley Cibber's daughter dressed as a man, imprisoned in a country town, singing the songs of Macheath from *The Beggar's Opera*, playing, that is, in drag, would undoubtedly have created a particularly titillating scandal for those interested in the lives and idiosyncrasies of the rich and famous. In her apparent effort to rescue her father from a reputation as hardened and unaffectionate parent, Charke actually emasculates him, entertaining the reader by making a fool of her father before his public. Forced to sell the body of her text to support herself, she sells his along with it.

The very writing of her life becomes a complex effort at holding her father up for ransom in an act of filial blackmail. It affects a roguish fish slap in her father's face. She professes in the opening pages her disinterested desire to recover her father's affection; but such profession is fundamentally duplicitous. In fact, the material purposes of her "small treatise" are assuredly very real. Writing her life is her latest scheme for making money and easing her destitution. If her narrative wins her reconciliation with her father, she can count on his financial support to relieve her. Like the other schemes she chronicles throughout her narrative, however, this one proves to be just another failure: Her father will not "buy" it. But her audience will; and so, when the first of her purposes fails, she continues to "sell" her life for her living, forced as she is by the economic exigencies she chronicles so effectively into an act of survival that, if it fails to earn her reconciliation with her father, at least earns her some money.

This middle-class daughter of a famous father seems, despite the very real destitution she experienced, to enjoy the writing of her autobiography, to take a perverse pleasure in recounting her romp through life as an outcast rogue, a woman defiant of all conventions, including the fundamental convention of sexual difference. The sexual cross-dressing that amplifies and thickens the pleasure of the text combines with the economic down-dressing, or cross-class dressing, to create an environment of intense disorder, social, sexual, and narrative. And yet Charke's autobiographical victory is a Pyrrhic one since the stories through which she fashions her life betray her in the end. While she provides her reader with a kind of autobiographical carnival, embedding in her story biographical fictions of her age, she does not recognize that the narrative patterns do not fit. Thus, as she cavorts with maternal and paternal narratives, they cavort with her. I noted above how the narrative of the sentimental penitent fails her. But Charke has always been more interested in paternal, rather than maternal, narratives; and it is the narratives of "masculine" selfhood that betray her most profoundly.

As Charke dons a man's story, cross-dressing narratively, she effectively unmasks her desire for a cultural life story that will bear significance, that will "speak" to her reader. In the story of the essentially good outcast who is thrown on the road to make "his" way in life, the narrative recalls that of Tom Jones. Yet, while she is like a Tom Jones thrown on the world as outcast, she is not a man, but a woman dressed as a man; and she is not a son who goes from bastardy to true filiality, but a daughter who falls from true filiality to a kind of metaphorical bastardy. Moreover, as a woman she cannot absorb the moral errancies of a Tom Jones into her tale. Tom is forgiven his healthy sexual desires. Charke must repress whatever desires she may have. There is no place for a female Tom Jones in her culture.

Nor do the stories of the prodigal and the criminal serve her any better. Playing the prodigal son, Charke informs her secular autobiography with typological references to the sacred text. Part of the "typological habits of mind" of the eighteenth century, this biblical type functioned as a popular cultural figure.[18] Yet the prodigal was a culturally valued figure of male selfhood, whose androcentric story fulfilled the culture's desire for both prodigality and reincorporation into community. In fact, rejection of the father and his authority became a sign of entry into the world of the fathers, a sign of manhood. It thereby became a figure of selfhood identified with formal autobiography. When Charke assumes the story line of the prodigal, therefore, she must wrench it to fit her story, "abstract[ing]" the biblical figure, "draw[ing it] away from the theological field of action" and embedding it in the detailed realism of a woman's sensational life story.[19] As the type is pressed through the specificities of Charke's strange story, it becomes too culturally distorted. In the end, the story of the prodigal wrapped around the story of a woman does not undermine the sanctity of the type so much as it undermines her attempt to add sanctity to her story. As a prodigal "son," she is more ridiculous than significant.

Her relationship to the story of "masculine" criminality is equally problematic. During the first half of the century especially, biographies of criminals and criminality itself captured the imagination of the English. In response to that cultural preoccupation and in turn promoting it, balladeers, pamphleteers, the new novelists (Defoe, Fielding, Smollet), prison officials—all wrote sensationalized biographies of rogues and criminals, both factual and fictional.[20] A source of great curiosity in an age enamored of the variety, eccentricities, and especially the excesses of human experience, such stories fed the culture's fascination for the narrative possibilities inherent in the lives of aberrant transgressors of social codes, laws, and relationships. Generally, however, criminal or rogue biographies of the eighteenth century served two disparate yet complementary purposes; and they told two stories. On the one hand, they spoke of grave yet exuberant transgression, ennobling the lives of figures rebellious against the laws of society and propriety. On the other, they spoke of penitence and eventual reintegration into community. After "threaten[ing] the world with disorder and with domination by the dark and often violent forces of evil," the criminal acknowledged his wrong ways and returned to the arms of social convention "so that society might be seen exercising its power to redeem the world and, in many cases, the criminal as well."[21] The structures of power within the church and the state were thereby reaffirmed, rebellion forestalled, subversiveness domesticated. Criminal biographies therefore fused titillating tales of the illicit with moralizing, sentimental tales of social rapprochement. Because they reflected both the prurient and the religious interests of the eighteenth century, criminal biographies and autobiographies "sold."[22]

Charke links her narrative explicitly to stories of criminality in the first passage of her text. She identifies herself as a female author who acknowledges the disadvantages of female authorship: "As the following History is the Product of a Female Pen, I tremble for the terrible Hazard it must run in venturing into the World, as it may very possibly suffer, in many Opinions, without perusing it" (11). Talking about the fate of female works, she alludes to the more general fate of females: For a woman (as for her work), "venturing into the World" is necessarily a "terrible Hazard" in the sense that such venturing is unconventional, improper, perhaps even illicit. Consequently, she pleads for special consideration: "I therefore humbly move for its having the common Chance of a Criminal, at least to be properly examin'd, before it is condemn'd" (11). Since Charke's grammar blurs the referent of "it," she forces an inelegant association between her "text" and a "criminal," the transgressor who, acting out of the ordinary, defies cultural codes.

Charke certainly challenges her culture's comfortable sense of its own order, revealing the fragilities of conventions and identities by providing an arena in which hierarchy is defied. Engaging in her masquerade she enters the arena of "transformation, mutability, and fluidity," where she becomes the amoral, sexually ambiguous protagonist defiant of social and sexual identities.[23] Further, her story insinuates a world of female-female relations into the text. After all, Charke describes how she traveled with a woman for many years; how they posed as man and wife; how various women fell in love with her.[24] The promise of female-female love masked by the male-female masquerade renders the life and the story even more disruptive of a social order founded on the patriarchal moralities of heterosexual relationship.

While Charke luxuriates in her "prodigal" and "criminal" masquerade, however, the story and the experience itself provide her with no illuminating moments. She is truly, as she claims in her dedication, "thoughtless" and intellectually "indolent." The masquerade in bit parts goes on and on, uninterrupted by any moment of truth before the gallows, any greater understanding of either her prodigality or her culture. The prodigal must understand the nature of prodigality, the inevitability of rebellion, and the relationship of son to father. Repentent criminals, seeing themselves for what they are, must acknowledge their crimes and seek forgiveness from society. Yet, because she plays them unself-consciously, cavalierly, neither the plot of the criminal nor that of the prodigal work for Charke. Incapable of anything more than a cavalier, unself-conscious performance, she leaves behind rhetoric with no understanding—a self-destructive bravado of language by which to declaim herself, quite entertaining but devastatingly vacuous. She becomes nothing but the polyglot of lines of stories fused together from the "orts and fragments" of her culture's stories. Narrative impersonation, the source of endless self-fabrication, becomes in Charke's life story the mechanism for self-cancellation, a dispersion of any idea of self into a series of bit parts played with rhetorical flourish.[25]

A Narrative of the Life of Mrs. Charlotte Charke offers its reader a voyeuristic romp through the disorders of male self-representation for woman. This woman who would be man leaves behind her a silence far greater than the silence signified in her father's blank page. She does not want to be woman. We see that in the repression of the mother's story, the suppression of the story of passion and sexual desire, the subversion of the story of sentimental penitent. She renders her sexual identity "impenetrable," erasing her female subjectivity from the story of man as she erases her female body in her man's clothes.[26] Yet as she becomes absorbed in male plots and masculine speaking postures, she loses her "self" precisely because she must erase the woman that she is. Self-denial is the price exacted of her in her flight toward male selfhood. Like the female figures of the nun and the queen, even the female rogue represses that which is the center of her being, her female sexuality, in pursuit of male autobiography. But she is not and cannot be man. Promising empowerment, male literary prototypes deliver only alienation, isolation, and self-delusion. Castle says of her that she is not only the victim of family, strangers, and fate, but also, and most important, a victim of literature.[27] More particularly, she is the victim of male "autobiography," in life and in her text.

A woman dressed as a man, Charke cannot place herself comfortably within the narratives of her culture. She is truly "peerless." With no self-illumination and self-reflectiveness, she cannot discover who and what she is. Charlotte Charke's autobiographical gesture is therefore a futile one. She fails in this narrative venture as she fails in venture after venture in life. She wins no emotional or financial reprieve from her father. But more significantly she wins through to no clearer understanding of her past, herself, or her sexuality. Betrayed by both maternal and paternal narratives and her own lack of reflectiveness about those narratives, she becomes only endless words strung together.

If Charlotte Charke had had more self-knowledge, less indolence and thoughtlessness, she might have pulled off a major subversion of the ideology of gender, a major disruption in the notion of autobiography. She certainly had the energy and spirit to do so. In embracing the "male" dress of narrative impersonation, however, Charke unwittingly affirms the priority of male autobiography, and thus the ordination of man over woman, of male storytelling over female storytelling. She may appear to be rebelling against a social ideology that constructs female selfhood in certain forms of dependency and passivity in her "male" fabrications; but in her flight from conventional "female" selfhood to "male" selfhood, she reaffirms the lineaments of the ideology of gender and thus serves the very fictions that confine her.

Charke's text is like the body of those prostitutes among whom she lived. Forced by fate and the waywardness of her own character to sell her self/text to make a living, she becomes to her culture the sign of misguided, fallen woman. Her "life" becomes one of those "exempla" her culture uses to secure the ideologies of gender on which it rests, to make sure that women do not aspire to empowering life scripts. To the extent that it dramatizes the fate of misguided womanhood, it confirms the patriarchal stories of her culture by dramatically showing the price woman pays for transgressing cultural conventions and patriarchal authority: the rootlessness, destitution, and eccentricity that attend the female outcast, especially the female outcast who "admitted and realized her desire to act forcefully."[28] The power of the sign is reflected in the words of the person who writes an introduction to the 1827 edition of her autobiography: Her "life will serve to shew what very strange creatures may exist, and the endless diversity of habits, tastes and inclinations which may spring up spontaneously, like weeds, in the hot-bed of corrupt civilization."[29] It is reflected also in the words of the "Sequel": "The fate of this victim to an innate taste for eccentricity and vagabondism may excite surprise, but scarcely sympathy. Born in affluence, educated with care and tenderness, and possessed of at least respectable talents, the misfortunes of this extraordinary woman were altogether of her own creating."[30] Instead of challenging convention, Charke's story ends up supporting it.

The body of the unself-conscious prostitute serves the desires of others rather than the desires of the self. Or, rather, the desires of the prostitute become so confused and problematic that she cannot see herself through the role she plays. Charke titillates, but she does not discover her own source of desire. As a rebellious "son" who lacks self-reflectiveness, Charke fails to escape her dependency on the father. Instead of throwing off the father's power and assuming her own independence, she remains disempowered psychologically, financially, narratively, ideologically. As a result, she ends up serving rather than challenging the pleasure of the patriarchs or the ordination of masculine autobiography.

SEVEN

Harriet Martineau's *Autobiography*

The Repressed Desire of a Life like a Man's

> I fully expect that both you and I shall
> occasionally feel as if I did not discharge a
> daughter's duty, but we shall both remind
> ourselves that I am now as much a citizen
> of the world as any professional *son* of
> yours could be.

—Harriet Martineau to her mother, July 8, 1833

Charlotte Charke dons the clothes and gestures of the man as she sets out on her adventures, virtually erasing the signature of her mother on her life. The fictions of "woman" that she does attend to as she plays the part of the sentimental heroine in her story are undermined by the bravado of the quixote. Centering her narrative attention on the father and the fictions of "man," she plays the prodigal "son," imitating and rebelling against the father as well as against his middle-class proprieties and conventions. Dressed up as a man in both life and text, she manages before her death to offer the reader a luxuriating romp through the margins of transgressive female selfhood. But her romp fails to eventuate in self illumination that might render it truly subversive. In the end Charke dies a silent death, alone in her poverty and marginality.

In the next century, Harriet Martineau also assumes the role of the "manly" woman, appropriating the prerogatives and privileges of male selfhood; but the dynamics of her "masculine" selfhood are entirely different from those of Charke's. When Martineau takes up the pen to write her autobiography, she looks back on a radically different experience. Having achieved public recognition for her intellectual and political accomplishments, she has secured her place in English life and history. Her writings are widely read; her opinions and advice are anxiously sought by political leaders; her knowledge of other cultures is extensive. An intellectually and financially independent woman, Martineau has become famous in her own right, not because she is someone else's daughter or wife. Thus, when Martineau writes her *Autobiography*, she assumes her authority to speak as an acknowledged figure of the time.

"From my youth upwards," she tells her reader,

> I have felt that it was one of the duties of my life to write my autobiography. I have always enjoyed, and derived profit from, reading that of other persons, from the most meagre to the fullest: and certain qualities of my own mind,—a strong consciousness and a clear memory in regard to my early feelings,—have seemed to indicate to me the duty of recording my own experience. When my life became evidently a somewhat remarkable one, the obligation presented itself more strongly to my conscience: and when I made up my mind to interdict the publication of my private letters, the duty became unquestionable.[1]

The tone of moral rectitude and self-confidence evident in that opening passage pervades both volumes of Martineau's life story. The insecurities, the ambivalent desires of a Charke, of a Kempe, or of a Cavendish, are tucked centuries away from the staunch certitudes of Martineau's speaking posture as she reviews her life from the security of a considerable public stature and from the psychological vantage point of self-satisfaction and intellectual confidence, not from the vantage point of failure, destitution, and cavalier rebellion that characterizes Charke's retrospective.

Confidence in the importance of her individual destiny derived from the culture's ideological preoccupations. The romantic poets had created in the reading public an appetite for the exploration of subjective experience, a fascination with psychology also promoted and satisfied by the nineteenth-century novel. Autobiography and biography mirrored that interest in the unfolding of individual destiny. Joining such works as John Stuart Mill's *Autobiography*, Mrs. Gaskell's *Life of Charlotte Brontë*, Brontë's *Jane Eyre*, and Dickens's *David Copperfield*, Martineau's *Autobiography* told in concert with them the evolutionary story of selfhood as it traced the curve of individual experience from a tormented childhood to the autumnal years of personal satisfaction and social integration.[2] Autobiography and biography simultaneously satisfied a reading public fascinated by the story of individualism. "In an increasingly competitive economy," notes Mary Poovey, "individual effort became the mark of past accomplishments and the guarantor of future success; this was the era of the 'self-made man,' when aristocratic privilege could finally be challenged on a wide scale by individuals with talent, opportunity, and the capacity for simple hard work."[3] Further, autobiography responded to the public's desire for information about the lives of famous people, those larger-than-life "Carlylian" figures whose influence on the unfolding of history was profound. In a time when traditional religious beliefs eroded before the onslaught of scientific discoveries and political and social theories, the writer and artist took on the role of prophet and truth-sayer. Of course, the famous romantics had lived lives of mythical dimensions as they defied social conventions in the name of creativity and freedom. But Victorian literary figures also assumed a prominent place in the English imagination, redefining as they did the way human beings situated themselves in relationship to God, to nature, to history, and to each other.

Martineau does indeed join a distinguished group of writers engaged in the autobiographical project. Yet the list just rehearsed underscores the fact that autobiography proper remained a male preserve. Women writers on the list wrote either biography (Gaskell) or autobiographical novel (Charlotte Brontë), not public autobiography. Women not on the list may have written about themselves but did so in socially acceptable, and more private, forms. As Linda H. Peterson suggests, they "turned to their private journals not because they desired to produce whitehot records of the moment, but because they were judged incapable of writing autobiography in its standard form."[4] Peterson goes on to describe how the arguments about women's unsuitability for the autobiographical enterprise derived from certain notions of woman's intellectual difference, a difference captured clearly in such works as Hannah More's influential *Strictures on the Modern System of Female Education*, published in 1799:

> Women have equal *parts*, but are inferior in *wholeness* of mind, in the integral understanding: that though a superior woman may possess single faculties in equal perfection, yet there is commonly a juster proportion in the mind of a superior man: that if women have in equal degree the faculty of fancy which creates images and the faculty of memory which collects and stores ideas, they seem not to possess in equal measure the faculty of comparing, combining, analysing, and separating these ideas; that deep and patient thinking which goes to the bottom of a subject; nor that power of arrangement which knows how to link a thousand connected ideas in one dependent train, without losing sight of the original idea out of which the rest grow, and on which they all hang.[5]

Descriptions of female difference such as More's reveal a cultural ideology that would have effectively discouraged women from writing in an autobiographical tradition associated in the mid-nineteenth century with an analytic, summative, retrospective practice. Furthermore, as Peterson suggests, women faced other obstacles in thinking about autobiography. The practice demands confidence in the significance of the narrator's life, a confidence that in women was weak or nonexistent, in part because they lacked the wide range of experience open to men and the sense of authority to write at all for public self-display.

"Martineau," writes Peterson, "had no desire to circumvent a primary literary tradition simply because she was a woman or to write autobiographical fiction because it was a typical form of feminine self-expression."[6] On the contrary, she maintained the prerogatives of male intellectuality and embraced the autobiographical purpose and practice in the face of imminent death.[7] Confident in her authority to speak publicly, she offered her narrative as a gift to a public that would know the significance of its heroes, those individuals who best exemplified the optimistic side of the Victorian imagination, its utilitarianism, its positivism, its belief in progress. In fact, conceiving of her life as a model for human development, she imagined herself as representative "man." Despite her confidence, despite her certitude, however, this representative "man" remained keenly aware of her precarious position as unrepresentative "woman." Like Charke, though to nowhere near the same extent, the controversial Martineau had experienced a certain alienation from society. She had been labeled "an ill-favoured dogmatizing, masculine spinster"; and she had been indicted as "[a] *woman* who thinks child-bearing a *crime against society!* An *unmarried woman* who declaims against *marriage!*"[8] Inevitably, the other story of her life, the muted drama of repression, disrupts the evolutionary line of "masculine" identity. For me, at least, the tension generated by competing fictions of selfhood tinges the stolid, verbose autobiography with a melancholy shadow. Martineau paid a high price for her unconventional life, a price whose effect permeates the very writing of her autobiography. Like Charke before her, she too is betrayed by the story of "man," by the very storytelling demanded of "autobiography."

For Victorians, autobiography commenced in childhood, that distant place of beginnings. Accordingly, the structural pattern that comes to define Martineau's *Autobiography* originates, as it does in so much fiction of the century, in the troubled state of infancy and childhood. Earlier autobiographers lingered far less critically on those years. Kempe never mentions them. Cavendish and Charke briefly describe some details of their early experiences; but both women do so as a way of suggesting the kind of young girls they were—the former raised in the sheltered environment of ideal femininity, the latter anxious to command the powers and attention of youthful male selfhood. Their real narrative interest lies in the experiences of adulthood. In contrast, the nineteenth-century autobiographer became fascinated by the idea that at birth the mind is effectively a *tabula rasa* and that the subsequent development of the "innocent" child depended intimately on environmental influences. The Victorians, Martineau among them, became acutely aware of the formal qualities of human development, especially important in an age so challenged by theories of evolution.

Throughout the seventeenth century the idea of childhood had changed radically as Locke's *Treatise on Education* altered the cultural understanding of human development. Emphasizing the importance of the senses as the original source of ideas and information about the world, Locke questioned the efficacy of educating the child through programs designed to proceed from abstract reasoning.[9] The new consciousness of childhood as a critical time in the development of the adult gained cultural currency through the writings of Rousseau *(Émile, Julie, Confessions)*, followed by the work of English romantics such as Wordsworth (whose *Prelude* "revealed that there *was* an epic dimension to childhood experience") and of German romantics such as Goethe *(Dichtung und Wahrheit* and *Wilhelm Meisters Lehrjahre).*[10] By the middle of the nineteenth century, stories of childhood fired the public's and the writer's imagination. "If childhood is in one sense a historical 'invention,'" comments Luann Walthur as she explores the representation of childhood in Victorian autobiography, "the Victorian autobiographical childhood is in another sense a literary one, since never before this period had so many English writers been interested in recalling their early lives at length within the form of sustained prose autobiography."[11] But two antithetical representations of childhood emerged: the nostalgic memory of idyllic belonging rendered powerfully in Wordsworth's *Prelude* and the haunting memory of physical and psychological deprivation. Many Victorian autobiographies and novels, galvanized by and grounded in evolutionary tropes, described in powerful scenes the constrictions of loveless and orphaned beginnings. Martineau's is one of those evocations of profound loneliness, remarkably similar to Brontë's *Jane Eyre*, Dickens's *David Copperfield*, Mill's *Autobiography*.

Her narrative of childhood establishes the origins of her desire to repress the vulnerable "woman" within and to live life like a man. Consequently, the early pages of the *Autobiography* invite detailed attention. Since she "really remember[s] little that was not painful at that time of my life" (I:17), the memories that the older woman pieces together re-create a story of intense suffering. The ambiance of a lonely, fearful, emotionally "orphaned" childhood overwhelms the early pages of the narrative, which remain of all the work the most compelling, vivid, memorable. She describes how, as an infant abandoned to a wet nurse, a common practice among the prosperous middle class, she literally starves because the wet nurse has no milk. When her mother discovers the undernourished Martineau, she forces milk on a child who ever after experiences nausea in response to it. (This is the first moment in the text when Martineau's mother is associated with her illnesses, but it will not be the last.) During childhood and adolescence the young Martineau, continuing to receive little nurturance from her mother, responds desperately to the kindnesses of occasional strangers or relatives.

Throughout the early pages of the story, Martineau portrays her mother as a strong-willed, distant, capricious, authoritarian figure. At once powerful and oppressive, her mother becomes the locus of emotional deprivation and physical disease.[12] (Of her father, Martineau says almost nothing except when she describes her response to his death.)

In that environment, the child's relationship to sensual experience became problematic. Particularly skilled in re-creating the kinds of experience that characterize early infancy and childhood, Martineau describes how she responded to every sensual impression with fear, pain, and shame: fear at the light of the magic lantern, pain at the grating sensation of a rough hand, the coarse feel of sheets, the repulsive taste of milk, the distressing sound of mattresses being beaten.[13] Seemingly innocuous moments of sight, sound, taste, touch, smell press unremittingly on the imagination of the supersensitive child with the result that her body becomes a constant source of displeasure and disgust. The only effective way she finds to protect herself from that discomfort is to repress her sensuality, so that, by nature or by psychological fiat, one sense after another is gradually taken from her. Moreover, sickly, lonely, fearful, ashamed, the young child becomes mute: "It never occurred to me to speak of anything I felt most" (I:9). "I went on for years together in a puzzle, for want of its ever occurring to me to ask questions," the older woman recalls (I:24). Intimidated by the world and by others, the young Martineau cannot articulate her own desires. Since she has no voice of her own, others perceive her to be "dumb," applying to her the maxim "slow and sure" (I:17).

Martineau recalls how, as she represses more and more of her adolescent desires, she engages, on the one hand, in self-destructiveness and, on the other, rebellion:

> While I was afraid of everybody I saw, I was not in the least afraid of God. Being usually very unhappy, I was constantly longing for heaven, and seriously, and very frequently planning suicide in order to get there. I was sure that suicide would not stand in the way of my getting there. I knew it was considered a crime; but I did not feel it so. I had a devouring passion for justice;— justice, first to my own precious self, and then to other oppressed people. Justice was precisely what was least understood in our house, in regard to servants and children. Now and then I desperately poured out my complaints; but in general I brooded over my injuries, and those of others who dared not speak and then the temptation to suicide was very strong. (I:14)

The autobiographer recognizes the self-destructiveness inherent in such childhood repression as she recalls the fantasy of self-erasure; but she also asserts the importance of the child's ability to name the situation as "injustice" and to identify with others silenced by the forces of authority and tyranny. In other words, she recognizes the child's effort to move beyond emotional responses to an intellectual analysis that occasions understanding. Acutely aware of injustice while yet too young to discover an effective means of combatting it, the young Martineau remains silent publicly but suffers privately: "The interior rebellion kept my conscience in a state of perpetual turmoil" (I:17). Such constant internal turmoil leads Martineau to live ever more centrally inside herself. Deprived of the body of the mother for nurturance and deprived of her own senses, the child turns inward to the quiet spaces of the mind in order to find a place of identity and meaning. Appearing "dumb" on the outside, she is on the inside alive, questioning, pursuing knowledge, grappling with injustice: "In an intellectual life I found then, as I have found since, refuge from moral suffering, and an always unexhausted spring of moral strength and enjoyment" (I:50). Promising empowerment, the intellectual life will relieve her of suffering, release her into self-confidence, and provide the interpretative patterns that invest experience with meaning. Unlike the self-erasure of suicide, the life of the mind gives the rebel a way to confront injustice and authoritarianism.

Influenced by evolutionary theory, especially by the belief that environment is central in shaping individual destiny, Martineau structures her story of childhood in terms of its relationship to her later intellectual development. Ironically, childhood suffering as it becomes the source of later accomplishment assumes a beneficial aspect. In fact, Martineau joins other Victorian novelists and autobiographers in affirming the ultimate efficacy of suffering.[14] She would not have recommended to parents that they model their relationships with children on her own life; and yet, had she not suffered from self-disgust and from an inner turmoil made more potent for lack of the ability to voice her sense of confusion, pain, and shame, she would not have sought sustenance in the intellectual life and thus achieved the public reputation she did.

Even more important, the young girl would not have developed the storytelling capacity that serves her intellectual and emotional purposes. Martineau describes how as a young girl she applied her "methodical" mind to the task of "distribut[ing] scripture instructions under the heads of the virtues and vices, so as to have encouragement or rebuke always ready at hand" (I:27). While she pokes fun at herself for the presumption of wrenching the Bible into her own maxims for good living, she nonetheless reveals the pattern-making, or hermeneutical, propensity that characterized her early response to life. Patterns provided a means of control, making life more coherent and tractable, less chaotic and threatening. Through pattern making the child could use her mind to overcome the pains of emotional deprivation. Early patterns of self-expression and identity, as suggested in the discussion of Charke, become paradigmatic. Further, "these self-defining acts," as Paul John Eakin notes, "may be re-enacted as the autobiographical narrative is being written."[15] In Martineau's case, the autobiographical project is another one of those attempts, first identified in the child, to control her life by imposing a pattern on it. In that way she would make her "life" a maxim, an edifying model for others to live and to learn by.

After describing a painful, stifled, repressive childhood and an adolescence spent withdrawing into religion and literature, Martineau goes on to chronicle her public career as an author, focusing on those first electrifying attempts at publication, then detailing the circumstances of her authorship of the Political Economy series, her journeys to America and the Middle East, and her subsequent literary work. Here is the exceptional woman at work, absorbed in a consequential vocation, surrounded in her text as in life with famous personages, involved in exciting adventures. But the *Autobiography* offers more than a retrospective summary of a life's work, more than glimpses at the famous people who surrounded her. Looking forward to death and backward over the past, Martineau finds, as she was wont to do from an early age, a clear pattern, what she calls "the progression of a mind." An evolutionary figure of selfhood, such progression reflected a pattern dear to the Victorian sensibility, one that seemed to satisfy a culture drawn to the idea of human progress, individual and social. In literature that cultural fascination crystallized in the emergence and maturity of what became known as the *Bildungsroman*. For Wilhelm Dilthey, a student of the structures of selfhood in the nineteenth century, the formal qualities of the *Bildungsroman* were specific: "A regulated development within the life of the individual is observed, each of its stages has its own intrinsic value and is at the same time the basis for a higher stage. The dissonances and conflicts of life appear as the necessary growth points through which the individual must pass on his way to maturity and harmony."[16] The structure of Martineau's autobiography parallels that fictive pattern, its idea of progressive selfhood, its developmental plot.

The overall design of the *Autobiography* is purposive. The autobiographer divides her narrative into discrete stages of growth, into chronological periods and sections within them. Characterized by its own unique preoccupations, each stage follows naturally from the previous one and prepares the way for the next. The autobiographer even provides the reader with signposts, projecting forward at certain points in the text, implanting in the story line expectations about the future and, in doing so, testifying to the inevitability of destiny. Moreover, all the difficulties (the hearing problems, the loss of financial security, the tumor that confines her to bed for five years) function as chastening and eventually energizing difficulties. Each

successive obstacle has a salutory effect on the line of her life, the development of her ideas, the movement toward mature vision. Each potentially
disempowering and imprisoning experience becomes paradoxically a liberating obstacle that leads her to the freedom she desires. Everything fits the
hermeneutical framework.

The fictive pattern of the *Bildungsroman* provides the general structure
for Martineau's story. But the specific characteristics of her journey derive
their definition from the epistemological categories Martineau adapted
from Auguste Comte, whose major work, *Cours de Philosophie Positive*, she
translated and abridged in 1853. Concerned from her earliest years about
the impact of familial tyranny embodied in the figure of her mother, increasingly aware of the importance of systematic education as an avenue for
escape from tyranny and injustice, Martineau found Comte's developmental categories the most powerful hermeneutical tool for understanding the
world and herself. According to Valerie Kossew Pichanick, "she seized hold
of its main elements: that humankind should seek to understand only the
phenomena of the knowable; that the West should be liberated from anach-
ronistic theologians and anarchic metaphysicians in order to constitute 'a
true sociocracy'; and that society should assume the responsibility for its
own education."[17] When in 1855 she looked back on the past, she subjected
her own life to a positivist analysis and, in the language of positivist philosophy, traced the observable law of its evolutionary development through the
theological, the metaphysical, and the scientific stages to "the open sky of
knowledge." At each of the first two stages, the younger Martineau is
trapped in an epistemological quagmire, confined first by theological and
later by metaphysical fictions through which she projects her own self-
absorbed desires for certitude and belonging onto the face of reality. Pro-
gressing from a childhood of mythological innocence and repression,
through Necessarian Unitarianism, with its metaphysical desire to discover
causal relationship, she finally reaches the intellectual freedom of a scientific rationalism grounded in empirical phenomenon. As she describes it,
her life becomes a series of successive deliveries from bondage until, in the
language of political euphoria, she finds herself "with the last link of my
chain snapped,—a free rover on the broad, bright breezy common of the
universe" (I:89). It is also a journey with psychological ramifications. A
slave to her early self-consciousness, her painful emotions, intellectual limitations, and mythologies, the maturing woman goes through a series of
awakenings and conversions. After long and difficult struggle, she arrives
via her intellectual journey at the psychological freedom of total selflessness, effectually escaping the bondage of self-reflecting interpretations or,
as she calls it, "the prison of my own self, wherein I had formerly sat trying
to interpret life and the world,—much as a captive might undertake to

paint the aspect of Nature from the gleams and shadows and faint colours reflected on his dungeon walls" (II:28–29).

The law of her life's unfolding and the consequent purposiveness of her storytelling testify to the legitimacy of her philosophical interpretation and of her positivist developmental paradigm.[18] Having arrived at the pinnacle of intellectual and personal freedom, she affirms for her reader the rightness of the intellectual, psychological, and vocational road she has traveled. But hers is not an isolated achievement. Since ontogeny recapitulates phylogeny, it is simultaneously an achievement of all humankind. The evolution of her intellectual development recapitulates the evolutionary progress of humanity (species life) itself, from its infancy of mythological beliefs, through its adolescence of metaphysical beliefs, to its maturity of scientific positivism. Her story is the story of civilization's advancement. Karl Joachim Weintraub suggests that this universalizing phenomenon is characteristic of nineteenth-century autobiography generally, remarking that the "full form of historical mindedness came to the fore when the trust in the power of genetic explanation became wedded to the fascination with individual specificity as a treasured thing."[19] The hero of her own *Bildungsroman*, Martineau gives narrative and cultural coherence to her life, locating its meaning in the ideology of the nineteenth century.

This evolutionary figure is decidedly a secular fiction, part of what Michel Foucault would call the century's increasingly secular *episteme*. Yet, while it cannot be construed as "spiritual" in a traditional sense, it nonetheless imitates a "spiritual" figure of selfhood in another. The language of the conclusion captures the eschatology of the quest:

> I am confident that a bright day is coming for future generations. Our race has been as Adam created at nightfall. The solid earth has been but dark, or dimly visible, while the eye was inevitably drawn to the mysterious heavens above. There, the successive mythologies have arisen in the east, each a constellation of truths, each glorious and fervently worshipped in its course; but the last and noblest, the Christian, is now not only sinking to the horizon, but paling in the dawn of a brighter time. The dawn is unmistakable; and the sun will not be long in coming up. The last of the mythologies is about to vanish before the flood of a brighter light. . . . In the extinction of that suspense, and the discrediting of that selfish quackery, I see the prospect, for future generations, of a purer and loftier virtue, and a truer and sweeter heroism than divines who preach such self-seeking can conceive of. When our race is trained in the morality which belongs to ascertained truth, all "fear and trembling" will be left to children; and men will have risen to a capacity for higher work than saving themselves,—to that of "working out" the welfare of their race, not in "fear and trembling," but with serene hope and joyful assurance.
>
> The world as it is is growing somewhat dim before my eyes; but the world as it is to be looks brighter every day. (II:123–24)

The language of selfhood is here infused with the prophetic voice of biblical hermeneutics as the autobiographer traces a "spiritual" pattern of development from early "bondage" to eventual release into the freedom of selflessness. But her narrative does not retell the "Christian" story, modeled after the Augustinian pattern of salvation so powerful an influence in the history of spiritual autobiography. Nor is it informed by the biblical typology that characterized so much life writing throughout the seventeenth, eighteenth, and nineteenth centuries.[20] Unlike other autobiographers of her culture, Martineau does not recover her life story through the typological enactments of biblical figures. She is no prodigal daughter. She is no Israelite lost in the wilderness. She is no Adam expelled from the garden into the knowledge of original sin. No David fighting Goliath. No Paul before and after conversion. And she is certainly no Eve. Moreover, the scenes of her life do not reenact the archetypal scenes of Christianity. Such scenes of selfhood are, in fact, the very scenes she has successfully escaped, as the passage above attests.

In language redolent of biblical prophesy, Martineau subverts biblical authority, turning the textures of its language against Christian pieties. Indeed, through her autobiography this woman would offer an alternative hermeneutics, a new way of interpreting the world and the self. Linda Peterson has argued persuasively that nineteenth-century women had a problematic relationship to the typological traditions of biblical hermeneutics. Because they were forbidden access to the priesthood, women were denied the formal training characteristic of that profession, including training in biblical hermeneutics. Additionally, hermeneutics required knowledge of classical languages, not included in the makepiece curriculum common to girls' education.[21] The education women did receive in biblical interpretation would have been personalized (as Martineau's description of her own relationship to the Bible attests), not systematic. Thus they could not bring to the writing of a spiritual autobiography the same kind of interpretative figures and speaking postures as could their male counterparts.

Self-trained and fiercely motivated, intellectual women began to appropriate bits and pieces of traditions, philosophical ideas, and political ideologies that best served their struggle toward a fuller selfhood. The struggle toward a satisfying hermeneutics is apparent in Martineau's *Autobiography;* for she recognized that, while the biblical tradition offered a template for individual conversion and spiritual growth, it could not clear a space for the figure of an empowered female selfhood. The Christian paradigm was inescapably engendered. Rejecting Christianity, therefore, she did more than reject an outdated mythology; she rejected specific fictions about herself as a woman. But if she did not appropriate the figures of Christian typology and biblical hermeneutics, she was nonetheless motivated by an analogous hermeneutical preoccupation. In that sense, as Peterson notes, her life story "echoes" the conventional patterns of androcentric self-writing—but with an important difference. She introduced a newer, alternative figure of selfhood, thinking her life through the Comtian paradigm, which she found responsive to female desire for a "spiritual" identity. That hermeneutics was as much Martineau as Comte since the two philosophers differed significantly in their vision of woman. "Biological analysis," asserts Comte, "presents the female sex, in the human species especially, as constitutionally in a state of perpetual infancy, in comparison with the other; and therefore more remote, in all important aspects, from the ideal type of the race."[22] Apparently Martineau blindfolded herself to whole areas of Comtian thought, adopting from him only those aspects of his philosophical system that resonated with her own analysis.[23] In doing so she wrenched his schema to her own purposes, as she had earlier wrenched the Bible, transforming it from an engendered vision of human possibility to one that gives woman a place of power, language, and expansive, rather than constricted, selfhood.

Perhaps the most critical freedom she came to know, then, was hermeneutical freedom.[24] Through access to an alternative interpretative pattern, she could escape the tyranny of cultural fictions condemning women to cultural insignificance and silence. Instead of being confined in the home as a Coventry Patmore "angel," that redemptive being nailed to the pedestal, Martineau joined the company of men as they marched on their progression toward mind. Refusing the worship even Comte would accord to woman as abstract idea rather than as flesh-and-blood reality, she descended from the pedestal and left the home to become her own interpreter. No guardian of the emotional life of man, she would become his intellectual equal. But, if her heroic life exemplifies the most advanced form of human life generally, it nonetheless exemplifies male rather than female selfhood. Philosopher, author, world traveler, political consultant, Martineau presents herself as the exceptional woman who lives the life of a man. Playing the "son" to her mother, she ventures into the world. Intellectually and economically independent, she speaks with the authority of man. Posterity and her own time, she is convinced, will accept the unconventional transvestism: "Whatever a woman proves herself able to do, society will be thankful to see her do,—just as if she were a man" (I:302).

The very form of her story reinforces that transvestism as she privileges an androcentric vision of autobiographical selfhood by telling a "public," rather than a "private," story, tracing in a causal line the empirically established "progression of a mind." The "exceptional woman" who is simultaneously the "representative man," Martineau gives her reader a story "just as if she were a man." Assuming the universal significance of her life, she educates her culture about the possibilities for female selfhood that would allow her, and other women who followed her lead, to live like men.

Speaking in a voice of "masculine" certainty, Martineau assumes the significance of her achievement and the authority of her self-asserting story. Yet she is no man, but a "manly" woman who is vulnerable to the cultural fictions about appropriate female behavior circulating through the lines of her narrative. As she participates in the celebration of individualism by speaking about herself forcefully, directly, autobiographically, she violates the prescriptive behavior constituting the ideology of female propriety and invites speculation about her immodest, transgressive behavior. Her very words become signs of contamination, reminding the public of the sexuality lying in wait beneath the veneer of the proper lady.[25] To avoid censure, to justify having lived her life and having narrated her story like a man, therefore, Martineau wraps a story of conventional female selfhood around the evolutionary story line.

Always, she maintains that, despite having lived an unconventional life, she has remained the "good" woman, taking care to define her idea of good woman through the stories of "good" and "bad" women with which she punctuates her text. On one side, she aligns women of public prominence who "think" like men but who act like proper Victorian ladies, with modesty, propriety, self-sacrifice. Intellectual but dispassionate, they effectively suppress passionate emotions and sexual desire. There is Mrs. Somerville: "It was delightful to see her always well-dressed and thoroughly womanly in her conversation and manners, while unconscious of any peculiarity in her pursuits" (I:269). There is Joanna Baillie. "I have solaced and strengthened myself with the image of Joanna Baillie, and with remembering the invulnerable justification which she set up for intellectual superiority in women, while we may hope that the injury done to that cause by blue stockings and coquettes will be scarcely more enduring than their own trumpery notoriety" (I:271). On the other side, she places those bluestockings whom she condemns for vulgar self-promotion, immodest self-display, because they flaunt their intellectual powers aggressively before the public. Her commentary on Margaret Fuller places the American woman in both categories: "She was then unconsciously approaching the hour of that remarkable regeneration which transformed her from the dreaming and haughty pedant into the true woman. In a few months more, she had loved and married; and how interesting and beautiful was the closing period of her life, when husband and child concentrated the powers and affections which had so long run to waste in intellectual and moral eccentricity" (I:518). Even more important, however, Martineau includes among the "bad" women the passionate ones. Fanny Kemble's "passionate nature" disturbs her (I:275).

So does Mary Wollstonecraft, that "poor victim of passion" (I:301). Such women call forth Martineau's fiercest (most passionate!) invective:

> Women who would improve the condition and chances of their sex must, I am certain, be not only affectionate and devoted, but rational and dispassionate, with the devotedness of benevolence, and not merely of personal love. But Mary Wollstonecraft was, with all her powers, a poor victim of passion, with no control over her own peace, and no calmness or content except when the needs of her individual nature were satisfied. . . . Nobody can be further than I am from being satisfied with the condition of my own sex, under the law and custom of my own country; but I decline all fellowship and co-operation with women of genius or otherwise favourable position, who injure the cause by their personal tendencies. . . . The best friends of that cause are women who are morally as well as intellectually competent to the most serious business of life, and who must be clearly seen to speak from conviction of the truth, and not from personal unhappiness. The best friends of the cause are the happy wives and the busy, cheerful, satisfied single women, who have no injuries of their own to avenge, and no painful vacuity or mortification to relieve. . . . The Wollstonecraft order set to work at the other end, and, as I think, do infinite mischief; and, for my part, I do not wish to have any thing to do with them. (I:301–303)

Applauding the woman who thinks and acts like a "man," dispassionately, rationally, Martineau condemns those who succumb to the winds of passion and remain imprisoned in the self. So imprisoned, they betray the cause of women because they cannot in their passion enact the scenario of male selfhood and thus affirm woman's right to the life of a man. Rejecting membership in the "Wollstonecraft order," claiming membership in the company of "best friends," Martineau presents herself as "the busy, cheerful, satisfied single" woman.

Because the figure of the happy single woman challenges the ideology of woman's proper life script, the process by which the autobiographer establishes textually the legitimacy of her role as a "spinster" unmoved by passion remains complex and fascinating. Early on, she re-creates herself as a rather unattractive little girl. The good Victorian, she assumes partial responsibility for her pain and suffering, despite the culpable actions of those around her, by characterizing herself as difficult. "Of course, my temper and habit of mind must have been excessively bad," she writes. "I have no doubt I was an insufferable child for gloom, obstinacy and crossness" (I:33). Later she comments: "I look back upon another scene with horror at my own audacity, and wonder that my family could endure me at all" (I:65).[26] While Martineau is not beyond suggesting that her parents, especially her mother, treated her inappropriately—"Still, when I remember my own placability,—my weakness of yielding every thing to the first word or tone of tenderness, I cannot but believe that there was grievous mistake in the case, and that even a little more sympathy and moral support would have spared me and others a hideous amount of fault and suffering" (I:33)—she nonetheless affirms that her personality was not a pleasant one. Repressed, ashamed, inwardly rebellious, serious, physically plain, the young Martineau did not conform to the fiction of the ideal little girl.

As she gradually loses her hearing, the adolescent Martineau becomes even more unattractive.[27] Yet the autobiographer neutralizes the real pain of that experience by placing the deafness in her eschatological framework: "This same deafness is about the best thing that ever happened to me" (I:59), she writes, because the suffering it caused and the resources it demanded strengthen her forebearance and make her more self-sufficient. The deafness also releases her from the conventional activities of the young lady, as the following passage suggests:

The great calamity of my deafness was now opening upon me. . . . My beloved hour of the day was when the cloth was drawn, and I stole away from the dessert, and read Shakspere by firelight in winter in the drawing-room. My mother was kind enough to allow this breach of good family manners; and again at a subsequent time when I took to newspaper reading very heartily. (I:53–54)

Deafness reinforces certain proclivities of character. It also provides both the occasion and the excuse for her to turn away from the social life expected of a young woman to the silent world of books and the uncharted space of intellect. Later it protects her from the fate of governess, the usual occupation for the middle-class woman without money. Moreover, as symbolic fortress, it also protects her from the social criticism her unconventional life invites.

The autobiographer describes a younger version of herself as personally unattractive, intellectually independent, socially unconventional. But significantly, she carefully defends herself against charges that she *chose* to live the unconventional life of the "masculine spinster." She could not control the devastating environment of her childhood. She could not control the ravages of her body. Before she launches into the story of her intellectual achievement and her public role as social prophet, she reassures her reader that she also did not choose to remain single. With the loss of the family fortune, she is denied the economic basis for securing her future as wife and mother. She becomes thereby unattractive as a marriage partner. Despite those circumstances, however, she becomes engaged to her brother's friend, a drama the older woman recreates as a brief, tragic love story: The young man pursues the engagement despite her poverty; then he becomes seriously ill, lapses into insanity, dies; and the promise of marriage fades into a memory of bittersweet happiness. As a young woman, then, she did not intentionally, willfully subvert the normal pattern of a woman's life. Providence intervened; and her fate as the happy, single woman became the inevitable outcome of the laws of Necessity. Through this story of ill-fated romance, Martineau attends to the conventional shape of female selfhood and upholds the Victorian values promoted in the discourse venerating home and family, reaffirming on one level the expectations of her reader about the appropriate life script for a young woman while, on the other, she justifies her own transgression of that natural pattern.

Confidence in Necessity permeates her narration of what must have been a traumatic experience (I reproduce this lengthy passage because it is so critical to an understanding of Martineau's autobiographical selfhood and because I will have occasion to return to it later):

> There has never been any doubt in my mind that, considering what I was in those days, it was happiest for us both that our union was prevented by any means. I am, in truth, very thankful for not having married at all. I have never since been tempted, nor have suffered any thing at all in relation to that matter which is held to be all-important to woman,—love and marriage. Nothing, I mean, beyond occasional annoyance, presently disposed of. Every literary woman, no doubt, has plenty of importunity of that sort to deal with; but freedom of mind and coolness of manner dispose of it very easily: and since the time I have been speaking of, my mind has been wholly free from all idea of love-affairs. My subsequent literary life in London was clear from all difficulty and embarrassment,—no doubt because I was evidently too busy, and too full of interests of other kinds to feel any awkwardness,—to say nothing of my being then thirty years of age; an age at which, if ever, a woman is certainly qualified to take care of herself. I can easily conceive how I might have been tempted,—how some deep springs in my nature might have been touched, then as earlier; but, as a matter of fact, they never were; and I consider the immunity a great blessing, under the liabilities of a moral condition such as mine was in the olden time. If I had had a husband dependent on me for his happiness, the responsibility would have made me wretched. I had not faith enough in myself to endure avoidable responsibility. If my husband had *not* depended on me for his happiness, I should have been jealous. So also with children. The care would have so overpowered the joy,—the love would have so exceeded the ordinary chances of life,—the fear on my part would have so impaired the freedom on theirs, that I rejoice not to have been involved in a relation for which I was, or believed myself unfit. The veneration in which I hold domestic life has always shown me that that life was not for those whose self-respect had been early broken down, or had never grown. Happily, the majority are free from this disability. Those who suffer under it had better be as

I,—as my observation of married, as well as single life assures me. When I see what conjugal love is, in the extremely rare cases in which it is seen in its perfection, I feel that there is a power of attachment in me that has never been touched. When I am among little children, it frightens me to think what my idolatry of my own children would have been. But, through it all, I have ever been thankful to be alone. My strong will, combined with anxiety of conscience, makes me fit only to live alone; and my taste and liking are for living alone. The older I have grown, the more serious and irremediable have seemed to me the evils and disadvantages of married life, as it exists among us at this time: and I am provided with what it is the bane of single life in ordinary cases to want,—substantial, laborious and serious occupation. My business in life has been to think and learn, and to speak out with absolute freedom what I have thought and learned. The freedom is itself a positive and neverfailing enjoyment to me, after the bondage of my early life. My work and I have been fitted to each other, as is proved by the success of my work and my own happiness in it. . . . Who could have believed, in the awful year 1826, that such would be my conclusion a quarter of a century afterwards! (I:100–102)

This passage is curious for its complexities and ambiguities. While she pays lip service to the conventional expectations of her culture, Martineau excuses herself from the expected pattern; and she does so, interestingly, by describing herself as unfit for conventional womanhood, unfit to be a wife and mother. Her habitual illnesses, her deafness, her childhood deprivations as they affect her character, all combine to make her a probable failure as wife and mother since the obstacles she experienced in her childhood, adolescence, and early adulthood render her both unattractive as a marriage partner and increasingly independent as a woman. But, of course, that character and those obstacles resulted from the environment that shaped her. She therefore denies her own role in choosing an unconventional life. In fact, she implies, her expansive powers of love lie dormant, untapped. She would have been even more fierce in her love of and loyalty to husband and children than other women. Passive before the forces of Necessity, Martineau renders unreasonable society's censure of her as a transgressive female.

Throughout the autobiography Martineau characterizes herself as the ideal, if single, woman. Uncontaminated by passion of the kind she associates with Wollstonecraft and other misdirected women, she remains pure, chaste, like the virgin queen or the nun. And the comparison is appropriate in other ways as well. The body is a constant source of discomfort to her, not the source of sensual or sexual pleasure: She is sickly as a child; she loses her hearing; she is easily exhausted from the trials of authorship; she must isolate herself in a small house for five years because of a tumor; she begins her autobiography in the face of impending death (and then lasts another twenty years). A chronic invalid, Martineau literally suffers the burdens of mortality. But there is more meaning in her invalidism than the physiological explanation assumes. The emphasis on infirmities, the apparent enthusiasm with which she talks about her bodily weaknesses, suggests that for Martineau physical disability functions psychologically in a variety of ways as it functions narratively to sustain the representation of herself as a certain kind of woman. For one, bodily displeasure in early infancy turns the child away from sensual delight and sexual desire to the privacies and certainties of the mind. It motivates her escape into intellect and pattern making as it reaffirms the utility of finding sources of sustenance other than the desires of the body.

Simultaneously, invalidism becomes one of the prices this independent woman pays for pleasures of the mind. Ashamed of her body from early childhood, she becomes a mind captured in a body that is decaying around her. And yet that price is a convenient protection: The damages of the body render her unfit to embrace a conventional life as wife and mother. They justify her choice of the single life in a culture enamored of the ideology of home and hearth, of domestic priorities and felicities. In fact, notes Gillian Thomas, "the status of invalid was a socially recognized one for Victorian women and one that enabled Martineau to pursue an important part of her literary career relatively undisturbed."[28] Her chronic invalidism allows her to present herself as the appropriately chaste, asexual being who has successfully escaped the downward drag of the body and its desires. Like the nun who embraced the body-denying practices of Catholicism, Martineau claims as the sign of her true purity the degree to which her body has been mortified. And like the nun, or the virgin queen of an earlier age, she presumes to speak authoritatively because she has effectively repressed her female nature. Like them, she remains a virgin, the single woman who does not become captive to the passions of earthly love, the dailiness of wifehood and motherhood.

Also like those predecessors, Martineau embraces a self-denying vocation, sacrificing her own desire to the call of a higher duty. Her role, she emphasizes, has been a passive, not an active, one:

> Authorship has never been with me a matter of choice. I have not done it for amusement, or for money, or for fame, or for any reason but because I could not help it. Things were pressing to be said; and there was more or less evidence that I was the person to say them. . . . What wanted to be said must be said, for the sake of the many, whatever might be the consequences to the one worker concerned. Nor could the immediate task be put aside, from the remote consideration, for ever pressed upon me, of lengthening my life. (I:143)

Denying any trace of complicating passion in favor of a procrustean Necessity, Martineau assures her reader that authorship has been a duty, not a pleasure. She followed an unconventional life, not out of any personal desire, but only out of altruistic motives fostered by external forces.[29] The sense that she has in fact literally sacrificed her life for her calling here echoes an earlier scene from childhood in which she describes how, as a lonely, unhappy child, she was drawn toward the idea of personal martyrdom. And indeed, the older woman, a martyr for truth, has been slandered, misunderstood, abused, threatened with death, ostracized. The piece on Thomas Malthus and population control through late marriage and family planning incites vicious personal attacks on her femininity. Outspoken opposition to slavery makes her American journey a life-threatening one. Great physical risks attend her as she travels to Egypt and the Middle East. The rejection of Christianity chronicled in the letters she exchanged (and subsequently published) with Henry G. Atkinson brings renewed attacks, from her brother among others.

Martineau sustains her role as an altruistic martyr, assuring her reader that she derives little personal pleasure from and risks great personal harm in a vocation foisted on her by Necessity. She purposefully avoids literary lionism, reinforcing that claim within the pages of her autobiography by incorporating a lengthy essay written many years earlier entitled "Literary Lionism." Again and again, she draws a picture of herself as uncomfortable and self-effacing in the midst of sycophants and devotees. Throughout she emphasizes her desire to escape from the crowds of admirers into the quietness and isolation of home. She takes pains, that is, to assure her reader that she has not suffered from the vanity that in woman is monstrous.[30] Sacrificing her personal life to the public duty demanded by her calling, she remains celibate, chaste, devoted to others rather than self. Precisely because she re-creates herself as ideal woman uncontaminated by sexuality or personal desire, she can play the representative man. Moreover, she can defend herself against those rumors and stories that circulate around her, characterizing her as a self-promoting, opinionated, aggressive woman.[31]

In her provocative study of the relationship of nineteenth-century women novelists to figurative and literal languages, Margaret Homans traces certain themes and structures by which women writers sought to "bear the word" in their texts:

> In a culture that was still essentially patrilineal, or at least that still subscribed to the ideology of patriliny, as mid-nineteenth-century England was and did, women's primary role was to afford the means of the transmission of inheri-

tance from father to son. It became incumbent upon women writers to convert the writing that they nevertheless felt driven to do into a version of these female duties of selfless transmission, just as, mythically, Mary facilitated the transmission of Word into flesh.[32]

Martineau participated in that tradition of self-sacrificing transmission even as she lived life as a man; and she did so in two ways. Her autobiography chronicles a life devoted to "bearing the word" of male philosophers (Jeremy Bentham, Thomas Malthus, Auguste Comte, among others). She literally translated Comte into English so that his word would be accessible to a wider audience. She translated the ideas of Bentham and Malthus into novels more accessible to the masses of people whom she sought to educate. But more than that, her very autobiography serves as a vessel through which she can "bear" the philosophical vision of Comtian positivism and thereby reaffirm the ordination of androcentric selfhood.

But. . . . The patterns of self-interpretation are too tight, too procrustean. "I am disposed to think it probable that I am casting back the light of a later time among the mists of an earlier, and supposing myself sooner capable than I really was of practically distinguishing between a conception and a conviction" Martineau comments at one point (I:82). In that dramatic aside the confident autobiographer qualifies the truthfulness of her story. Drawing on earlier sources to refresh her memory—the article "Literary Lionism," the journals of her American tour, the letters to Atkinson—she reveals the uncertainty of memory as a source of truth. Throughout, she punctuates the narrative with muted references to experiences not included in her official story for various reasons: She would appear too self-promoting; she has recounted them elsewhere; she considers them inconsequential; propriety demands their omission. In all these ways, Martineau sustains the tentative nature of the autobiographical project, hinting at stories left untold, life left unrepresented, ultimately unmasking the fictive nature of her pattern making.

Actually, Martineau's narrative remains overdetermined. In his study of memory and writing, Philip Davis argues that in most nineteenth-century autobiographies "memory proposes itself as the end of time and therefore aptly summative and conclusive of it. Everything falls into line, becoming in the life's story what, with hindsight, it turned out to be."[33] For those autobiographers who wrote their stories when they believed death to be near, as Martineau did, that tendency is especially pronounced. For someone who, like Martineau, is drawn to the Necessarian Solution, the summative tendency of memory is further exacerbated: Having embraced the ideology of evolutionary progress, the autobiographer looks back on a life that seems destined to have evolved along the lines it did. Thus, as Davis notes, Martineau's *Autobiography* embodies a disturbing fatedness.[34] Since all human desire, emotion, tentativeness, ambivalence have apparently been erased from the text, the self-satisfying acceptance of her destiny takes its toll on the very truthfulness of her "life." The following passage, quoted also by Davis, captures the static nature of Martineau's vision:

> I think I may sum up my experience of this sort by saying that this book [the Atkinson letters] has been an inestimable blessing to me by dissolving all false relations, and confirming all true ones. No one who would leave me on account of it is qualified to be my friend; and all who, agreeing or disagreeing with my opinions, are faithful to me through a trial too severe for the weak are truly friends for life. I early felt this. (II:46–47)

Suppressing the experience of disappointment, betrayal, and loss that must have characterized that period in her life, Martineau insists that there were from the beginning only two kinds of people—the friends and the not-friends. Davis calls the kind of thinking evidenced in such passages "the logic of retrospection," wherein all "interim meanings" are suppressed, giving way to the authority of summative meanings.[35]

Yet that approach toward autobiography served Martineau in profound psychological ways. As already noted, in constructing a story of fatedness, she defended herself against those critics, real and imagined, who charged her with arrogant female transgression. But the same sense of fatedness allows her to overcome the ravages of conventional female selfhood. To explore this aspect of fatedness, let me return to the passage quoted at length above. The language she uses to describe the loss of a fiancé is terse, cold, controlled, entirely void of emotion. "Love" becomes "that matter." Her feelings are an "occasional annoyance, presently disposed of." Mind and manner overcome the emergencies and indeterminacies of passion. Everything, all possible "interim meanings" are contained within the carefully structured language of a system. As Davis suggests, the grammatical past tense assigns everything, including her emotions, to the finality of fact.[36] The Necessarian Solution provided this woman a system of belief through which to subdue, then to escape the entanglements of passion, those swirling and stifling pains and pangs of doubt and shame and self-disgust that kept the child constantly on the edge of desire.[37] The language of autobiographical selfhood betrays the desire to repress all the confusion of life and fire inside. Mind exerts control over emotion, that seething stressful wind of passion, rebellion, and shame. And that control is piercingly evident in the patterns language imposes on the past, in the auto-biographer's allegiance to memory rather than to what Davis calls "the

provisional nature of time."[38] Martineau's suppression of interim meanings, her desire to repress her passional experience within the public, official story of her life, recapitulates the childhood scene she so vividly recreates in the opening pages of her text: "It never occurred to me to speak of
anything I felt most" (I:9). Evading feeling, she develops a fierce need to
find patterns for living (by wrenching the Bible into her own maxims, by
embracing "solutions"). She flees toward pattern making in order to escape
the emotional life. Fundamentally, that escape from the world of emotions
becomes an escape from the "feminine" life of feeling and sensitivity, from
"female" autobiography as defined by the ideology of gender in the nineteenth century. Embracing the story of a man as she embraces the life of a
man, Martineau, like Charke before her, literally gives her self up to the
exactions of male autobiography.

Identifying with the "father" and his world of public action, Martineau
grounds her authority to write about herself in the fit of her life to the story
of male selfhood. In doing so, she suppresses the story of emotional turmoil, the story of sexual difference and desire. Giving her allegiance to the
ideology of male selfhood, she silences the "feminine" story of her identity
as daughter. Yet the suppressed story of thwarted emotion and desire disturbs the placid surfaces of the stolid and carefully structured narrative of
representative man; and it does so through the glimpses of her experience
as daughter to her mother. For in the portrait she draws of her mother,
Martineau unmasks her ambivalence about domestic life and ideal womanhood by indirectly revealing the underside of domesticity and motherhood.
On the one hand, she would be the "ideal" daughter, dutifully imitating the
model of filiality dear to her mother. She emphasizes how much she has
enjoyed sewing, an occupation forced on her by her mother in their early
days of financial distress. She presents herself as a woman to whom the
comfort and retirement of home is sustaining. She describes how, contrary
to her wishes, she obeys her mother, returning home after her first successful trip to London. She represents herself as obedient toward her mother,
domestically oriented, chaste, self-sacrificing. But this mother is fundamentally a figure of overpowering dominance and gloom. In fact, the last and
most fundamental form of imprisonment Martineau suffers and flees is the
imprisonment within her relationship as daughter to this mother. Buried
inside her official life, therefore, lies a story of rebellion against the tyranny
of the mother and the tyranny of female life scripts.

Unlike Cavendish, this daughter presents the mother as a tarnished,
rather than as an ideal, figure. Her childhood memories resonate with the
vision of a mother remote, capricious, insensitive, harsh. Dramatically, she
admits that, when she left home and escaped the daily influence of her
mother, her habitual tendency to tell untruths ceased (I:68). And yet she

did not really escape the presence of her mother until much later; for when the family loses its money, when her favorite older brother dies, when Martineau begins to support herself from the proceeds of her career as a writer, she and her mother become the new household. Reconfigured in a complex way, the domestic drama casts Martineau as the "husband/son" who supports the household financially while her mother plays the "wife" by assuming responsibility for all domestic arrangements. Critically, the arrangement in part reverses the dynamics of the earlier, parent-child relationship: The mother is dependent on a daughter formerly dependent on her. Moreover, the daughter achieves public recognition and authority "like a man."

Apparently Martineau's mother had difficulty accepting the change in power relations that attended her daughter's rise to public stature. Jealous of her daughter's prominence, driven by what appeared to be her own will to control, she asserted her emotional authority within the new household:

> My mother, who loved power and had always been in the habit of exercising it, was hurt at confidence being reposed in me, and distinctions shown, and visits paid to me; and I, with every desire to be passive, and being in fact wholly passive in the matter, was kept in a state of constant agitation at the influx of distinctions which I never sought, and which it was impossible to impart. What the meddlers and mischief-makers did was to render my old ladies, and especially my mother, discontented with the lowliness of our home. They were ever suggesting that I ought to live in some sort of style. . . . Their officiousness proved their vulgarity: and my mother saw and said this. Yet, every word told upon her heart; and thence, every word helped to pull down my health and strength. (I:188)

Characteristically, the daughter's posture toward her mother's will to power remained a "passive" one. She silenced her own desires before the mother's presence. But she paid a price for that passivity—"a state of constant agitation"—as the pressure of her mother's personality makes the daughter literally ill.

This passage, which connects her mother's wilfullness to her own ill health, echoes those earlier passages in which the older woman recalls how her mother's remoteness, her inability to nurture her daughter, created the childhood environment in which the young Martineau developed ill health and a morbid personality. Later in the autobiography, she associates her five-year illness with her mother's oppressive presence. The disease, she writes,

> was unquestionably the result of excessive anxiety of mind,—of the extreme tension of nerves under which I had been living for some years, while the three

anxious members of my family were, I may say, on my hands,—not in regard to money, but to care of a more important kind. My dear aunt, the sweetest of old ladies, was now extremely old, and required shielding from the anxiety caused by the other two. My mother was old, and fast becoming blind; and the irritability caused in her first by my position in society, and next by the wearing trial of her own increasing infirmity, told fearfully upon my already reduced health. My mother's dignified patience in the direct endurance of her blindness was a really beautiful spectacle: but the natural irritability found vent in other directions; and especially was it visited upon me. Heaven knows, I never sought fame; and I would thankfully have given it all away in exchange for domestic peace and ease: but there it was! and I had to bear the consequences. (I:441)

The doubled language permeating this passage betrays the profound ambiguity in Martineau's feelings toward her mother. Her mother is admirable and irritable, but more irritable than admirable since that word is repeated, underscoring the real emphasis in Martineau's imagination and memory. Attempting to serve her mother by playing the "son" to her, the daughter only undermines the mother's sense of her own authority. (The ability of the mother to make her daughter sick, literally and figuratively, will become the very subject of Maxine Hong Kingston's twentieth-century work, *The Woman Warrior.*)

The daughter's response to such emotional tyranny erupts in little passages. For instance, Martineau describes how her increasing deafness served to disappoint her mother: "My mother loved music, and, I know, looked to me for much gratification in this way which she never had" (I:41). While the language is that of apology tinged with regret, the comment strikes a kind of ironic pose. Something about it suggests the degree to which the young woman derived subversive pleasure from causing disappointment to a mother who had so profoundly disappointed her. Having separated from her mother in order to live in Tynemouth much later in her life, Martineau describes for the reader the recurrent nightmare in which "my mother had fallen from a precipice, or over the bannisters, or from a cathedral spire; and that it was my fault" (I:442). Revealing more than she probably would after Freud, Martineau captures in that dream the fierce desire for her mother's death and the deep edge of guilt about that repressed desire.

Her final and most consequential gesture of rebelliousness comes in the very narrating of her life story. Characterizing her mother as an uncaring, harsh, demanding, and "sickening" figure, the daughter actually offers an indictment of the woman whom she would serve in the name of truthfulness. She becomes a negative model of parenthood in the work of a daughter who spent much of her professional life promoting an enlightened conception of education. She becomes a negative model of interpersonal relations, the most powerful figure of tyranny for a daughter who spent a lifetime writing about various kinds of slavery. She becomes a negative model of the enslaved self, an individual absorbed in her own projections of reality, for a daughter who spent a lifetime struggling toward the philosophic vision of selflessness. Martineau aspires to everything her mother is not, refusing to imitate her "female" model by embracing the male scenario of selfhood. (Her brother, alarmed at the portrait of his mother in the *Autobiography*, denied its facticity. And yet, as critics have noted, he would have had as a son a different experience of his mother.)[39]

Her rejection of her mother's role emerges forcefully in her careful indictment of marriage. In the passage quoted at length above, Martineau describes her constitutional inadequacy for marriage. Going beyond a tribute to the sanctity of marriage and the family, she challenges the ideology of marriage itself by equating the institution with "bondage." Looking back on her life, the older woman tellingly reveals that, had she married, she would never have been able to accomplish what she did since she would not have had the freedom to pursue her own independent growth and to assume her own philosophical voice. Only "widowhood" left her free to pursue her calling. Thus, despite her admiration for the happy wife and her attempt to play the good daughter to her mother, it is clear that for her the demands of marriage are antithetical to intellectual growth and independent accomplishment for women. While she may want to convince her reader that she did not intentionally subvert the expected pattern of female development, the language and force of the passage controverts that intention. Identifying marriage as another one of those forms of bondage and injustice against which she railed her entire life, this Victorian woman betrays her own fundamental abhorrence of the very institution she would support. Martineau is glad to have escaped the fate of her mother and of women generally. The intensity with which she repudiates marriage and her mother as embodiment of womanhood testifies to the abhorrence she felt for emotional bondage. Only the ideal of male autobiography promised her deliverance.

With the death of her mother, the dutiful but quietly rebellious daughter escapes the tyranny of maternal presence to begin a new life as man. In the final pages of the *Autobiography* Martineau describes how she broke out of the old patterns of domestic arrangements and reconstituted her own, alternative arrangements, building her new household in the Lake District. The liberating language here suggests the degree to which she valued that reconstitution of domestic life, all the more because of the "disease" inherent in her previous domestic arrangements: "No true woman, married or single, *can* be happy without some sort of domestic life;—without having somebody's happiness dependent on her; and my own ideal of an innocent and happy life was a house of my own among poor improvable neighbours, with young servants whom I might train and attach to myself" (I:497–98). While she identifies the desires as those of a "true woman," she betrays in her evocation of that idyllic homestead the desire for masculine authority. The "dependents" of the earlier household, her mother and aunt, are here replaced by other dependents. While the configuration is similar, however, the dynamics of power are different in critical ways. Martineau is no longer tied to her dependents by the repressive bonds of filiality. Nor are the dependents competing with her for authority and power. As poor neighbors and servants, they are situated "beneath" her. She has all the power of money, public stature, class, intelligence, age, land. She suffers no dependencies that spawn frustrated demonstrations of tyranny. She enjoys fully the prerogatives of the patriarchs, transforming what she represents as the negative power of female tyranny into the more positive power of male beneficence. A female "patriarch," this woman has brought everything under her control, including her "life."

In the introduction Martineau announces a theory of autobiography as she defends her decision to have her personal letters burned. "Bear[ing] emphatic practical testimony on behalf of the principles of the privacy of epistolary intercourse," she maintains for a variety of reasons that personal correspondence should be held from public scrutiny. She herself has acted to restore confidence in the integrity of personal correspondence "by a stringent provision in my will against any public use whatever being made of my letters, unless I should myself authorize the publication of some, which will, in that case, be of some public interest, and not confidential letters" (I:3). Establishing a distinction between official and unauthorized versions of selfhood, she suggests at the outset of her story that the work the reader has just begun to read is only one version of the real Martineau, the public version. Revealingly, she acknowledges that public versions are not always the most truthful: "The most valuable conversation, and that which best illustrates character, is that which passes between friends, with their feet on the fender, on winter nights, or in a summer ramble" (I:3). Nonetheless, public versions are the most carefully controlled, the most rational, authoritative, legitimate. They are, that is, the most "masculine."

For Harriet Martineau male autobiography served public and private purposes. If her autobiography denies interim meanings "because she felt her emotions to be pre-empted by the laws of Necessity and silenced by the law of Justice," it defends by proving inevitable the law of Harriet Martineau's evolutionary selfhood.[40] She lived her life like a man because it was inevitable that her life be lived that way. Thus the controversial woman could defend herself publicly before those critics who condemned her for her unfeminine life and personality. Privately, male autobiography, as text and context, provided her a medium through which to escape the emotional vulnerability that characterized the "life" of this psychologically damaged nineteenth-century woman. Repressing the "private," "maternal" story of desire in service to a male ideal of dispassionate intellectuality, Martineau gained control over both her own suffering and subsequent interpretations of her life. She did so at the price of her own passional life.

EIGHT

Maxine Hong Kingston's
Woman Warrior

Filiality and Woman's Autobiographical Storytelling

> It is hard to write about my own mother.
> Whatever I do write, it is my story I am
> telling, my version of the past. If she were
> to tell her own story other landscapes
> would be revealed. But in my landscape or
> hers, there would be old, smoldering
> patches of deep-burning anger.
>
> —Adrienne Rich, *Of Woman Born*

Since Harriet Martineau wrote her autobiography in 1856, many hundreds of women have contributed the story of their lives to the cultural heritage. Writers, artists, political figures, intellectuals, businesswomen, actors, athletes—all these and more have marked history in their own way, both as they lived their lives and as they wrote about them. A tradition so rich and various presents a challenge to the critic of twentieth-century autobiography. There is much to be written about the works; indeed, studies of twentieth-century autobiography are beginning to emerge. Articles now abound. I do not want to conclude this study of women's autobiographies without attention to a contemporary work; but I also realize that there are many choices that would have served my critical purposes. Nonetheless, for me at least, no single work captures so powerfully the relationship of gender to genre in twentieth-century autobiography as Maxine Hong Kingston's *Woman Warrior*.

And so it is fitting to conclude this discussion of women's autobiography with *The Woman Warrior: Memoirs of a Girlhood among Ghosts*, which is, quite complexly, an autobiography about women's autobiographical storytelling. A postmodern work, it exemplifies the potential for works from the marginalized to challenge the ideology of individualism and with it the ideology of gender. Recognizing the inextricable relationship between an individual's sense of "self" and the community's stories of selfhood, Kingston self-consciously reads herself into existence through the stories her culture tells about women. Using autobiography to create identity, she breaks down the hegemony of formal "autobiography" and breaks out of the silence that has bound her culturally to discover a resonant voice of her own. Furthermore, as a work coming from an ethnic subculture, *The Woman Warrior* offers the occasion to consider the complex imbroglios of cultural fictions that surround the autobiographer who is engaging two sets of stories: those of the dominant culture and those of an ethnic subculture with its own traditions, its own unique stories. As a Chinese American from the working class, Kingston brings to her autobiographical project complicating perspectives on the relationship of woman to language and to narrative.

Considered by some a "novel" and by others an "autobiography," the five narratives conjoined under the title *The Woman Warrior* are decidedly five confrontations with the fictions of self-representation and with the autobiographical possibilities embedded in cultural fictions, specifically as they interpenetrate one another in the autobiography a woman would write.[1] For Kingston, then, as for the woman autobiographer generally, the hermeneutics of self-representation can never be divorced from cultural representations of woman that delimit the nature of her access to the word and the articulation of her own desire. Nor can interpretation be divorced from her orientation toward the mother, who, as her point of origin, commands the tenuous negotiation of identity and difference in a drama of filiality that reaches through the daughter's subjectivity to her textual self-authoring.

Preserving the traditions that authorize the old way of life and enable her to reconstitute the circle of the immigrant community amidst an alien environment, Kingston's mother dominates the life, the landscape, and the language of the text as she dominates the subjectivity of the daughter who writes that text. It is Brave Orchid's voice, commanding, as Kingston notes, "great power" that continually reiterates the discourses of the community in maxims, talk-story, legends, family histories. As the instrument naming filial identities and commanding filial obligations, that voice enforces the authority and legitimacy of the old culture to name and thus control the place of woman within the patrilineage and thereby to establish the erasure of female desire and the denial of female self-representation as the basis on which the perpetuation of patrilineal descent rests. Yet that same voice gives shape to other possibilities, tales of female power and authority that seem to create a space of cultural significance for the daughter; and the very strength and authority of the material voice fascinates the daughter because it "speaks" of the power of woman to enunciate her own representations. Hence storytelling becomes the means through which Brave Orchid passes on to her daughter all the complexities of and the ambivalences about both mother's and daughter's identity as woman in patriarchal culture.[2]

Storytelling also becomes the means through which Kingston confronts those complexities and ambivalences. In dialogic engagement with her mother's word, she struggles to constitute the voice of her own subjectivity, to emerge from a past dominated by stories told to her, ones that inscribe the fictional possibilities of female selfhood, into a present articulated by her own storytelling. Her text reveals the intensity of that struggle throughout childhood and adolescence and the persistance of those conflicts inherent in self-authoring well into adulthood; for, not only is that effort the subject in the text; it is also dramatized by the text. In the first two narratives she re-creates the stories about women and their autobiographical possibilities passed on to her by her mother: first the biographical story of no-name aunt, an apparent victim and thus a negative model of female life scripts, and then the legendary chant of the warrior woman Fa Mu Lan, an apparent heroine and positive model. But as she explores their fates, Kingston questions the very basis on which such distinctions are predicated. Uncovering layer by layer the dynamics and the consequences of her mother's interpretations as they resonate with the memories of her past, the daughter, as she too passes them on to posterity, circles around them, critiquing them, making them her own. Next she reconstructs out of the autobiographical fragments of Brave Orchid's own Chinese experience a biography of her mother, discovering by the way the efficacies of powerful storytelling for the woman who has fallen in status with her translation to another culture. In the fourth piece, an elaborate fabrication played on actual events, she becomes even more keenly attentive to all autobiographical and biographical representations, including her own. Looking back to the beginnings of her own struggle to take a voice, she traces in the final narrative the origins of her own hermeneutics. The apparent line of progress, which as it ends returns us to the beginning, becomes effectively a circle of sorts, a textual alternative to the constricting patriarchal circle Kingston has had to transgress.

" 'You must not tell anyone,' my mother said, 'what I am about to tell you. In China your father had a sister who killed herself. She jumped into the family well. We say that your father has all brothers because it is as if she had never been born.' "[3] With that interdiction of female speech, uttered in the name of the father, Kingston's mother succinctly elaborates the circumstances of the sister's suicide. The concise maternal narrative concludes with forceful injunctions and powerful maxims inscribing the filial obligations of daughters in the patriarchal order: " 'Don't let your father know that I told you. He denies her. Now that you have started to menstruate, what happened to her could happen to you. Don't humiliate us. You wouldn't like to be forgotten as if you had never been born. The villagers are watchful' " (5). Kingston thus situates the origins of her autobiography in her recollection of the story her mother used to contextualize the moment of transition ineradicably marking female identity and desire. That event, as it proclaims woman's sexual potency, proclaims also woman's problematic placement within the body social, economic, politic, and symbolic.[4] While her body, the locus of patrilineal preservation, will be contracted out to male authority to serve as the carrier of legitimate sons and of the order those sons perpetuate, it will always remain a potential source of disruption and disintegration in the community: It may provide no sons for the line of descent; or it may entertain strangers and thus introduce illegitimate children and an alternative genealogy into the order.[5] Should a daughter opt for the latter (unfilial) alternative, warns the mother, the patriarchal order will work efficiently to punish her transgression of the contract, eliminating her body and name from the world of things and of discourse. Kingston's aunt has suffered this fate: Her family, like the villagers, has enacted its own cleansing ritual; and Kingston's mother has perpetuated the ritual in the very way she tells the story. The aunt's name remains unuttered; and her interpretation of events is sacrificed, within the mother's text, to concern for the villagers' actions. Only her body assumes significance as it reveals the sign of its transgression, as it plugs up the family well.

The mother's cautionary tale at once affirms and seeks to cut off the daughter's kinship with a transgressive female relative and her unrepressed sexuality.[6] Kingston acknowledges the effectiveness of that strategy by revealing later in the narrative that for a long time she accepted her mother's interpretation and kept her counsel, thereby colluding in the perpetuation of both her own silencing and the erasure of her aunt's name:

> I have believed that sex was unspeakable and words so strong and fathers so frail that "aunt" would do my father mysterious harm. I have thought that my family, having settled among immigrants who had also been their neighbors in the ancestral land, needed to clean their name, and a wrong word would incite the kinspeople even here. But there is more to this silence: they want me to participate in her punishment. And I have. (18)

Now, however, at the moment of autobiographical writing, Kingston resists identification with mother and father by breaking the silence, returning to the story that marked her entrance into sexual difference and constituting her own interpretation of events. She comes to tell another story, seeking to name the formerly unnamed—the subjectivity of her aunt. As she does so, she imagines her aunt in a series of postures toward that excess of sexuality signified by the growth of her womb. Initially dismissing the probability that "people who hatch their own chicks and eat embryos and the heads for delicacies and boil the feet in vinegar for party food, leaving only the gravel, eating even the gizzard lining—could . . . engender a prodigal aunt" (7), she imagines her aunt the victim of rape, fearful, silent, and vulnerable before her victimizer. But she suspends that narrative line, apparently dissatisfied with its unmitigated emphasis on female powerlessness and willlessness. Beginning again, Kingston enters her aunt's subjectivity from another perspective, preferring to see her as a willful woman after "subtle enjoyment." Contemplating this posture, she finds herself increasingly aware of the gaps in her mother's tale, which motivate her to ask further questions of the story and to piece together an alternative textual genealogy.[7]

Instead of imagining her aunt as one of "the heavy, deep-rooted women" who "were to maintain the past against the flood, safe for returning" (9), and thus as victim, she imagines her as a woman attuned to "a secret voice, a separate attentiveness" (13), truly transgressive and subversive. The fruit of her womb becomes the mark exposing the priority of her desire for sexuality and autobiographical inscription. Indeed, the expansion of her very body and of her sense of her own authority to define herself ultimately challenges the ontological roots of her culture—"the real"; for publicized female subjectivity points to the fundamental vulnerability of the patrilineage by exposing it as a sustained fiction.[8] The alternative genealogy thus engendered breaks the descent line, subverting the legitimacy of male succession that determines all lines in patriarchy—descent lines, property lines, and lines of texts.[9] "The frightened villagers, who depended on one another to maintain the real," writes Kingston, "went to my aunt to show her a personal, physical representation of the break she had made in the 'roundness.' Misallying couples snapped off the future, which was to be embodied in true offspring. The villagers punished her for acting as if she could have a private life, secret and apart from them" (14).

While her journey across the boundaries that circumscribe the patriarchal order takes the aunt into the unbounded spaces of self-representation, Kingston acknowledges also that this "rare urge west" (9) leads her into the vast spaces of alienation, fearfulness, and death. Expelled from the family circle, her aunt becomes "one of the stars, a bright dot in blackness, without home, without a companion, in eternal cold and silence" (16). While the endless night proposes limitless identities beyond the confining borders of repetitious patriarchal representations, it promotes the "agoraphobia" attending any move beyond the carefully prescribed boundaries of ancestral, familial, and community paradigms of female self-representation. Overwhelmed by the vast spaces of possibility, the aunt returns to the genealogical source, reestablishing her cultural "responsibility" by giving birth in the pigsty—"to fool the jealous, pain-dealing gods, who do not switch piglets" (16)—and then by killing herself and her child—"a child with no descent line would not soften her life but only trail after her, ghostlike, begging her to give it purpose" (17). From one point of view, then, the aunt enacts on her own body and her own alternative genealogical text the punishment of the tribe, fulfilling her filial responsibilities to her circle by eliminating the source of contamination from its center and thereby restoring it to its unbroken configuration. She thus returns to the silence that defines her condition and her identity. From another point of view, however, the aunt's suicide continues her rebellion in a congeries of ways.[10] First, she brings back with her to the center of her natal circle the two loci of greatest pollution in Chinese culture—the moments of birth and death.[11] Second, by jumping back into the circle—the family well—she contaminates, in a recapitulated gesture of disruption, the water that literally and symbolically promises the continuance of patrilineal descent and the symbolic order it nourishes. Third, she takes with her the secret of paternal origins, never revealing the name of the father. Saving the father's face, she paradoxically erases the paternal trace, betraying in yet another way the fundamental fragility of undisputed paternal authority. Finally, by withholding from her natal family the name of the offender whose actions have caused such disgrace, she denies them the means to recover face by enacting their own revenge on the violator.[12] Thus, while she seems to capitulate before the monolithic power of the order against which she has transgressed, Kingston envisions her as a "spite suicide," an antiheroine whose actions subvert the stability of an order that rests on the moral imperatives of filial obligations, including sexual repression. Her very silence becomes a powerful presence, a female weapon of vengeance. Toward the end of this imaginative portrait, Kingston returns once again to her mother's tale by repeating the earlier refrain: "'Don't tell anyone you had an aunt. Your father does not want to hear her name. She has never been born'" (18). Yet while Kingston repeats her mother's words, she does so with a critical difference. Unlike her mother, she engenders a story for her aunt, fleshing out the narrative and incorporating the subjectivity previously denied that woman. Individualizing her mother's cautionary and impersonal tale, she transforms in the process both her aunt's text and her aunt's body from a maxim (a mere vessel to hold patriarchal signifiers) into a "life." Moreover, she ensures that she herself becomes more than a mere vessel preserving her mother's maxims, however deeply they may be embedded in her consciousness. For the story of this "forerunner," her "urge west" and her agoraphobia, becomes a piece in the puzzle of her own erased and erasable identity: "Unless I see her life branching into mine, she gives me no ancestral help" (10). And so, the filiations of her own story stretch backward to her aunt's, and the filiations of her aunt's story stretch forward to her own, as the two lives interpenetrate, crossing narrative boundaries in the text as Kingston interweaves her childhood experiences in the immigrant community encircling her with the imaginative biography of her aunt.

Kingston retrieves her aunt from the oblivion of sexuality repressed and textuality erased by placing her in an alternative narrative: the line of matrilineal descent to which she traces her origins and through which she gives voice to her subjectivity. Like her aunt's before her, this transgression of the injunction to filial silence challenges the priority of patrilineal descent. Allowing her imagination to give voice to the body of her aunt's text, Kingston expresses in her own way the excess of narrative (textuality) that links her intimately to that earlier excess of sexuality she identifies in her aunt. Indeed, her aunt becomes her textual "child," product of the fictions through which Kingston gives "birth" to her, and, by the way, to herself. Her story thus functions as a sign, like her aunt's enlarging belly, publicizing the potentially disruptive force of female textuality and the matrilineal descent of texts.

On the level of her mother's tale, then, the originating story of Kingston's autobiography testifies to the power of the patriarchy to command through mothers the silence of daughters, to name and to unname them, and thereby to control their meaning in discourse itself. On another level the opening piece displaces the mother's myth with the daughter's, thereby subverting the interpretations on which patrilineal descent and filial responsibilities are predicated and establishing a space in which female desire and self-representation can emerge. Yet Kingston concludes with a word of caution:

> My aunt haunts me—her ghost drawn to me because now, after fifty years of neglect, I alone devote pages of paper to her, though not origamied into houses and clothes. I do not think she always means me well. I am telling on her, and she was a spite suicide, drowning herself in the drinking water. The Chinese are always very frightened of the drowned one, whose weeping ghost, wet hair hanging and skin bloated, waits silently by the water to pull down a substitute. (19)

As the final sentence suggests, the identification may not be fortuitous, for autobiographical journeys and public self-representations are problematic adventures for daughters to pursue. Kingston does not yet know her aunt's name; and the subjectivity she has created for her remains only another interpretation, a fiction. Nor, by implication, can she be sure that she will ever know the truth about her own past. Her name is never uttered in the text; and her memories and stories may only be fictions too. This maternal trace, disruptive of the patriarchal order, may be potentially as threatening to Kingston as it was to her aunt. Indeed, she may be the child—"it was probably a girl; there is some hope of forgiveness for boys" (18)—that her aunt takes with her to the grave. Ultimately, the full, the "real" story of woman may lead to madness and to self-destruction rather than to legitimate self-representation.

Kingston in the second piece engages another of her mother's representations of female autobiography, a story from which she learned that Chinese girls "failed if we grew up to be but wives and slaves." Here she does not distinguish in quotation marks the words of her mother; rather, she moves directly to her own elaboration of Fa Mu Lan's chant.[13] But she goes further, appropriating not only the chant but also the very body of that legendary woman warrior: The identities of woman warrior and of woman narrator interpenetrate until biography becomes autobiography, until Kingston and Fa Mu Lan are one.[14] Through this fantasy of mythic identification, the adult daughter inscribes an autobiography of "perfect filiality" through which she fulfills her mother's expectations and garners her mother's unqualified love. Simultaneously, this "life" enables her to escape confinement in conventional female scripts and to enter the realm of heroic masculine pursuits—of education, adventure, public accomplishment, and fame. Ironically, however, Kingston's mythical autobiography betrays the ontological bases on which that love, power, and compliance with perfect filiality rest.

The woman warrior gains her education beyond the engendered circle of community and family in a magical, otherworldly place where male and female difference remains undelineated. Her educators are a hermaphroditic couple beyond childbearing age whose relationship appears to be one of relative equality; and the education they offer encourages her to forge an identity, not through conventional formulations of woman's selfhood, but through a close identification with the creatures of nature and the secrets of natural space.[15] In such a space female sexuality, signaled by the onslaught of puberty, remains a "natural" event rather than a cultural phenomenon situating the girl in a constellation of attitudes toward female pollution and contamination. Nonetheless, that education, while it appears to be liberating, presupposes Fa Mu Lan's total identification with the desires of her family, ubiquitously present even in its absence. For instance, she passively watches in the gourd as her own wedding ceremony takes place despite her absence, the choice of husband entirely her parents' prerogative. Ultimately, woman can be trained as warrior only in a space separate from family; but she can enter that space only because her sacrifice to the circle is the basis on which her education takes place at all. Consequently, her empowerment does not threaten to disrupt the representations of the patriarchal circle; on the contrary, it serves both the family and the discourse of gender.

When she returns home, Fa Mu Lan takes her place, not as "woman," but as extraordinary woman—as, that is, man: "My parents killed a chicken and steamed it whole, as if they were welcoming home a son" (40). As surrogate son, she replaces her father in battle, eventually freeing her community from the exploitation and terrorization of the barons. Yet she must do more than enact the scenario of male selfhood. She must erase her sexual difference and publicly represent herself as male, a "female avenger" masquerading in men's clothes and hair styles. And while her sexual desire is not repressed altogether, as in the case of the virginal Joan of Arc to whom Kingston alludes, it must remain publicly unacknowledged. Hidden inside her armor and her tent, her "body" remains suppressed in the larger community.[16] It also bears the marks of her textual and sexual appropriation by man: "Now when I was naked, I was a strange human being indeed—words carved on my back and the baby large in front" (47). The lines of text on her back are not her own creation: They are the words by which the father has inscribed his law on her body, wounding her in the process. And her belly is full of a male heir whose birth will ensure the continuance of the patrilineage she serves in her heroism.[17] Finally, and most telling, the narrative's closure asserts the ultimate limitations of the warrior woman's autobiographical possibilities. Fa Mu Lan's story breaks roughly into two parts: the narratives of preparation and public action. It thus reinscribes the traditional structure of androcentric self-representation, driven by a linear-causal progression. Once the revenge carved on her back has been enacted, however, both her life as woman warrior and her autobiography end. Having returned home to unmask herself and to be recuperated as publicly silenced wife and slave, she kneels before her parents-in-law: " 'Now my public duties are finished. . . . I will stay with you, doing farmwork and housework, and giving you more sons' " (53–54). There is nothing more to be said by her and of her.

Fa Mu Lan's name, unlike the name of no-name aunt, is passed on from generation to generation, precisely because the lines of her story as woman warrior and the lines of her text as woman autobiographer reproduce an androcentric paradigm of identity and selfhood and thereby serve the symbolic order in "perfect filiality." Since both life and text mask her sexual difference and thereby secure her recuperation in the phallic order by inscribing her subjectivity and her selfhood in the law of the same representation, they legitimate the very structures man creates to define himself, including those structures that silence women.[18]

The heroic figure of Fa Mu Lan thus represents a certain kind of woman warrior, a culturally privileged "female avenger." Embedded in Kingston's fantasy autobiography, however, lies a truly subversive "story" of female empowerment. Imaged as tiny, foot-bound, squeaky-voiced women dependent on male authority for their continued existence, the wives of warriors, barons, and emperors who haunt the interstices of the textual landscape are, in one sense, conventional ghosts. Yet those apparently erased ciphers become, in another sense, the real female avengers:

> Later, it would be said, they turned into the band of swordswomen who were a mercenary army. They did not wear men's clothes like me, but rode as women in black and red dresses. They bought up girl babies so that many poor families welcomed their visitations. When slave girls and daughters-in-law ran away, people would say they joined these witch amazons. They killed men and boys. I myself never encountered such women and could not vouch for their reality. (53)

Such "witch amazons" are figures of all that is unrepressed and violent in ways both sexual and textual, in the narrator herself as well as in the social order. Wielding unauthorized power, they do not avenge the wrongs of fathers and brothers; they lead daughters against fathers and sons, slaying the source of the phallic order itself.[19] Moreover, they do so, not by masking, but by aggressively revealing their sexual difference. Paradoxically, Fa Mu Lan has liberated the women who subvert the order she serves, just as Kingston the narrator has released the rumor that subverts the story she tells.

Kingston's memories of the real, rather than mythical, childhood also subvert the fiction she has created out of her mother's expectations. Juxtaposing to this autobiography of androcentric selfhood another self-representation that undermines the priority of the fantasy of "perfect filiality," Kingston betrays Fa Mu Lan's story as a fragile fiction only coterminous with the words that inscribe it as myth. And the jarring texture of her recollected experience—its nervous, disjointed, unpoetic, frustrated prose—calls into question the basis for the seamless elegance and almost mystical lyricism of Fa Mu Lan's poetic autobiography.

Kingston recalls the repetition of commonplace maxims that deny female significance ("Feeding girls is feeding cowbirds"; "When you raise girls, you're raising children for strangers"; "Girls are maggots in the rice"); the pressures of a language that conflates the ideographs representing the female "I" and "slave"; the images "of poor people snagging their neighbors' flotage with long flood hooks and pushing the girl babies on down the river" (62). All these signs and stories of her culture equate her identity as "girl" with failed filiality and engender in her a profound sense of vulnerability and lack. Thus she remembers how she tried to fulfill her filial obligations in the only way imaginable to her: She works at being a "bad" girl—for, as she asks, "Isn't a bad girl almost a boy?" (56). She rejects the traditional occupations of femininity: refusing to cook, breaking dishes, screaming impolitely as maxims are mouthed, defiantly telling her parents' friends that she wants to become a lumberjack, bringing home straight A's, those signs from another culture of her extraordinary public achievements. She adopts, that is, the cultural postures of a "son" by generating signs imitative of male selfhood. But her efforts to be the phallic woman do not earn the love and acceptance of her mother and community, as they do Fa Mu Lan. And so her experience gives the lie to that other autobiography: Everywhere the legend is betrayed as a misleading fiction.[20]

In the end, there remains only one residual locus of identity between Kingston and Fa Mu Lan: "What we have in common are the words at our backs. The ideographs for revenge are 'report a crime' and 'report to five families.' The reporting is the vengeance—not the beheading, not the gutting, but the words. And I have so many words—'chink' words and 'gook' words too—that they do not fit on my skin" (63). Her appropriation of the pen, that surrogate sword, and her public inscription of the story of her own childhood among ghosts become the reporting of a crime—the crime of a culture that would make nothing of her by colonizing her and, in so doing, steal her authority and her autobiography from her as her mother's legend would do. In the tale the forces of exploitation remain external to her family; but in her own experience they remain internal, endemic to the patriarchal family whose existence is founded on the colonization and erasure of women in service to the selfhood of men and boys and whose perpetuation is secured through the mother's word. By simultaneously enacting and critiquing that legendary story of female power, Kingston manages to shatter the complacencies of cultural myths, problematic heroines, and the illusory autobiographical possibilities they sanction. By "slaying" the stories of men and boys and phallic women warriors, she allies herself with the true female avengers of her tale. Fa Mu Lan may have denied her identity with such women; Kingston does not.

Whereas the first two narratives explore the consequences of Kingston's appropriation of her mother's stories, the third goes through the stories to the storyteller herself. Three scrolls from China serve as the originating locus of this biography of her mother pieced together with "autobiographical" fragments. Texts that legitimate her mother's professional identity as doctor, the scrolls stimulate biography because they announce public achievements, a life text readable by culture. They also announce to the daughter another mother, a mythic figure resident in China who resisted the erasure of her own desire and who pursued her own signifying selfhood. In her daughter's text, Brave Orchid becomes a kind of "woman warrior," whose story resonates with the Fa Mu Lan legend: both women leave the circle of the family to be educated for their mission and both return to serve their community, freeing it through many adventures from those forces that would destroy it. Both are fearless, successful, admired.

Kingston's biography accretes all varieties of evidence testifying to her mother's bravery and extraordinariness. Portrayed as one of the "new women, scientists who changed the rituals" (88), Brave Orchid bears the "horizontal name of one generation" that truly names her rather than the patronym signifying woman's identity as cipher silently bonding the patrilineage. Thus Kingston's awe-filled narration of her mother's confrontation with the Sitting Ghost takes on such synecdochic proportions in the text: "My mother may have been afraid, but she would be a dragoness ('my totem, your totem'). She could make herself not weak. During danger she fanned out her dragon claws and riffled her red sequin scales and unfolded her coiling green stripes. Danger was a good time for showing off. Like the dragons living in temple eaves, my mother looked down on plain people who were lonely and afraid" (79). The ensuing battle between woman and ghost unfolds as a primal struggle with the dynamics and the rhythms of an attempted rape. A physically powerless victim of the palpably masculine presence who "rolled over her and landed bodily on her chest" (81), Brave Orchid is initially unable to challenge his strength. But she ultimately prevails against the Boulder, defeating him with the boldness of her word and the power of the images she voices to taunt him into submission and cowardice. Such fearlessness and verbal cunning characterize subsequent adventures the daughter invokes: the coexistence with ghosts and strange monsters populating the countryside through which she travels on her way to administer to the sick; the bargain she drives with the slave dealer; her response to the birth of monster babies; and her bold orientation toward food.[21]

Embedded in the daughter's representation of her mother's extraordinariness, however, lies another, a palimpsest that tells of her mother's preoccupation with autobiographical interpretation. Even more important than the story of Brave Orchid's confrontation with the Sitting Ghost is the re-creation of her narrative of the encounter. Skillful in creating compelling stories of her experience, Brave Orchid makes of the ghost a vividly ominous antagonist, thereby authoring herself as powerful protagonist. Such imaging ensures the emboldening of her presence in the eyes and imaginations of the other women (and of her daughter): " 'I am brave and good. Also I have bodily strength and control. Good people do not lose to ghosts' " (86). Kingston also suggests that her mother secured the same admiration in other ways. By studying in secret, "she quickly built a reputation for being brilliant, a natural scholar who could glance at a book and know it" (75). Returning to her village, she "wore a silk robe and western shoes with big heels"; thereafter she maintained that posture by never dressing "less elegantly than when she stepped out of the sedan chair" (90). By avoiding treatment of the terminally ill, she ensured that her powers as doctor were magnified. In linguistic and behavioral postures, Brave Orchid orchestrates her public image, inscribes, that is, her own autobiography as extraordinary woman.

The mother's mode of self-authoring complicates the daughter's effort to reconstruct her mother's biography. Brave Orchid's stories about China become the only archival material out of which Kingston can create that "life"; and yet the stories are already "representations" or "fictions" of her experiences before she reaches an America where she is no doctor, where she works daily washing other people's laundry or picking fruit and vegetables in the fields, where she is no longer woman alone but a wife and mother, where she is no woman warrior dressed elegantly in silk. "You have no idea how much I have fallen" (90), she confesses and therein suggests the efficacy of stories and storytelling as means to preserve her extraordinariness. Significantly, the dynamics of the mother's fate recall those of Fa Mu Lan's: Adventures concluded, both return to the home of the husband as wife and slave, there to become the subject of wonderful tales of an earlier glory in a faraway place.

Kingston's narrative, as it interpenetrates her autobiography with her mother's biography, reveals how problematic such stories can become for the next generation. From one point of view, they can be exhilarating, creating in children the admiration that is so apparent in Kingston's text. But from another, they generate confusions and ambiguities, since as a child Kingston inflected the narratives with her own subjectivity, attending to another story within the text of female heroism. For Brave Orchid's tales of bravery and exoticism are underwritten by an alternative text of female vulnerability and victimization. The story elaborating the purchase of the slave girl reaffirms the servile status of women and actually gives legitimacy to Kingston's fears her parents will sell her when they return to China. The stories of babies identify femaleness with deformity and suggest to the daughter the haunting possibility that her mother might actually have practiced female infanticide. The story of the crazy lady, scurrying directionless on bound feet, encased in the mirror-studded headdress, caught in her own self-destructive capitulations, dramatizes communal fear of the anomalous woman who embodies the threat of uncontrolled female sexuality and sub-versive alliances between women—always strangers within the commu-nity—and the enemy outside.

All these tales from her mother's past, by reinforcing the representation of women as expendable, resonate with Kingston's sense of displacement in her family and in the immigrant community in America, her confusion about her sexuality, and her fears of her own "deformities" and "mad-nesses." They leave her with food that suffocates her, a voice that squeaks on her, and nightmares that haunt the long nights of childhood. They also complicate Kingston's sense of identification with her mother by betraying the basis on which her tales of extraordinariness are founded, that is, the powerlessness of ordinary women and children and their cruel and insensi-tive victimization, even at the hands of Brave Orchid herself. In fact, in her self-representation Kingston identifies herself with the "lonely and afraid," a victim of her mother's stories, and thus no true heroine after her mother's model. Paradoxically, her mother, the shaman with the power of word and food, has, instead of inspiring her daughter to health and heroism, made the daughter sick, hungry, vulnerable, fearful.

In the closing passage of this third narrative, Kingston re-creates her most recent encounter with her mother and, through it, her continuing resistance to her mother's victimizing presence. Ironically, the scene re-capitulates the earlier scene of her mother's biography. The dark bedroom, the late hour recall the haunted room at the medical school. Here Brave Orchid is herself the ghost who would continue to haunt her daughter: "My mother would sometimes be a large animal, barely real in the dark; then she would become a mother again" (118). Like Brave Orchid before her, King-ston grasps the only weapon effective in overcoming that ghost—the words with which she resists her. In the syncopated rhythm of statement and rebuttal, she answers her mother's vision of things with her own, challeng-ing unremittingly the power of her mother to control interpretations. She also offers an alternative representation of her mother in this closing scene, portraying her as an old woman, tired, prosaic, lonely, a woman whose illusions of returning to China have vanished, whose stories have become peevish, repetitious. In creating a portrait of her mother as neither fearless nor exotic, the daughter demystifies Brave Orchid's presence and diffuses the power of her word.

For all the apparent rejection of her mother as ghost, the final passage points to a locus of identification between mother and daughter and a momentary rapprochement between the two. In saying goodnight, King-ston's mother calls her Little Dog, a name of endearment unuttered for many years, and, in that gesture of affection, releases her daughter to be who she will. As a result, Kingston experiences the freedom to identify with her; for, as the daughter makes evident in her biography, her mother before her had strayed from filial obligations, leaving her parents behind in pursuit of her own desire: "I am really a Dragon, as she is a Dragon, both of us born in dragon years. I am practically a first daughter of a first daughter" (127). At this moment of closure, Kingston affectionately traces her genealogy as woman and writer to and through her mother in a sincere gesture of filiality, acknowledging as she does so that her autobiography cannot be inscribed outside the biography of her mother, just as the biography of her mother cannot be inscribed outside her own interpretations. Mother and daughter are allied in the interpenetration of stories and storytelling, an alliance captured in the ambiguous reference of the final sentence: "She sends me on my way, working always and now old, dreaming the dreams about shrinking babies and the sky covered with airplanes and a Chinatown bigger than the ones here" (127). As the motifs of the final pages suggest, both mother and daughter are working always and now old.

In the fourth narrative Kingston does not take the word of her mother as her point of narrative origin. She will reveal at the inception of the next piece that the only information she received about the events narrated in the fourth piece came from her brother through her sister in the form of an abrupt, spare bone of a story: "What my brother actually said was, 'I drove Mom and Second Aunt to Los Angeles to see Aunt's husband who's got the other wife'" (189). Out of a single factual sentence, Kingston creates a complex story of the two sisters, Brave Orchid and Moon Orchid. She admits that "his version of the story may be better than mine because of its bareness, not twisted into designs" (189); but the "designs" to which she alludes have become integral to her autobiographical interpretations.

In Kingston's designs Moon Orchid, like Brave Orchid in "Shaman," embodies her name: She is a flower of the moon, a decorative satellite that revolves around and takes its definition from another body, the absent husband. Mute to her own desire, attendant always on the word of her husband, she represents the traditional Chinese wife, a woman without autobiographical possibilities. "For thirty years," comments her niece, "she had been receiving money from him from America. But she had never told him that she wanted to come to the United States. She waited for him to suggest it, but he never did" (144). Unlike Brave Orchid, she is neither clever nor shrewd, skilled nor quick, sturdy nor lasting. Demure, self-effacing, decorative, tidy, refined—she is as gracefully useless and as elegantly civilized as bound feet, as decoratively insubstantial as the paper cutouts she brings her nieces and nephews from the old country. Having little subjectivity of her own, she can only appropriate as her own the subjectivity of others, spending her days following nieces and nephews through the house, describing what they do, repeating what they say, asking what their words mean. While there is something delightfully childlike, curious, and naive about that narration of other people's lives, there is a more profound sadness that a woman in her sixties, unformed and infantile, has no autobiography of her own.

When her husband rejects her, giving his allegiance to his Chinese-American wife, who can speak English and aid him in his work, he denies the very ontological basis on which Moon Orchid's selfhood is predicated and effectually erases her from the lines of descent. He also undermines with his negation of her role what autobiographical representations she has managed to create for herself. " 'You became people in a book I read a long time ago' " (179), he tells the two sisters, dramatically betraying the elusiveness of the "fictions" on which Moon Orchid has sustained her identity as first wife. Once having been turned into a fairy-tale figure from a time long past, this woman loses the core of her subjectivity and literally begins to vanish: She appears "small in the corner of the seat" (174); she stops speaking because the grounds for her authority to speak have been undermined—"All she did was open and shut her mouth without any words coming out" (176); later she stops eating, returning to Brave Orchid's home "shrunken to the bone." Ultimately, she vanishes into a world of madness where she creates repetitious fictions, variations on a story about vanishing without a trace. Thus she fantasizes that Mexican "ghosts" are plotting to snatch her life from her, that " 'they' would take us in airplanes and fly us to Washington, D.C., where they'd turn us into ashes. . . . drop the ashes in the wind, leaving no evidence" (184). The tenuousness, evanescence, and elusiveness of identity press on her so that everywhere she sees signs (secs, that is, evidence of the legitimacy of her own interpretations) that alien males threaten to erase her from the world, leaving no trace of her body as her husband has left no trace of her patrilineal existence. To protect herself she withdraws into the "house" of her sister, that edifice that has supported her construction of an identity as first wife. There she literally makes of the house what it has always been metaphorically—a living coffin—windows shut and darkened, "no air, no light," and she makes of storytelling itself a living coffin. As Brave Orchid tells her children, " 'The difference between mad people and sane people . . . is that sane people have variety when they talk-story. Mad people have only one story that they talk over and over' " (184). Only after Brave Orchid commits her to a mental institution does she find a new fiction to replace the old one, a renewed identity as "mother" to the other women ("daughters") who can never vanish. In the end the story of vanishing without leaving a trace becomes the only trace that is left of her, an impoverished autobiographical absence.

Her mother Kingston now represents, not as the "new woman" of "Shaman," but as a traditional woman intent on preserving her family from harm by maintaining the old traditions against the erosions of American culture. Through the conventions of speaking (Chinese), eating, greeting, chanting, storytelling, she keeps China drawn around her family in a linguistic and gustatory circle. More particularly, she seeks to preserve the old family constellation and, with it, the identity of woman. Thus, from Brave Orchid's "Chinese" perspective, her sister is a first wife, entitled to certain privileges and rights, even in America. Yet, in her allegiance to the old traditions of filial and affinal obligations, Brave Orchid becomes shortsighted, insensitive, and destructive. She succeeds only in making other women (her niece, who remains trapped in a loveless marriage; her sister, who dies in a mental institution) unhappy, sick, even mad; and she does so because, failing to anticipate just how misplaced the traditions and myths have become in the new world, she trusts her word too well. The stories she tells create illusions that fail of reference to any reality.

The story of the Empress of the Western Palace is a case in point. " 'A long time ago,' " Brave Orchid tells her sister on the drive to Los Angeles,

> "the emperors had four wives, one at each point of the compass, and they lived in four palaces. The Empress of the West would connive for power, but the Empress of the East was good and kind and full of light. You are the Empress of the East, and the Empress of the West has imprisoned the Earth's Emperor in the Western Palace. And you, the good Empress of the East, come out of the dawn to invade her land and free the Emperor. You must break the strong spell she has cast on him that has lost him the East." (166)

The myth, however, is an inappropriate text through which to interpret Moon Orchid's experience. The Empress of the West is not conniving; the Emperor does not want freeing; and the Empress of the East cannot break the spell. Moreover, for all Brave Orchid's forceful narratives of the projected meeting among Moon Orchid, the husband, and the second wife, the actual scene is pitifully humorous, squeezed as it is in the backseat of the car. " 'What scenes I could make' " (146), she tells her sister; but the only scenes she makes are in her fantasies of them (and her daughter the storyteller is the one who actually makes the scene). Though she is not entirely speechless when they confront Moon Orchid's husband, she is obviously awed by the wealthy, successful, and much younger man, and by the pressure of his young, efficient wife. Kingston creates a Brave Orchid bested in the game of fictionalizations. The husband has turned the two sisters into characters from a book read long ago, a devastating recapitulation of their efforts to turn him into the fictional Emperor. While the power of her myths to help define and situate identities has been eroded by another cultural tradition, Brave Orchid herself has not been destroyed because, unlike Moon Orchid, she is willful, hardworking, clever, intelligent, shrewd, stubborn, "brave"—all those qualities that have enabled her to cope with and to survive in her translation to another cultural landscape. Moreover, she can always fabricate another story, as she does when she urges her children to sabotage any plans her husband, now in his seventies, might have to marry a second wife. Nonetheless, other women are victimized by her words, their autobiographical possibilities cut off.

Through the "designs" in "At the Western Palace," Kingston confronts explicitly the problematics of autobiographical "fictions." Both Moon Orchid and Brave Orchid serve as powerful negative models for the perils of autobiography. Moon Orchid, bereft of the husband who defines her place and who sets the limits of her subjectivity within the structures of the patrilineage, succumbs to an imagination anchored in no-place, an imaginative rootlessness threatening Kingston herself. Overwhelmed by repetitious fantasies, her aunt vanishes into a world where alien males continually plot to erase her from existence, a preoccupation that resonates with Kingston's childhood fears of leaving no culturally significant autobiographical trace. A woman of no autobiography, Moon Orchid cannot find a voice of her own, or, rather, the only subjectivity that she finally voices is the subjectivity of madness. Brave Orchid, too, serves as a powerful negative model. She would write a certain biography of her sister, patterned after traditional interpretations of the identity of a first wife. In preserving her interpretations, however, she victimizes other women by failing to make a space in her story for female subjectivity in unfamiliar landscapes, by remaining insensitive to her sister's fears and desires, as she remains insensitive to her daughter's desires. Giving her unquestioning allegiance to language, she fails to recognize the danger in words, the perils inherent in the fictions that bind.

In the end Kingston, too, has created only a fiction, an elaborate story out of the one sentence passed by her brother through her sister; and she, too, must beware the danger in words as she constructs her stories of those other women, more particularly her mother. To a certain extent she seems to do so in this fourth narrative. For all the negative, even horrifying, aspects of Brave Orchid's fierce preservation and Moon Orchid's repetitious fantasies, both women come across in this section as fully human. Her mother, especially, does so; and that is because, releasing her mother to be her own character, under her own name "Brave Orchid," rather than as "my mother," the daughter penetrates her mother's subjectivity with tender ironies and gentle mercies. In doing so, she effaces her own presence in the text as character, her presence implied only in the reference to Brave Orchid's "children." Unlike her mother, then, who does not imagine the contours of her sister's subjectivity, Kingston here tries to think like her mother and her aunt. Yet even as she creates the fullness of her mother out of her word, she recognizes the very fictionality of her tale—its "designs" that serve her own hermeneutical purposes. She, too, like her mother within her story, negotiates the world by means of the fictions that sustain interpretations and preserve identities. In the persistent reciprocities that characterize Kingston's storytelling, her mother becomes the product of her fictions, as she has been the product of her mother's.

Kingston represents in the final piece, "A Song for a Barbarian Reed Pipe," her adolescent struggle to discover her own speaking voice and autobiographical authority. This drama originates in the memory of her mother's literally cutting the voice out of her: "She pushed my tongue up and sliced the frenum. Or maybe she snipped it with a pair of nail scissors. I don't remember her doing it, only her telling me about it, but all during childhood I felt sorry for the baby whose mother waited with scissors or knife in hand for it to cry—and then, when its mouth was wide open like a baby bird's, cut" (190). Notably, Kingston remembers, not the actual event, but the reconstruction of the event in language, a phenomenon testifying to the power of the mother's word to constitute the daughter's history, in this case her continuing sense of confusion, horror, deprivation, and violation. Her mother passes on a tale of female castration, a rite of passage analogous to a clitoridectomy, that wounding of the female body in service to the community, performed and thereby perpetuated by the mother.[22] It is a ritual that results in the denial to woman of the pleasure of giving voice to her body and body to her voice, the pleasure of autobiographical legitimacy and authority.

In her re-creation of the confrontation with the Chinese-American girl in the bathroom of the Chinese school, Kingston evokes her childhood confusion about speechlessness: "Most of us," she comments, "eventually found some voice, however faltering. We invented an American-feminine speaking personality, except for that one girl who could not speak up even in Chinese school" (200). A kind of surrogate home, the Chinese school functions as the repository of old traditions and conventional identities within the immigrant community; and the bathroom is that most private of female spaces—only for girls, only for certain activities, which, as it locates the elimination of matter from the body, ultimately becomes associated with female pollution and shame. In that space, Kingston responds cruelly, even violently, to the female image before her, abhorring the girl's useless fragility: her neat, pastel clothes; her China-doll haircut; her tiny, white teeth; her baby-soft, fleshy skin—"like squid out of which the glassy blades of bones had been pulled," "like tracing paper, onion paper" (206). Most of all, she abhors her "dumbness," for this girl, who cannot even speak her name aloud, is ultimately without body or text. " 'You're such a nothing,' " Kingston remembers yelling at her. " 'You are a plant. Do you know that? That's all you are if you don't talk. If you don't talk, you can't have a personality. You'll have no personality and no hair. You've got to let people know you have a personality and a brain. You think somebody is going to take care of you all your stupid life?' " (210).

Yet, while the girl stands mute before the screaming Kingston, they both weep profusely, wiping their snot on their sleeves as the seemingly frozen scene wraps them both in its embrace. Kingston remembers feeling some comfort in establishing her difference from the girl, taking pride in her dirty fingernails, calloused hands, yellow teeth, her desire to wear black. But the fierceness with which she articulates her desire for difference only accentuates her actual identity with the nameless girl: Both are the last ones chosen by teams; both are silent and "dumb" in the American school. An exaggerated representation of the perfect Chinese girl, this girl becomes a mirror image of Kingston herself, reflecting her own fears of insubstantiality and dumbness (symbolized for her in the zero intelligence quotient that marks her first-grade record). In the pulling of the hair, the poking of the flesh, Kingston captures the violence of her childhood insecurity and self-hatred. Striking the Chinese-American girl, she strikes violently at her own failure to take a voice and at all her mother's prior narratives of female voicelessness. Tellingly, her aggressive attack on that mirror image eventuates, not in the girl's utterance of her name, but in Kingston's eighteen-month illness, which ensures that she indeed does become like the other girl. Confined to bed, isolated inside the house, she is literally silenced in the public space, a fragile and useless girl. Attended always by her family, she too becomes a plant, a nothing. Ironically, she says of that time. "It was the best year and a half of my life. Nothing happened" (212). The admission betrays the tremendous relief of not having to prove to people she has "a personality and a brain," the powerful enticement of succumbing to the implications of her mother's narratives and her culture's maxims, the confusing attractiveness of not having to find a public voice, of not struggling with shame.

For, as her narrative recollection reveals, taking a voice becomes complicated by her sense of guilt. She is ashamed to speak in public with a voice like those of the immigrant women—loud, inelegant, unsubtle. She is ashamed to speak the words her mother demands she say to the druggist ghost because she considers her mother's words, as they exact compliance with traditional beliefs, to be outdated. She is ashamed to keep the same kind of silences and secrets her mother would keep because such secrets command her duplicity before the teachers she respects. For all these reasons she would not speak like her mother (and Chinese women) in her American environment; but her own efforts to take the appropriate American-feminine voice fail, and that failure too gives her cause for shame. In public her voice becomes "a crippled animal running on broken legs" (196), a duck voice; her throat "cut[s]" off the word; her mouth appears "permanently crooked with effort, turned down on the left side and straight on the right" (199). Her face and vocal chords continue to show the signs of her prior castration, the physical mutilation and discomfort that mark her relationship to language and to any public enunciation of subjectivity.

The landscape of her childhood, as she reconstructs it, reveals the underlying logic in Kingston's failure to overcome her symbolic disability. Seeing around her the humiliating representations of woman, hearing words such as "maggots" become synonyms for "girls," suspecting that her mother seeks to contract her out as the wife and slave of some young man, perhaps even the retarded boy who follows her around with his box full of pornographic pictures, she negotiates a nightmare of female victimization by adopting the postures of an unattractive girl, the better to foil her mother's efforts and to forestall her weary capitulation. Cultivating that autobiographical signature, she represents herself publicly as the obverse of her mother's image of the charming, attractive, practical young girl by becoming clumsy, vulgar, bad-tempered, lazy, impractical, irreverent, and stupid "from reading too much" (226). She becomes, that is, a kind of fiction; and the psychic price she pays for orchestrating such a public posture is high. Publicly appearing as the "dumb" and awkward girl, she does not earn the affection and respect of her family and community. Moreover, she must convince herself of the reality of her mind by constantly attending to the grades she earns in the American school, those signs, unrecognized in her Chinese culture, that signal her access to other discourses. She remains "dumb" in another sense, for she recognizes even in childhood that "talking and not talking made the difference between sanity and insanity," in that "insane people were the ones who couldn't explain themselves" (216). Since she cannot give voice to her subjectivity except by indirection and dissimulation, externalizing in an awkward masquerade the text of publicly unexpressed desires, she finds commonality with the anomalous women such as Pee-A-Nah and Crazy Mary, who retreat into imaginary worlds, there to haunt the outskirts of the immigrant community and the imaginations of its children.

The culmination of this struggle with voice comes when Kingston finally attempts to "explain" her silenced guilts, the text of which lengthens daily, and to represent her repressed desires to her mother, believing that by doing so she will establish some grounds for identification and overcome her profound isolation and dumbness: "If only I could let my mother know the list, she—and the world—would become more like me, and I would never be alone again" (230). Recapitulating the earlier castration, her mother cuts her tongue by refusing to acknowledge the daughter's stories as legitimate: "'I can't stand this whispering,' she said looking right at me, stopping her squeezing. 'Senseless gabbings every night. I wish you would stop. Go away and work. Whispering, whispering, making no sense. Madness. I don't feel like hearing your craziness'" (233). In response, Kingston swallows her words, but only temporarily. The tautness of her vocal cords increasing to a breaking point, she later bursts the silence, uttering in a cathartic moment the text of her inner life before her mother. Finally, this girl takes of voice, albeit in great confusion, and thereby authors a vision, textualizes her subjectivity, and legitimizes her own desires. She embarks, that is, on the autobiographical enterprise, articulating her interpretations against her mother's.

In this battle of words, mother and daughter, products of different cultural experiences, systems of signs, and modes of interpretation, speak two different "languages" and inscribe two different stories—graphically imaged in the sets of quotation marks that delimit their separate visions and betray the gap in the matrilineage as the circle of identity, of place and desire, is disrupted. Unable to understand the mother, unwilling to identify with her, the daughter would, in ironic reciprocity, cut off her mother's word: "'I don't want to listen to any more of your stories; they have no logic. They scramble me up. You lie with stories. You won't tell me a story and then say, 'This is a true story,' or 'This is just a story'" (235). But her mother's reluctant admission—"'We like to say the opposite'" (237)—forces Kingston to question, at the moment of their origin, her own interpretations and thus the "truth" or "fictiveness" of the autobiography she would inscribe through her memories of the past. As a result, the young Kingston comes to recognize the relativity of truth, the very elusiveness of self-representation that drives the autobiographical enterprise. "Ho Chi Kuai" her mother calls her; and, even to the moment in her adult life when she writes her autobiography, she cannot specify, can only guess, the meaning of the name her mother gave her from that culture she would leave behind. In the end she can only try to decipher the meaning of her past, her subjectivity, her desire, her own name: "I continue to sort out what's just my childhood, just my imagination, just my family, just the village, just movies, just living" (239).

Kingston closes *The Woman Warrior* with a coda, returning it to silence after telling two brief stories, one her mother's, one hers. She starts with the former: "Here is a story my mother told me, not when I was young, but recently, when I told her I also talk-story. The beginning is hers, the ending, mine" (240). Notably, her mother's story is now a gift. Passed from one storyteller to another, it signals the mother's genuine identification with the daughter. Yet the two-part story also functions as a testament to difference, the simple juxtaposition of two words rather than the privileging of one before the other. Here, at last, Kingston lets her mother's word stand without resisting it.

Her mother's story, set in the China of the previous generation, presents Kingston's grandmother as a willful and powerful woman who, convinced "that our family was immune to harm as long as they went to plays" (241), loves to attend theater performances. Unfolding in the ironies of the unexpected, the contingencies of opposites, the absense of linear logic, the story is emblematic of Brave Orchid's individual narrative style and vision, of the kinds of stories she tells. It speaks both of the horrifying vulnerability of women and of their fierce and commanding power; and it tells of the power of art to sustain the continuity of life and the power of interpretations to turn adversity and victimization to triumph. Through her "gift," mother places daughter in the line of powerful "Chinese" women whose source of inspiration and whose very survival in the midst of vulnerability lie in the word of the creative imagination.

Kingston follows her mother's words with what she imagines might be the story on the stage at one of those performances. Turning toward rather than resisting her Chinese roots, she takes as her protagonist a Chinese poet who lived in the second century.[23] Forced to live among barbarians for twelve years, during which time she bears two children who cannot speak Chinese, Ts'ai Yen remains isolated beyond the boundaries that sustain her sense of place and identity. Nonetheless, she eventually discovers that even barbarians make music of life and longing, reflecting civilized, rather than merely primitive, sensibilities. In the midst of cultural difference, the poet finds a commonality of experience and subjectivity through the language of art, which enables her to give voice to her own desire for self-representation and, in doing so, to join the circle of humanity. Eventually, Ts'ai Yen is ransomed, returning to her home "so that her father would have Han descendants" (243); but the more momentous "birth" she contributes to posterity is the song of sadness, anger, and wandering created out of her experience in the alien land. Speaking of human yearning, it "translates well" through the generations and across communal boundaries. Ultimately, the story of Ts'ai Yen, the woman of words, is the tale of Brave Orchid, who finds herself hostage in the barbarian land of America where even her children, born like Ts'ai Yen's among the aliens, cannot "speak" her native language, cannot understand her. Yet the tale is simultaneously that of Kingston herself, whose sense of alienation is doubly complicated, since, as a product of two cultures, she remains outside the circle of both. Mother and daughter sing the songs of sadness, loneliness, and displacement, finding their common sustenance in the word. Thus through her storytelling Kingston can create the total identification of mother and daughter as they both become Ts'ai Yen, woman poet.

In that final juxtaposition of two stories, Kingston asserts the grounds of identification with her mother, affirming continuities rather than disjunctions in the line.[24] She is her mother's daughter, however much she may distance herself geographically and psychologically, learning from her the power and authority that enable her to originate her own storytelling. Carrying on the matrilineal trace, she becomes like her mother a mistress of the word in a culture that would privilege only the lines, textual and genealogical, of patrilineal descent.[25] With her text she gives historical "birth" to Brave Orchid, creating for her a textual space in the genealogical record, and she gives "birth" to herself as the daughter who has passed through the body and the word of the mother.

Coda

Until the twentieth century women who chose to write public autobiography—as Kempe, Cavendish, Charke, and Martineau did—appropriated androcentric fictions as their templates for self-expression. Bringing their experiences as women and their attentiveness to cultural fictions of woman to the autobiographical forms developed and privileged by patriarchal authorities (literary, ecclesiastical, political), these women responded to their own desires as well as to the expectations of their cultural reader. They sometimes brought an unbridled vitality to the formal rigidities of androcentric structures of signification. They sometimes brought too unself-conscious a desire to make the form and voice of their selfhood fit the androcentric model, as did Charke and Martineau.

In the twentieth century the woman who writes autobiography becomes more self-conscious of her place as woman and as narrator. Certainly, modernism and postmodernism have precipitated that self-consciousness. Profoundly influencing the direction of generic possibilities, postmodernism has effectively subverted the ideology of individualism, demystified the idea of a metaphysical self and its relationship to language and literature. The ideas of psychology and psychoanalysis have shattered comfortable assumptions about the integrity of consciousness; the challenges of twentieth-century philosophy have forcefully questioned the relationship of knowledge and power. Poststructuralism, with its critique of the metaphysics of presence, has disrupted the notion of the author and of authority itself. Language, we have come to understand, speaks us even as we speak through it. The ideology of gender that so carefully structured the way men and women conceived of themselves and their place in the universe has been bombarded from all kinds of ideological and methodological points of view. For both men and women, then, the teleological conception of selfhood has given way before experimental explorations of experience, memory, language, sexuality, social and political engagements. In this time of destabilization, however, women (and other culturally disempowered people) have been able to promote their own vision of empowering selfhood, with more variety, volubility, and authority than in earlier centuries. For voices from the margins are louder at the moment of cultural instability.

Moreover, the breakdown of a hegemonic conception of selfhood has fostered the collateral breakdown of canonical literature's hegemony. "Autobiography" no longer makes sense culturally. Its structural, rhetorical, and imagistic rigidities have been fractured by the heteroglossic possibilities inherent in new ideologies of selfhood. Thus, as women have taken their own voices as the source of autobiographical truth, they have engaged the genre of autobiography with more inventiveness and ingenuity than did their foremothers. With more freedom and possibilities, women writing autobiography in the twentieth century explore alternative scenarios of textuality and sexuality. Kingston provides one avenue for expressive selfhood, discovering her own voice through the overpowering voices of her culture. But others have also experimented with formal autobiography, fracturing it beyond recognition as they fracture conventional fictions of female desire beyond recognition. Gertrude Stein invests herself in another's voice to talk about her own life in *The Autobiography of Alice B. Toklas*. Later she becomes "Everybody" of *Everybody's Autobiography*. Virginia Woolf pursues narratively those "moments of being" that imprinted themselves through the imagination of a sensitive, talented girl who came of age at the nexus of the nineteenth and twentieth centuries. Dorothy Richardson diffuses her rhetorical persona throughout long volumes of semiautobiographical narrative. Anaïs Nin literally lives her life in the multivolume outpouring of language and desire. For these women all, the masculine autobiographical mode is passé. Rejecting the universalizing ideology of the essential self that erases male and female difference on the one hand and that illegitimizes female forms of self on the other, they pursue a vision of their own.

Yet twentieth-century daughters share a heretical posture with their foremothers. For, ultimately, every woman who writes autobiography ends up interrogating the prevailing ideology of gender, if only unconsciously and clumsily. In her engagement with the fictions of the dominant discourse, the autobiographer who is a woman pushes against the boundaries of cultural patterns of verisimilitude and significance. Inevitably, as she represents herself to the world, the woman autobiographer rereads the stories of man and of woman. She greets, identifies with, rebels against, cannibalizes, and ultimately transforms public forms of selfhood. Cannabalizing the forms of selfhood embedded in the ideology of gender, she turns the female "self" and female storytelling into some amalgam, something neither conventionally male nor female, some energizing mutation played on autobiographical possibilities. Fashioning her own voice within and against the voices of others, she performs a selective appropriation of stories told by and about men and women. Subversively, she rearranges the dominant discourse and the dominant ideology of gender, seizing the language and its powers to turn cultural fictions into her very own story.

From the interiors of her subjectivity, she presses against the flat-surfaced panes of patriarchal figures of female desire, selfhood, and life stories. And, from outside the experience of man, she presses against the comfortable interiors of male-identified selfhood and autobiography. She also looks from within and without through another pair of eyes, if often dimmed by the dark glasses of language's conventions. In reenvisioning cultural figures of selfhood through the perspectives of her own experience, she ends up questioning the complacencies of culture itself, exposing both the limitations on and the possibilities of self-invention in the symbolic order of patriarchy and unmasking for her reader her own, often qualified, empowerment within the words and narratives that would silence her. Sometimes, in the wonderful ingeniousness of her effort, she performs a critical unraveling of the hegemonic figures of selfhood. Always she ends up creating herself once again in a medium that will hold her forever still but not silenced.

In that creative gesture, woman speaks to her culture from the margins. While margins have their limitations, they also have their advantages of vision. They are polyvocal, more distant from the centers of power and conventions of selfhood. They are heretical. Perhaps that is why I have found women's autobiographies to be both eccentric and alive, whatever their limitations. There is a theatricality about them, but of the regional stage. Characterized by dysphoria, by the restlessness and anxieties of self-authorship, women's stories frustrate expectations and thoroughly enchant the reader because they are vital, unconventional. From them erupt, however suppressed they might be, rebellion, confusion, ambivalence, the uncertainties of desire. But always there is that voice, close to the surface of the story, telling about woman's life, negotiating the stories of man and woman.

The inventiveness and originality of women's autobiographies in the history of the genre and the source of their fate at the hands of traditionally minded critics (those arbiters of the symbolic order and its ideology of gender) lie in that very attempt to reconcile sometimes irreconcilable readings of the self, to sustain and to subvert comfortable fictions. They lie in that quarrel with one kind of significance or the other's.

Notes

1. AUTOBIOGRAPHY CRITICISM AND THE PROBLEMATICS OF GENDER

1. James Olney, "Autobiography and the Humanities," proposal submitted to the National Endowment for the Humanities, June 1, 1980, p. 3. Olney offered this seminar for college teachers at the University of North Carolina at Chapel Hill, summer 1981.

2. William C. Spengemann, *The Forms of Autobiography: Episodes in the History of a Literary Genre* (New Haven and London: Yale Univ. Press, 1980), pp. 170–246; James Olney, "Autobiography and the Cultural Moment," in *Autobiography: Essays Theoretical and Critical*, ed. James Olney (Princeton: Princeton Univ. Press, 1980), pp. 3–27. Both essays provide a far more comprehensive overview than I intend to provide here.

3. Spengemann, pp. 175–76.

4. Georg Misch, *A History of Autobiography in Antiquity*, trans. E. W. Dickes (Cambridge: Harvard Univ. Press, 1951), pp. 8–13.

5. Georges Gusdorf, "Conditions et limites de l'autobiographie," *Formen der Selbstdarstellung: Analekten zu einer Geschichte des literarischen Selbstportraits* (Festgabe fur Fritz Neubert), ed. Gunther Reichenkron and Erich Hasse (Berlin: Duncker & Humblot, 1956); Francis R. Hart, "Notes for an Anatomy of Modern Autobiography," *New Literary History* 1 (1970): 485–511. An English translation of Gusdorf's article is included in *Autobiography*, ed. Olney, pp. 28–48.

6. Olney, "Autobiography and the Cultural Moment," p. 20.

7. Wayne Shumaker, *English Autobiography: Its Emergence, Materials, and Forms* (Berkeley and Los Angeles: Univ. of California Press, 1954); Margaret Bottrall, *Every Man a Phoenix: Studies in Seventeenth-Century Autobiography* (Chester Springs, Pa: Dufour, 1958); Paul Delany, *British Autobiography in the Seventeenth Century* (London: Routledge & Kegan Paul, 1969); Daniel B. Shea, *Spiritual Autobiography in Early America* (Princeton: Princeton Univ. Press, 1968); Hart; Roy Pascal, *Design and Truth in Autobiography* (Cambridge: Harvard Univ. Press, 1960); Spengemann; William L. Howarth, "Some Principles of Autobiography," *New Literary History* 5 (1974): 363–81. For more comprehensive bibliographies, see also Olney, "Autobiography and the Cultural Moment"; and Spengemann.

8. Ultimately, as both Olney and Spengemann suggest, the typologies have proliferated and generic definition has remained elusive; they have proven neither coherent nor exhaustive.

9. See the discussion of "classical autobiography theory" in Elizabeth W. Bruss, "Eye for I: Making and Unmaking Autobiography in Film," in *Autobiography*, ed. Olney, pp. 296–320. See also Janet Varner Gunn, *Autobiography: Toward a Poetics of Experience* (Philadelphia: Univ. of Pennsylvania Press, 1982), pp. 6–10.

10. This brief description of recent theories is adapted from Sidonie Smith and Marcus Billson, "Toward a Structuralist Poetics of Autobiography," paper presented at the annual meeting of the Modern Language Association, Houston, December 1980.

11. Michael Sprinker, "Fictions of the Self: The End of Autobiography," in *Autobiography*, ed. Olney, p. 342.

12. Barbara Johnson, *The Critical Difference: Essays in the Contemporary Rhetoric of Reading* (Baltimore: Johns Hopkins Univ. Press, 1980), p. 5. For an analysis of modernity's subversion of the West's paternal narratives, see Alice Jardine, *Gynesis: Configurations of Woman and Modernity* (Ithaca: Cornell Univ. Press, 1985), esp. ch. 3.

13. Nelly Furman, "Textual Feminism," in *Women and Language in Literature and Society*, ed. Sally McConnell-Ginet, Ruth Borker, and Nelly Furman (New York: Praeger, 1980), pp. 49–50.

14. Nancy K. Miller, "Women's Autobiography in France: For a Dialectics of Identification," in *Women and Language*, ed. McConnell-Ginet, Borker, and Furman, p. 271.

15. Gunn, p. 8.

16. Spengemann, p. 189. If we need to rely on linear conceptions of the history of autobiography criticism, we might, as Spengemann suggests, more appropriately set those approaches along a continuum with historiography on the one end and poetics on the other.

17. Spengemann, p. 205.

18. Olney, "Autobiography and the Cultural Moment," pp. 13–17.

19. Misch, p. 14.

20. Ibid., p. 12

21. Chapter two elaborates these issues in more detail. Let me note briefly here that, within the order of patriarchy, the realm of domesticity has been associated literally and symbolically with biological determinism and therefore with nature and necessity; the realm of public life is valued as the higher arena in which full humanity can be earned and the realm of necessity and nature, transcended. Many social scientists and theorists explore that aspect of patriarchy. See, for instance, Michelle Zimbalist Rosaldo, "Woman, Culture, and Society: A Theoretical Overview," in *Women, Culture, and Society*, ed. Michelle Zimbalist Rosaldo and Louise Lamphere (Stanford: Stanford Univ. Press, 1974), pp. 17–42; and Sherri Ortner, "Is Female to Male as Nature Is to Culture?" in ibid., pp. 67–87. Simone de Beauvoir explores the same phenomenon in the language of existentialist philosophy in Simone de Beauvoir, *The Second Sex*, trans. and ed. H. M. Parshley (New York: Knopf, 1953). For a variety of discussions of women's relationship to language and to the institution of literature in patriarchal culture, see such recent works as Sandra M. Gilbert and Susan Gubar, *The Madwoman in the Attic: The Woman Writer and the Nineteenth-Century Literary Imagination* (New Haven: Yale Univ. Press, 1979), esp. pp. 3–104; Margaret Homans, *Women Writers and Poetic Identity: Dorothy Wordsworth, Emily Brontë, and Emily Dickinson* (Princeton: Princeton Univ. Press, 1980); Elaine Showalter, *A Literature of Their Own: British Women Novelists from Brontë to Lessing* (Princeton: Princeton Univ. Press, 1977); Ellen Moers, *Literary Women: The Great Writers* (Garden City: Doubleday, 1976); and Patricia Meyer Spacks, *The Female Imagination* (New York: Knopf, 1975).

22. Jardine, pp. 118–19.

23. Elaine Showalter, "Feminist Criticism in the Wilderness," *Critical Inquiry* 8 (Winter 1981): 200. For a discussion of women's writing as lying on "the other side of the border," see also Myra Jehlen, "Archimedes and the Paradox of Feminist Criticism," *Signs: Journal of Women in Culture and Society* 6 (Autumn 1981): 582.

24. Karl Joachim Weintraub, *The Value of the Individual: Self and Circumstance in Autobiography* (Chicago: Univ. of Chicago Press, 1978), p. xv.

25. Ibid., pp. xvi–xvii.

26. Jehlen (pp. 593–94) also makes this point as she contrasts the vision of senti-

mentality embodied in Melville's *Pierre* with that embodied in the popular novels written by women during the nineteenth century.

27. Weintraub, p. 211.

28. From a certain point of view, the essence of mysticism allies itself with medieval notions of the feminine principle generally. Male mystics manifested traits similar to those of female mystics. Yet men were freer to choose mysticism as a form of religious experience; for women it may have remained a necessity. And men might assume its traits while assured of their identity as men; women seemed to be assuming the only form of worship they were generally suited to assume. Such possible differences and others not elaborated here suggest the complexity of the relationship of mysticism to the feminine. See also Marie-Florine Bruneau, "The Writing of History as Fiction and Ideology: The Case of Madame Guyon," *Feminist Issues* 5 (Spring 1985): 27–38.

29. Delany, p. 158.

30. Ibid., pp. 158, 159.

31. Shumaker, p. 24.

32. Ibid., p. 20.

33. Other critics bring to their reading of women's autobiographies similarly conventional expectations of and pronouncements about appropriately "feminine" heroism and narrative perspective. Bottrall devotes a good deal of space to Anne Lady Halkett's autobiography, although she does so only at the end of her study of seventeenth-century works. She pronounces with confidence that the work is "a thoroughly feminine document," by which she means: "It is neither reflective nor speculative; it is concerned with persons and actions, not with ideas" (p. 149). Yet she also notes that Halkett's work adumbrates the novels of Samuel Richardson in the eighteenth century.

34. Hart, p. 492.

35. Nancy Chodorow, *The Reproduction of Mothering: Psychoanalysis and the Sociology of Gender* (Berkeley and Los Angeles: Univ. of California Press, 1978), pp. 126–27, 169. See also Nancy Chodorow, "Family Structure and Feminine Personality," in *Women, Culture, and Society*, ed. Rosaldo and Lamphere, pp. 43–66; and Nancy Julia Chodorow, "Feminism and Difference: Gender, Relation and Difference in Psychoanalytic Perspective," *Socialist Review* 46 (July-August 1979): 51–69, repr. in *The Future of Difference*, ed. Hester Eisenstein and Alice Jardine (Boston: G. K. Hall, 1980), pp. 3–19. See also Dorothy Dinnerstein, *The Mermaid and the Minotaur: Sexual Arrangements and the Human Malaise* (New York: Harper & Row, 1976); Jane Flax, "Mother-Daughter Relationships: Psychodynamics, Politics, and Philosophy," in *The Future of Difference*, ed. Eisenstein and Jardine, pp. 20–40; and Jean Baker Miller, *Toward a New Psychology of Women* (Boston: Beacon Press, 1976). For an excellent review essay on literature about motherhood and daughterhood, see Marianne Hirsch, "Mothers and Daughters," *Signs: Journal of Women in Culture and Society* 7 (Winter 1981): 200–222.

36. Chodorow, *The Reproduction of Mothering*, p. 127.

37. Ibid., p. 169.

38. Ibid.

39. Madeleine Gagnon, "Body I," in *New French Feminisms*, ed. Elaine Marks and Isabelle de Courtivron (Amherst: Univ. of Massachusetts Press, 1980), p. 179; Hélène Cixous, "The Laugh of the Medusa," trans. Keith Cohen and Paula Cohen, *Signs: Journal of Women in Culture and Society* 1 (Summer 1976): 881. This too brief summary glosses over the very significant differences among the prominent French

theorists. Moreover, it does not address the relationship of the male writer to "feminine" writing. For further discussions of French feminism, see Josette Féral, "Antigone or the Irony of the Tribe," *Diacritics* 8 (September 1978): 2–14; Ann Rosalind Jones, "Writing the Body: Toward an Understanding of *l'Écriture féminine*," *Feminist Studies* 7 (Summer 1981): 247–63; Michele Richman, "Eroticism in the Patriarchal Order," *Diacritics* 6 (Spring 1976): 46–53; Michele Richman, "Sex and Signs: The Language of French Feminist Criticism," *Language and Style* 13 (1980): 62–80; Barbara Charlesworth Gelpi, ed., "French Feminist Theory," *Signs: Journal of Women in Culture and Society* 7 (Fall 1981): 1–86; Eisenstein and Jardine, eds., *The Future of Difference;* and Julia Kristeva, *Desire in Language: A Semiotic Approach to Literature and Art*, trans. Leon S. Roudiez, Alice Jardine, and Thomas Gora (New York: Columbia Univ. Press, 1980).

40. Chodorow ("Family Structure," p. 56) quotes this conclusion from R. Carlson, "Sex Differences in Ego Functioning: Exploratory Studies of Agency and Communion," *Journal of Consulting and Clinical Psychology* 37 (1971): 270. For explorations of the implications of feminist psychological theory in discussions of the female *Bildungsroman*, see Elizabeth Abel, Marianne Hirsch, and Elizabeth Langland, eds., *The Voyage In: Fictions of Female Development* (Hanover: Univ. Press of New England, 1983), esp. the introduction.

41. Margaret Homans, *Bearing the Word: Language and Female Experience in Nineteenth-Century Women's Writing* (Chicago: Univ. of Chicago Press, 1986), p. 13.

42. Willis R. Buck, Jr., "Reading Autobiography," *Genre* 13 (Winter 1980): 477–98.

43. Sandra M. Gilbert and Susan Gubar, "Sexual Linguistics: Gender, Language, Sexuality," *New Literary History* 16 (Spring 1985): 517.

44. Nancy K. Miller, "Emphasis Added: Plots and Plausibilities in Women's Fiction," *PMLA* 96 (January 1981): 46.

45. For a discussion of the process of misreading in general and as a theme in fiction by women, see Annette Kolodny, "A Map for Rereading: Or, Gender and the Interpretation of Literary Texts," *New Literary History* 11 (1980): 451–67.

46. Domna C. Stanton, "Autogynography: Is the Subject Different?" in *The Female Autograph*, ed. Domna C. Stanton (New York: New York Literary Forum, 1984), pp. 8–9.

47. Ibid., pp. 6–7.

48. Ibid., p. 18.

49. See, for instance, Cynthia S. Pomerleau, "The Emergence of Women's Autobiography in England," in *Women's Autobiography: Essays in Criticism*, ed. Estelle C. Jelinek (Bloomington: Indiana Univ. Press, 1980), pp. 21–39; and Carol Edkins, "Quest for Community: Spiritual Autobiographies of Eighteenth-Century Quaker and Puritan Women in America," in ibid., pp. 39–52.

50. Jelinek makes this argument for difference in Estelle C. Jelinek, "Introduction: Women's Autobiography and the Male Tradition," in ibid., pp. 1–20.

51. Stanton, p. 13.

52. Ibid., p. 14.

53. Cixous, p. 878.

54. Xavière Gauthier, "Existe-t-il une écriture de femme?" [Is there such a thing as women's writing?], trans. Marilyn A. August, in *New French Feminisms*, ed. Marks and de Courtivron, pp. 162–63. See also Gilbert and Gubar, "Sexual Linguistics," pp. 515–43.

55. Nancy K. Miller, "Arachnologies: The Woman, the Text, and the Critic," in

The Poetics of Gender, ed. Nancy K. Miller (New York: Columbia Univ. Press, 1986), pp. 270–96.

56. Virginia Woolf, *A Room of One's Own* (New York: Harcourt, Brace & World, 1957), p. 33.

2. RENAISSANCE HUMANISM AND THE MISBEGOTTEN MAN: A TENSION OF DISCOURSES IN THE EMERGENCE OF AUTOBIOGRAPHY

1. Georges Gusdorf, "Conditions and Limits of Autobiography," in *Autobiography: Essays Theoretical and Critical*, ed. James Olney (Princeton: Princeton Univ. Press, 1980), p. 30. Gusdorf opposes this historical consciousness to a mythical consciousness governed by such principles as eternal recurrence and repetition.

2. Ibid., p. 33.

3. G. A. Starr, *Defoe and Spiritual Autobiography* (New York: Gordian Press, 1971), pp. 13–14.

4. Michel Foucault, *The History of Sexuality*, vol. 1, *An Introduction* (New York: Pantheon, 1978), pp. 58–59.

5. Paul Delany, *British Autobiography in the Seventeenth Century* (London: Routledge & Kegan Paul, 1969), pp. 19–22. Economic historians would emphasize that the rise of early capitalism, with its demands for dependable sources of labor and new productive relationships, effectively subordinated the family unit (the family of the aristocracy included) to the state and to the forces of production. Moreover, this centralized state authority was served by an institutionally trained, rather than family trained, professional class that received its education in universities.

6. Basil Willey, *The Seventeenth Century Background: Studies in the Thought of the Age in Relation to Poetry and Religion* (Garden City: Doubleday, 1953), p. 15. See also Gusdorf, p. 31.

7. Willey, pp. 38–41.

8. For a discussion of the darker consequences of the scientific revolution, see Marjorie Hope Nicolson, *The Breaking of the Circle: Studies in the Effect of the "New Science" on Seventeenth-Century Poetry*, rev. ed. (New York: Columbia Univ. Press, 1960).

9. Wayne Shumaker, *English Autobiography: Its Emergence, Materials, and Forms* (Berkeley and Los Angeles: Univ. of California Press, 1954), p. 90.

10. Gusdorf, pp. 32–33. Delany (pp. 12–13) also notes the significance of the new Venetion mirrors and discusses Renaissance portraiture, including self-portraiture.

11. See Lennard J. Davis, *Factual Fictions: The Origins of the English Novel* (New York: Columbia Univ. Press, 1983), esp. chs. 1–8.

12. Ian P. Watt, *The Rise of the Novel: Studies in Defoe, Richardson, and Fielding* (Los Angeles and Berkeley: Univ. of California Press, 1957), p. 13. Josephine Donovan refers to Watt's analysis when she explores the influence of the Cartesian world vision on the novel in Josephine Donovan, "The Silence Is Broken," *Women and Language in Literature and Society*, ed. Sally McConnell-Ginet, Ruth Borker, and Nelly Furman (New York: Praeger, 1980), p. 208.

13. Delany, p. 167.

14. Ibid., p. 11. See also Stephen Jay Greenblatt, *Renaissance Self-Fashioning: From More to Shakespeare* (Chicago: Univ. of Chicago Press, 1980).

15. Of course, as Misch evidences so persuasively (Georg Misch, *A History of Autobiography in Antiquity*, trans. E. W. Dickes [Cambridge: Harvard Univ. Press,

1951]), autobiographical inscriptions existed. But they do not represent self-conscious attempts to capture a life in text. The problem of Augustine's *Confessions* remains, however: It appeared approximately one thousand years before autobiography emerged as a common phenomenon. Not only has autobiography criticism been riddled by a flurry of competing and complementary typologies that attempt to define the ever elusive form; it has also been riddled with disagreements about when the first autobiography was written. As Olney remarks (James Olney, "Autobiography and the Cultural Moment," in *Autobiography*, ed. Olney, pp. 5–7), the word *autobiography* was first introduced into the English language at the end of the eighteenth century. Yet such literal dating helps no one to define the genre or to name the first autobiography. Ultimately, the two issues are related: The designation of the first true autobiography will depend on the generic definition and typology that motivate a particular critical study.

16. Donovan, p. 209. Donovan comments on the new novel that "there were really no classical models nor critical rules that one would have to know in order to practice its writing" (ibid.). The same absence of models and rules characterized autobiographical practice.

17. Elizabeth W. Bruss, "Eye for I: Making and Unmaking Autobiography in Film," in *Autobiography*, ed. Olney, p. 298.

18. Ibid.; Michael Sprinker, "Fictions of the Self: The End of Autobiography," in ibid., p. 326.

19. Literary history becomes one more discourse that maintains the power of the patriarchal order. For forceful analyses of the relationship of discourse to power, see Foucault, *The History of Sexuality*; and Michel Foucault, *Discipline and Punish: The Birth of the Prison*, trans. Alan Sheridan (New York: Pantheon, 1977). For theories of narrative as an institution constituted by inscriptions of paternal genealogies, see representative works such as Roland Barthes, *The Pleasure of the Text*, trans. Richard Miller (New York: Hill and Wang, 1975); Harold Bloom, *The Anxiety of Influence* (New York: Oxford Univ. Press, 1973); and Edward Said, *Beginnings: Intention and Method* (New York: Basic Books, 1975). Although such works do not take as their focus the narrative of literary history, they do presume to discuss a general theory of narrative; certainly literary histories could be expected to manifest the same paradigmatic dramas. More to the point, see the critique of such theories of patrilineal descent put forth forcefully in Sandra M. Gilbert and Susan Gubar, *The Madwoman in the Attic: The Woman Writer and the Nineteenth-Century Literary Imagination* (New Haven: Yale Univ. Press, 1979). For more comments on the patrilineal preoccupation of autobiography criticism, see Annette Kolodny, "The Lady's Not for Spurning: Kate Millett and the Critics," in *Women's Autobiography: Essays in Criticism*, ed. Estelle C. Jelinek (Bloomington: Indiana Univ. Press, 1980), p. 240.

20. Luce Irigaray, *Speculum de l'Autre Femme* (Paris: Editions de Minuit, 1974), p. 92, quoted in Josette Féral, "Antigone or the Irony of the Tribe," *Diacritics* 8 (Fall 1978): 6.

21. See Eleanor Commo McLaughlin, "Equality of Souls, Inequality of Sexes: Woman in Medieval Theology," in *Religion and Sexism: Images of Woman in the Jewish and Christian Traditions*, ed. Rosemary Radford Reuther (New York: Simon & Schuster, 1974), pp. 213–66; Ian Maclean, *The Renaissance Notion of Woman: A Study in the Fortunes of Scholasticism and Medical Science in European Intellectual Life* (Cambridge: Cambridge Univ. Press, 1980), pp. 6–27.

22. See Maryanne Cline Horowitz, "Aristotle and Woman," *Journal of the History of Biology* 9 (Fall 1976): 183–213; and Christine Garside Allen, "Can a Woman Be

Good in the Same Way As a Man?" *Dialogue* 10 (September 1971): 534–44. For a more elaborate discussion of Renaissance notions of woman's physiology and anatomy as they imitated, rejected, and modified Aristotelian conceptions, see Maclean, pp. 28–46.

23. For a more extended discussion of Aquinas's interpretation of the story of the creation and the fall, see McLaughlin, "Equality of Souls," pp. 215–21. For a discussion of Renaissance interpretations of Genesis, see Maclean, pp. 8–14. And think about the implications of the Cartesian *cogito* as it resonates with the matter-form or the nature-intellect dualism inherent in classical philosophy and in Scholastic theology. For a discussion of Descartes's "ego," see Jane Flax, "Mother-Daughter Relationships: Psychodynamics, Politics, and Philosophy," in *The Future of Difference*, ed. Hester Eisenstein and Alice Jardine (Boston: G. K. Hall, 1980), pp. 26–29.

24. Maclean, pp. 15–16. Women, under the Judaic law embodied in the Pentateuch and perpetuated rather than rejected by Christian theology, were considered polluted during menstruation and directly after childbirth; at such times they could not take communion or touch holy vessels. This physiological pollution puts women at a distinct disadvantage to men since men experience no such comparable periods of uncleanliness. Not that Jewish laws do not specify times of uncleanliness for men—they cannot enter a holy sanctuary with running sores or "discharges." But those states are considered diseases in men. The unclean states of women are the normal, not diseased, result of human physiology; thus they are much more frequent and inevitable.

25. McLaughlin, "Equality of Souls," p. 236.

26. According to the *Apostolic Constitutions*, a woman was to be "meek, quiet, gentle, sincere, free from anger, not talkative, not clamorous, not hasty of speech, not given to evil-speaking, not captious, not double-tongued, not a busybody. If she see or hear anything that is not right, let her be as one that does not see, and as one that does not hear . . . and when she is asked anything by anyone, let her not easily answer, excepting questions concerning the faith, and righteousness, and hope in God, remitting those that desire to be instructed in the doctrines of godliness to the governors" (*Ante-Nicene Christian Library*, ed. Alexander Roberts and James Donaldson [Edinburgh: T. and T. Clark, 1868–72], vol. 17, bk. 3, sec. 5, pp. 95–96, quoted in JoAnn McNamara and Suzanne F. Wemple, "Sanctity and Power: The Dual Pursuit of Medieval Women," in *Becoming Visible: Women in European History*, ed. Renate Bridenthal and Claudia Koonz [Boston: Houghton Mifflin, 1977], p. 94).

27. Claude Lévi-Strauss articulates his version of exchange theory, a theory influenced by the earlier work of Marcel Mauss, particularly Mauss's *Essai sur le don* (1925), in Claude Lévi-Strauss, *Elementary Structures of Kinship*, rev. ed., trans. James Harle Bell, John Richard von Sturmer, and Rodney Needham, ed. Rodney Needham (Boston: Beacon Press, 1969). In elaborating the incest taboo, Lévi-Strauss offers a model of cultural origination that focuses on the importance of the exchange of three kinds of signs—goods and services, words, and women. The recognition of these three commodities as items of exchange signaled the emergence of symbolic thought itself; by exchanging words, women, and things, men communicated with other groups of men beyond the kinship core. In that way social, economic, and political structures emerged. For the crucial role marriage plays in Vico's vision of the development of human culture, see Tony Tanner's provocative analysis of *The New Science of Giambattista Vico* in Tony Tanner, *Adultery in the Novel: Contract and Transgression* (Baltimore: Johns Hopkins Univ. Press, 1979), pp. 58–66. For Vico, marriage became the social form that replaced the earlier, bestial, "infamous

promiscuity of things and women." For feminist critiques of Lévi-Strauss's theory see Gayle Rubin, "The Traffic in Women: Notes on the 'Political Economy' of Sex," in *Toward an Anthropology of Women*, ed. Rayna R. Reiter (New York: Monthly Review Press, 1975), pp. 157–210; Michele Richman, "Eroticism in the Patriarchal Order," *Diacritics* 6 (Spring 1976): 46–53; and Michele Richman, "Sex and Signs: The Language of French Feminist Criticism," *Language and Style* 13 (1980): 62–80.

28. The consequences of Eve's entrance into language can be redeemed only by the Word of God made Flesh, in other words, by the Son of God. For representative discussions of the impact of this central myth of origins and woman's relationship to language and literary production, see Gilbert and Gubar, *Madwoman*, esp. chs. 1, 2, and 6; and Margaret Homans, *Women Writers and Poetic Identity: Dorothy Wordsworth, Emily Brontë, and Emily Dickinson* (Princeton: Princeton Univ. Press, 1980), esp. pp. 29–33 and ch. 4.

29. Jean Bethke Elshtain, "Feminist Discourse and Its Discontents: Language, Power, and Meaning," *Signs: Journal of Women in Culture and Society* 7 (1982): 606. For an extended discussion of the figure of woman and the feminine in the philosophies of Plato and Aristotle, see Luce Irigaray, *Speculum of the Other Woman*, trans. Gillian C. Gill (Ithaca: Cornell Univ. Press, 1985).

30. Walter J. Ong describes classical rhetoric in these terms in a book review in *College English* 33 (February 1972): 615.

31. Elshtain, p. 606. For an exploration of the means by which the Greek citizen achieved his freedom and full humanity in the polis, away from the realm of necessity inhabited by women, slaves, and laborers who had no formal or authorized access to public discourse, see Hannah Arendt, *The Human Condition* (Chicago: Univ. of Chicago Press, 1958).

32. See Sarah B. Pomeroy, *Goddesses, Whores, Wives, and Slaves: Women in Classical Antiquity* (New York: Schocken, 1975), esp. ch. 1; and Marilyn Arthur, "'Liberated' Women: The Classical Era," in *Becoming Visible*, ed. Bridenthal and Koonz, pp. 60–89. See also Simone de Beauvoir, *The Second Sex*, trans. and ed. H. M. Parshley (New York: Knopf, 1953). The final scenes of Aeschylus's *Oresteia* are particularly suggestive in this context. Anthene signals the transformation from the law of blood revenge to the universal system of justice with the following claim: "There is no mother anywhere who gave me birth,/ and, but for marriage, I am always for the male/ with all my heart, and strongly on my father's side" (*The Eumenides*, in *Aeschylus I*, ed. David Grene and Richmond Lattimore [New York: Modern Library, 1942], 11.736–38).

33. See Féral, "Antigone," esp. pp. 2–3.

34. McLaughlin, "Equality of Souls," p. 221. For a discussion of the attitude of the church fathers to the virginal life for women, see Eleanor Commo McLaughlin, "Misogynism and Virginal Feminism in the Fathers of the Church," in *Religion and Sexism*, ed. Ruether, pp. 150–83. For further discussions of women in the convent, see also Lina Eckenstein, *Woman under Monasticism* (Cambridge: Cambridge Univ. Press, 1896); Mary Bateson, "Origin and Early History of Double Monasteries," *Transactions of the Royal Historical Society* 13 (1899): 137–98; and Eileen Power, *Medieval English Nunneries* (Cambridge: Cambridge Univ. Press, 1922).

35. "To this very day, mankind has always dreamed of seizing and fixing the fleeting moment when it was permissible to believe that the law of exchange could be evaded, that one could gain without losing, enjoy without sharing. At either end of the earth and at both extremes of time, the Sumerian myth of the golden age and the Andaman myth of the future life correspond, the former placing the end of

primitive happiness at a time when the confusion of languages made words into common property, the latter describing the bliss of the hereafter as a heaven where women will no longer be exchanged" (Lévi-Strauss, pp. 496–97). One might well ask, do women then become unnecessary?

36. McLaughlin, "Equality of Souls," pp. 236–37.

37. McNamara and Wemple, pp. 110–11. McNamara and Wemple also note that the Gregorian revolution of the twelfth century radically curtailed the power of laywomen in the church by introducing priestly celibacy and by eliminating lay participation in the awarding of church offices, thereby wresting power from secular authorities, some of whom were women.

38. McLaughlin, "Equality of Souls," p. 234. McLaughlin discusses the theological arguments informing the church's attitude toward female religious in more detail in ibid., pp. 233–45.

39. Ibid., p. 243.

40. Marina Warner uses this phrase as the title for Marina Warner, *Alone of All Her Sex: The Myth and the Cult of the Virgin Mary* (New York: Knopf, 1976).

41. Perhaps the elevation of Mary and her "feminine" qualities functioned to legitimize certain aspects of woman's nature in an otherwise bleak, misogynistic tradition of theology and sermon. Or perhaps, as McLaughlin suggests, the veneration of the Virgin Mary fulfilled the need of newly celibate priests to imagine a legitimate focus of otherwise illegitimate sexual fantasies; they could meditate on the Virgin Mary in the comfortable knowledge that she was a perfect, therefore unnatural, woman. This focus of interest in medieval culture is one ripe for speculation.

42. McLaughlin, "Equality of Souls," p. 243.

43. McNamara and Wemple, p. 113. See also Joan Kelly-Gadol, "Did Women Have a Renaissance?" in *Becoming Visible*, ed. Bridenthal and Koonz, pp. 137–64. Kelly-Gadol argues that the centralization of state power during the late Middle Ages led to a Renaissance for men, "yet precisely these developments affected women adversely" (p. 139), for the Renaissance ushered in a period of more conservative, more prescriptive visions of women and their appropriate social roles (pp. 160–61).

44. Maclean, p. 78.

45. Maclean discusses the issue of female succession and the theories of various commentators, including Tasso (pp. 61–63). See also Hilda L. Smith, *Reason's Disciples: Seventeenth-Century English Feminists* (Urbana: Univ. of Illinois Press, 1982), pp. 47–48. For further discussion of the discourse surrounding the "female prince," see Margaret W. Ferguson, Maureen Quilligan, and Nancy J. Vickers, eds., *Rewriting the Renaissance: The Discourses of Sexual Difference in Early Modern Europe* (Chicago: Univ. of Chicago Press, 1986), esp. Sheila Elliott, "Catherine de Medici as Artemisia: Figuring the Powerful Woman," in ibid., pp. 227–41; and Constance Jordan, "Feminism and the Humanists: The Case of Sir Thomas Elyot's *Defense of Good Women*," in ibid., pp. 242–58.

46. See Richard T. Vann, "Toward a New Lifestyle: Women in Preindustrial Capitalism," in *Becoming Visible*, ed. Bridenthal and Koonz, pp. 192–216.

47. Jane Dempsey Douglass, "Women and the Continental Reformation," in *Religion and Sexism*, ed. Ruether, p. 297.

48. *D. Martin Luthers Werke: Kritische Gesamtausgabe (Weimarer Ausgabe)* (Weimar: Hermann Böhlaus Nachfolger, 1883ff), vol. 43, p. 344, ll. 4–6, quoted in ibid.

49. See Walter Ong, "Latin Language Study as a Renaissance Puberty Rite," in

Rhetoric, Romance, and Technology: Studies in the Interaction of Expression and Culture (Ithaca: Cornell Univ. Press, 1971), pp. 113–41.

50. Juan Luis Vives, *The Instruction of a Christian Woman*, in *Vives and the Renascence Education of Women*, ed. Foster Watson (New York: Longmans, Green, 1912), p. 34. Smith (pp. 39–48) also quotes this passage from Vives in her analysis of the attitudes of Renaissance humanists to the education of women. She also suggests that while some humanists, such as Sir Thomas More, included intellectual instruction as part of the education of girls and young women, they always reaffirmed the natural subordination of woman to man and limited woman's influence to the domestic and private sphere and to the realm of domesticity. Her education was to be used in private service to father, children, and husband. For a more detailed discussion of the education of Renaissance women, see Ruth Kelso, *Doctrine for the Lady of the Renaissance* (Urbana: Univ. of Illinois Press, 1956), esp. chs. 3, 4, 5.

51. For a discussion of the "word" of woman as always potentially disruptive of the phallic order, see Susan Hardy Aiken, "Dinesen's 'Sorrow-acre': Tracing the Woman's Line," *Contemporary Literature* 25 (Summer 1984): 156–86.

52. Ann Rosalind Jones, "Surprising Fame: Renaissance Gender Ideologies and Women's Lyric," in *The Poetics of Gender*, ed. Nancy K. Miller (New York: Columbia Univ. Press, 1986), p. 76. Along these lines it is interesting to note Luther's impact on the potential uses of language in Western discourse; for he did help to liberate public discourse from the confining hold of the polite, classical languages, ones that could be learned only in academic institutions that denied access to most men and all women. According to Elshtain, "he transformed the possibilities of meaningful public and private discourse by demonstrating that serious attention should be paid to important and vital questions through the vehicle of the vernacular, the down-to-earth language of the ordinary person" (p. 608). By means of that liberation, more authority came to be vested in more speaking subjects who could give voice to and make public the private language of desire and of discontent. But, as Elshtain goes on to comment, "the truculent, irrepressible speech of one person (the brave man) is from another (the uncontrollable or slatternly woman) brazen, irrational, immoral speech" (p. 608). Thus women did not necessarily experience the same liberation, since an androcentric double standard applied to them. Christian women's use of the vernacular—the language they had always spoken—remained defined by such concepts as proper piety and housewifery. In the continued repression of their use of private language to articulate private experience was perpetuated the repression of their identities.

53. Vives, p. 56.

54. Jones, p. 79.

55. Aiken, p. 168.

56. A variety of reasons for the outbreak of the witch craze has been put forward. Some scholars point to the changing patterns of family organization and the shifting nature of economic relationships as sources of the concern about unattached women. Some point to the threat of depopulation that attended the great plague during the late medieval period as a source of the concern that all women become producers of the new generation. Gunnar Heinsohn and Otto Steiger suggest that the power of midwives, most often working-class women, over the dispensation of medicines and of medical education, was broken with the witch trials (Gunnar Heinsohn and Otto Steiger, "The Elimination of Medieval Birth Control and the Witch Trials of Modern Times," *International Journal of Women's Studies* 5 [May/June 1982]: 193–214). Male doctors, aided by the new technology of the forceps, gained

public authority for the control of birth and births. That erasure of knowledge about birth control ensured woman's greater subordination to the dictates of biological necessity and the roles of wife and mother. See Carolyn Merchant, *The Death of Nature: Women, Ecology, and the Scientific Revolution* (San Francisco: Harper & Row, 1980), pp. 152–55. See also Barbara Ehrenreich and Deirdre English, *Witches, Midwives, and Nurses: A History of Women Healers* (Old Westbury: Feminist Press, 1973); Clarke Garrett, "Women and Witches: Patterns of Analysis," *Signs: Journal of Women in Culture and Society* 3 (Winter 1977): 792–98; Claudia Honegger, "Comment on Garrett's 'Women and Witches,'" *Signs: Journal of Women in Culture and Society* 4 (Summer 1979): 792–98; and Nelly Moia, "Comment on Garrett's 'Women and Witches,'" *Signs: Journal of Women in Culture and Society* 4 (Summer 1979): 798–802.

57. *Malleus Maleficarum*, ed. Montague Summers (New York: B. Blom, 1970), p. 47.

58. Ibid., p. 48. Merchant argues that the disorder of witches and the disorder of nature coincide in the very language Bacon uses to describe the new scientific method noted earlier as important to the emergence of autobiography: "The interrogation of witches as symbol for the interrogation of nature, the courtroom as model for its inquisition, and torture through mechanical devices as a tool for the subjugation of disorder were fundamental to the scientific method as power" (p. 172). Although Merchant does not claim a direct relationship between the new attitude toward nature that emerged during the Renaissance and the outbreak of the witch craze, such a relationship is implied in her approach to both phenomena.

59. Heinsohn and Steiger, p. 205.

60. Féral (p. 3) makes this point about witches.

61. See Peter Stallybrass, "Patriarchal Territories: The Body Enclosed," in *Rewriting the Renaissance: The Discourses of Sexual Difference in Early Modern Europe*, ed. Margaret W. Ferguson, Maureen Quilligan, and Nancy J. Vickers (Chicago: Univ. of Chicago Press, 1986), pp. 123–42.

62. Marina Warner referred to these figures and their licit powers in "Personification and the Idealization of the Feminine," paper presented at the Medieval and Renaissance Studies Conference, State University of New York at Binghamton, November 1984.

63. Féral, p. 7. Woolf writes: "Women have served all these centuries as looking-glasses possessing the magic and delicious power of reflecting the figure of man at twice its natural size" (Virginia Woolf, *A Room of One's Own* [New York: Harcourt, Brace & World, 1957], p. 35).

64. Woolf, p. 36.

65. "Autobiography," in quotation marks, signifies autobiography as written by men.

66. For a discussion of the agentic and communal modes of being in the world see Nancy Chodorow, "Family Structure and Feminine Personality," in *Women, Culture, and Society*, ed. Michelle Zimbalist Rosaldo and Louise Lamphere (Stanford: Stanford Univ. Press, 1974), pp. 55–58. Chodorow quotes from David Bakan, *The Duality of Human Existence: Isolation and Communion in Western Man* (Boston: Beacon Press, 1966): "I have adopted the terms 'agency' and 'communion' to characterize two fundamental modalities in the existence of living forms, agency for the existence of an organism as an individual and communion for the participation of the individual in some larger organism of which the individual is part. Agency manifests itself in self-protection, self-assertion, and self-expansion; communion manifests itself in the sense of being at one with other organisms. Agency manifests itself in the formation of separations; communion in the lack of separations. Agency manifests

itself in isolation, alienation, and aloneness; communion in contact, openness, and
union. Agency manifests itself in the urge to master; communion in noncontractual
cooperation. Agency manifests itself in the repression of thought, feeling, and
impulse; communion in the lack and removal of repression" (p. 15).

67. Chodorow, p. 50.

68. For a provocative discussion of the disorder that is woman, see Carole Pate-
man, "'The Disorder of Women': Women, Love, and the Sense of Justice," *Ethics* 91
(October 1980): 20–34. See also Rosaldo; and the writings by French feminists cited
above, chapter one, note 36.

69. The term "stealing the language" comes from the title of Alicia Suskin Os-
triker, *Stealing the Language: The Emergence of Women's Poetry in America* (Boston:
Beacon Press, 1986).

70. See Lévi-Strauss, p. 496; and Sandra M. Gilbert and Susan Gubar, "Sexual
Linguistics: Gender, Language, Sexuality," *New Literary History* 16 (Spring 1985):
516.

71. Alice Jardine, *Gynesis: Configurations of Woman and Modernity* (Ithaca: Cornell
Univ. Press, 1985), p. 93.

72. Joan Kelly-Gadol, "Early Feminist Theory and the Querelle des Femmes,
1400–1789," *Signs: Journal of Women in Culture and Society* 8 (Autumn 1982): 5. Also
quoted in Jardine, p. 95.

73. While women's education in particular and their cultural status in general
excluded them from the sphere of literary discourse, with its prerequisite grounding
in the classical tradition of rhetoric, they could engage in what became a popular
activity in the seventeenth century, amateur letter writing. As Donovan notes, letter-
writing manuals of the century "provided correspondents with models of letters and
style to be used in stock situations. Because of these models it was no longer necessary to receive formal rhetorical training in order to write acceptable, if informal,
prose" (p. 210). Like letter writing, writing autobiography could remain a private,
family-oriented, and therefore equally acceptable, because conventionally feminine,
form of literary activity for women—if, that is, the actual work remained unpublished and did not make claims on or enter into public circulation.

74. Nancy K. Miller, "Women's Autobiography in France: For a Dialectics of
Identification," in *Women and Language in Literature and Society*, ed. Sally McConnell-
Ginet, Ruth Borker, and Nelly Furman (New York: Praeger, 1980), p. 266.

75. Ibid., p. 260.

76. For a provocative discussion of canonical authority, see Christine Froula,
"When Eve Reads Milton: Undoing the Canonical Economy," *Critical Inquiry* 10
(December 1983): 321–47.

3. WOMAN'S STORY AND THE ENGENDERINGS OF
SELF-REPRESENTATION

1. A recent conference brought together scholars from a variety of disciplines to
discuss the interconnections between gender, text, and context in life writing: "Autobiography and Biography: Gender, Text and Context," Stanford University, April
11–13, 1986 (subsequent references are to "the Stanford Conference"). I am grateful to the conference organizers, Susan Groag Bell and Marilyn Yalom, and to many
of the participants for stimulating discussions that have enriched the following
critique of women's autobiography.

2. Avrom Fleishman, *Figures of Autobiography: The Language of Self-Writing in*

Victorian and Modern England (Berkeley and Los Angeles: Univ. of California Press, 1983), p. 33.

3. The summary discussion of the poetics of autobiography in this paragraph and the next derives from Sidonie Smith and Marcus Billson, "Toward a Structuralist Poetics of Autobiography," paper presented at the annual meeting of the Modern Language Association, Houston, December 1980.

4. See Elizabeth W. Bruss, *Autobiographical Acts: The Changing Situation of a Literary Genre* (Baltimore: Johns Hopkins Univ. Press, 1976), pp. 33–92.

5. Francis R. Hart, "Notes for an Anatomy of Modern Autobiography," *New Literary History* 1 (1970): 492.

6. Ibid., p. 488.

7. For a provocative exploration of the relationship of self-writing, fiction, and truthfulness, with reference by the way to Foucault, Lacan, Vico, Kierkegaard, Nietzsche, and Freud, see Michael Sprinker, "Fictions of the Self: The End of Autobiography," in *Autobiography: Essays Theoretical and Critical*, ed. James Olney (Princeton: Princeton Univ. Press, 1980), pp. 321–42. See also Barrett J. Mandel, "Full of Life Now," in ibid., pp. 49–72; and Louis A. Renza, "The Veto of the Imagination: A Theory of Autobiography," in ibid., pp. 268–95.

8. Renza, p. 270.

9. Hart, p. 500.

10. Renza, p. 278.

11. Domna C. Stanton, "Autogynography: Is the Subject Different?" in *The Female Autograph*, ed. Domna C. Stanton (New York: New York Literary Forum, 1984), p. 11.

12. For an extended discussion of the problematic relationship of "identity" and "discourse" in autobiography, see Paul L. Jay, "Being in the Text: Autobiography and the Problem of the Subject," *Modern Language Notes* 97 (December 1982): 1045–1063.

13. Both Renza and Mandel emphasize the priority of the present, as opposed to the past, "self" in autobiography.

14. See E. H. Gombrich, *Art & Illusion: A Study in the Psychology of Pictorial Representation* (New York: Pantheon, 1960). I still find Gombrich's analysis the provocative forerunner of later deconstructionist variations on certain of his themes.

15. For a discussion of the relationship of "doxa of socialities" and the readability of the plots of women's novels, see Nancy K. Miller, "Emphasis Added: Plots and Plausibilities in Women's Fiction," *PMLA* 96 (January 1981): 36–48.

16. Fleishman, p. 49.

17. Sprinker, p. 325.

18. P. N. Medvedev/Bakhtin, *The Formal Method in Literary Scholarship: A Critical Introduction to Sociological Poetics*, trans. Albert J. Wehrle (Baltimore: Goucher College Series, 1978), p. 14.

19. Wayne Booth, "Freedom of Interpretation: Bakhtin and the Challenge of Feminist Criticism," *Critical Inquiry* 9 (September 1982): 51.

20. Mikhail Bakhtin, *The Dialogic Imagination*, trans. Caryl Emerson and Michael Holquist (Austin: Univ. of Texas Press, 1981), p. 294.

21. For a provocative challenge to the notion of gender as essential to identity, see Elizabeth L. Berg, "Iconoclastic Moments: Reading the *Sonnets for Helene*, Writing the *Portuguese Letters*," in *The Poetics of Gender*, ed. Nancy K. Miller (New York: Columbia Univ. Press, 1986), pp. 219–20.

22. Terry Eagleton, *Literary Theory: An Introduction* (Minneapolis: Univ. of Minnesota Press, 1982), p. 132.

23. Toril Moi, *Sexual/Textual Politics: Feminist Literary Theory* (London: Metheun, 1985), p. 166. Moi is discussing the theory of Julia Kristeva.

24. Berg, p. 220.

25. Nancy K. Miller, "Women's Autobiography in France: For a Dialectics of Identification," in *Women and Language in Literature and Society*, ed. Sally McConnell-Ginet, Ruth Borker, and Nelly Furman (New York: Praeger, 1980), p. 262.

26. See Michel Foucault, *The History of Sexuality*, vol. 1, *An Introduction* (New York: Pantheon, 1978), pp. 61–62. I thank Susan Hardy Aiken for making this point in Susan Hardy Aiken, "Caprice de femme enciente: Isak Dinesen and the Conceptions of Feminist Criticism," paper presented at the annual meeting of the Modern Language Convention, Washington, D.C., December 1984.

27. For another approach to the thematics of women's autobiography, see Albert E. Stone, *Autobiographical Occasions and Original Acts* (Philadelphia: Univ. of Pennsylvania Press, 1982), ch. 6. Stone focuses on "the peeling away of layers of a false social identity" in works by American women. For him, "to grow into new awareness of one's body and mind as parts of a distinct entity, to leave home and engage in independent occupations, are attitudes and actions answering the special, secret, often dimly perceived needs of a woman" (p. 225).

28. "Sexual difference—which is at once biological, physiological, and relative to production—is translated by and translates a difference in the relationship of subjects to the symbolic contract which *is* the social contract; a difference, then, in the relationship to power, language, and meaning" (Julia Kristeva, "Women's Time," *Signs: Journal of Women in Culture and Society* 7 [Autumn 1981]: 21).

29. For a discussion of the relationship between consciousness of gender and of race and nationality in contemporary fiction by women novelists, see Margaret Homans, "'Her Very Own Howl'": The Ambiguities of Representation in Recent Women's Fiction," in *Signs: Journal of Women in Culture and Society* 9 (Winter 1983): 186–205, esp. pp. 197–205. For a discussion of the relationship between what Elaine Showalter calls, via Shirley and Edwin Ardener, dominant and muted cultures, in particular the possibility of situating women in more than one muted culture, see Elaine Showalter, "Feminist Criticism in the Wilderness," *Critical Inquiry* 8 (Winter 1981): 197–205, esp. pp. 202–203.

30. Ann Rosalind Jones, "Surprising Fame: Renaissance Gender Ideologies and Women's Lyric," in *The Poetics of Gender*, ed. Miller, p. 79.

31. Miller, "Women's Autobiography in France," p. 267.

32. Much recent feminist literary criticism has explored this double-voiced reading in the works of women, most particularly in fiction. See Showalter, p. 204; Miller, "Emphasis Added"; and Sandra M. Gilbert and Susan Gubar, *The Madwoman in the Attic: The Woman Writer and the Nineteenth-Century Literary Imagination* (New Haven: Yale Univ. Press, 1979).

33. Julia Kristeva, *About Chinese Women*, trans. Anita Barrows (London: Boyars, 1977), p. 28.

34. Josette Féral, "Antigone or the Irony of the Tribe," *Diacritics* 8 (Fall 1978): 4.

35. Féral, pp. 6–7.

36. Gilbert and Gubar, *Madwoman*, p. 50.

37. For a discussion of Madame de Lafayette's central problem of trying simultaneously "to assert her power and protect her person" from the fictions of female passion, see Joan DeJean, "Lafayette's Ellipses: The Privileges of Anonymity," *PMLA* 99 (October 1984): 884–902, esp. 887. The autobiographer even more acutely than the novelist faces this problem.

38. Showalter, p. 193.

39. Christiane Olivier, *Les Enfants de Jocaste* (Paris: Denoël/Gonthier, 1980), p. 143, quoted in a translation by Elyse Blankley in Sandra M. Gilbert and Susan Gubar, "Sexual Linguistics: Gender, Language, Sexuality," *New Literary History* 16 (Spring 1985): 535.

40. Carolyn G. Burke, "Report from Paris: Women's Writing and the Women's Movement," *Signs: Journal of Women in Culture and Society* 3 (Summer 1978): 844.

41. Gilbert and Gubar, "Sexual Linguistics," p. 531.

42. Moi (pp. 133–34) is here paraphrasing the theory of Luce Irigaray. For a discussion of "a thematics of language" as it captures woman's problematic status as speaker in the hegemonic discourse of the dominant culture, see Homans, pp. 186–205. The essay is particularly significant in that Homans tries to bridge the gap between the Anglo-American and French feminist traditions by focusing on "the ambiguity entailed in the representation of unrepresentability" as "an instance in which French and American assumptions are equally correct—but only when taken together" (p. 205). For an exploration of the implications of Mikhail Bakhtin's theories of dialogism reread to incorporate the thematics of gender, see Patricia S. Yaeger, "'Because a Fire Was in My Head': Eudora Welty and the Dialogic Imagination," *PMLA* 99 (October 1984): 955–73.

43. Gilbert and Gubar, "Sexual Linguistics," p. 527.

44. Margaret Homans, *Bearing the Word: Language and Female Experience in Nineteenth-Century Women's Writing* (Chicago: Univ. of Chicago Press, 1986), pp. 1–29.

45. Nancy Chodorow, *The Reproduction of Mothering: Psychoanalysis and the Sociology of Gender* (Berkeley and Los Angeles: Univ. of California Press, 1978), p. 169.

46. For a variety of discussions of maternal *jouissance* and its relationship to the semiotic and the possibilities for an *écriture féminine*, see Julia Kristeva, *Desire in Language: A Semiotic Approach to Literature and Art*, trans. Leon S. Roudiez, Alice Jardine, and Thomas Gora (New York: Columbia Univ. Press, 1980); Hélène Cixous, "The Laugh of the Medusa," trans. Keith Cohen and Paula Cohen, *Signs: Journal of Women in Culture and Society* 1 (Summer 1976): 875–93; Féral; Michelle Richman, "Eroticism in the Patriarchal Order," *Diacritics* 6 (Spring 1976): 46–53; Michele Richman, "Sex and Signs: The Language of French Feminist Criticism," *Language and Style* 13 (1980): 62–80; Ann Rosalind Jones, "Writing the Body: Toward an Understanding of *l'Écriture féminine*," *Feminist Studies* 7 (Summer 1981): 247–63; Domna C. Stanton, "Language and Revolution: The Franco-American Disconnection," in *The Future of Difference*, ed. Hester Eisenstein and Alice Jardine (Boston: G. K. Hall, 1980), pp. 73–87; Domna C. Stanton, "Difference on Trial: A Critique of the Maternal Metaphor in Cixous, Irigaray, and Kristeva," in *The Poetics of Gender*, ed. Miller, pp. 157–82; Jane Gallop and Carolyn G. Burke, "Psychoanalysis and Feminism in France, in *The Future of Difference*, ed. Eisenstein and Jardine, pp. 106–21; Christiane Makward, "To Be or Not to Be. . . . A Feminist Speaker," in ibid., pp. 95–105; and Elaine Marks and Isabelle de Courtivron, eds., *New French Feminisms* (Amherst: Univ. of Massachusetts Press, 1980). For a review article on literature about mothers and daughters, see Marianne Hirsch, "Mothers and Daughters," *Signs: Journal of Women in Culture and Society* 7 (Summer 1981): 200–222. Both Miller ("Emphasis Added," p. 37) and Showalter (p. 186) allude to the provisional and promisory status of *écriture féminine*.

47. Moi, p. 105.

48. I am especially grateful to Julia Watson, whose paper "The Theory of Autobiography: Challenges from the Margin," presented at the Stanford conference,

required my rethinking of certain parts of this chapter; and to Caren Kaplan, whose pointed criticism of my own paper forced me to rearrange and place different emphases on parts of this chapter.

49. Virginia Woolf, *A Room of One's Own* (New York: Harcourt, Brace & World, 1929), p. 65.

4. *THE BOOK OF MARGERY KEMPE:* THIS CREATURE'S UNSEALED LIFE

1. *The Book of Margery Kempe: A Modern Version by W. Butler-Bowdon* (London: Jonathan Cape, 1936), p. 23. Subsequent citations appear in the text.

2. Medieval Christians were required to confess their sins at least once a year in order to remain in good standing in the church.

3. As Foucault remarks, "Confession is . . . a ritual that unfolds within a power relationship, for one does not confess without the presence (or virtual presence) of a partner who is not simply the interlocutor but the authority who requires the confession, prescribes and appreciates it, and intervenes in order to judge, punish, forgive, console, and reconcile; a ritual in which the truth is corroborated by the obstacles and resistances it has had to surmount in order to be formulated; and finally, a ritual in which the expression alone, independently of its external consequences, produces intrinsic modifications in the person who articulates it; it exonerates, redeems, and purifies him; it unburdens him of his wrongs, liberates him, and promises him salvation" (Michel Foucault, *The History of Sexuality,* vol. 1, *An Introduction* [New York: Pantheon, 1978], pp. 61–62).

4. For a discussion of the properties and values associated with virginity by the medieval church, see Marina Warner, *Alone of All Her Sex: The Myth and the Cult of the Virgin Mary* (New York: Random House, 1983), ch. 5.

5. For an exploration of the "mothering" qualities associated with Christ in the tradition of affective piety, see Caroline Walker Bynum, *Jesus as Mother: Studies in the Spirituality of the High Middle Ages* (Berkeley and Los Angeles: Univ. of California Press, 1982), esp. pt. 4. I am also indebted to Richi Cohn, "God and Motherhood in *The Book of Margery Kempe,*" paper presented at the annual meeting of the Modern Language Association, Washington, D.C., December 1984.

6. Clarissa Atkinson discusses the conventional stages in the life of the medieval mystic in Clarissa Atkinson, *Mystic and Pilgrim: The Book and the World of Margery Kempe* (Ithaca: Cornell Univ. Press, 1983), pp. 39–48.

7. Ibid., p. 160.

8. For extended discussions of the development of affective piety, see ibid., ch. 5; and Bynum, pt. 4.

9. For discussions of female mysticism and the influence of the cult of the Virgin on medieval piety, see Atkinson, ch. 6; and Warner.

10. For discussions of the Continental tradition, see Atkinson, ch. 6; Warner, ch. 12; and *The Book of Margery Kempe*, ed. Stanford B. Meech, with annotation by Hope Emily Allen, EETS orig. ser. 212 (London: Humphrey Milford, 1940), appendix 5.

11. See *The Ancrene Riwle*, trans. M. B. Salu (Notre Dame: Univ. of Notre Dame Press); and *Hali Meidenhad*, ed. Frederick James Furnivall (London: Oxford Univ. Press, 1922), p. 14.

12. Rosemary Radford Reuther, *New Woman/New Earth: Sexist Ideologies and Human Liberation* (New York: Seabury Press, 1975), p. 17.

13. Ibid., p. 17.

14. For a discussion of the economics of medieval nunneries, see Eileen Power,

Medieval Women (Cambridge: Cambridge Univ. Press, 1975), pp. 89–99. For further details of the life of enclosed religious, see Eileen Power, *Medieval English Nunneries: 1275–1535* (Cambridge: Cambridge Univ. Press, 1922).

15. On Christina of Markyate, and her escape to the convent, see Atkinson, p. 185.

16. Kempe's home city, Lynn, was an important port of exchange between England and the Continent.

17. Atkinson mentions parallels and notes similarities but is reticent about venturing further in her discussion of Kempe's text.

18. Sheila Delany, "Sexual Economics, Chaucer's Wife of Bath, and *The Book of Margery Kempe*," *Minnesota Review* (Fall 5 1975): 112. Indeed, according to medieval law, Kempe is able to run her own initially lucrative businesses and to own and dispose of her own property; yet neither she nor her husband is in possession of that most personal resource that is the body.

19. Allen determined that Kempe begins her story when she was about twenty and brings it up to the time of narration at age sixty.

20. Warner argues that "in times of persecution, martyrdom made amends for nature's wrongs, and proved the faith of the victim; and in untroubled times the equivalent of the arena was the cell, and the equivalent of the wild beast was the renunciation of worldly happiness and the practices of the hair shirt, the waterbowl, and the scourge. Through virginity and self-inflicted hardship, the faults of female nature could be corrected" (p. 69). Warner, of course, is discussing the cloistered virgin in her analysis; but with later medieval piety such characteristics could appropriately be associated with the religious woman who, like Kempe, sought chastity.

21. Luce Irigaray, *Speculum of the Other Woman*, trans. Gillian C. Gill (Ithaca: Cornell Univ. Press, 1985), p. 199.

22. Cohn discusses this aspect of Kempe's mysticism. For a stimulating analysis of the writing woman as bearer of the word, see Margaret Homans, *Bearing the Word: Language and Female Experience in Nineteenth-Century Women's Writing* (Chicago and London: Univ. of Chicago Press, 1986), p. 30. Also, Janel M. Mueller has suggested—I would argue overstated—a coherency to this story of spiritual motherhood in Janel M. Mueller, "Autobiography of a New 'Creatur': Female Spirituality, Selfhood, and Authorship in *The Book of Margery Kempe*," in *The Female Autograph*, ed. Domna C. Stanton (New York: New York Literary Forum, 1984). Mueller maintains that Kempe brings words, dialogues, scenes, events together in order to assure her reader as Christ has assured her that "there is no inherent incompatibility between becoming a bride of God and being acknowledged as the wife of John Kempe, burgess of Lynn, and the mother of his fourteen children" (p. 67).

23. On the place of tears in medieval mysticism see Atkinson, esp. ch. 6; Bynum; and Warner, pp. 221–23.

24. For a discussion of this aspect of the Virgin's story, see Warner, ch. 14.

25. See *The Book of Margery Kempe*, ed. Meech, pp. 257–58, note 4/4.

26. The second amanuensis begins to rewrite the *Book* the day after St. Mary Magdalen's day, 1436. He then adds the second, shorter volume to the first to bring the narrative up to date.

27. A. E. Goodman, "The Piety of John Brunham's Daughter, of Lynn," in *Medieval Women*, ed. Derek Baker (Oxford: Basil Blackwell, 1978), p. 349.

28. Deborah S. Ellis, "Margery Kempe & the Virgin's Hot Caudle," *Essays in Arts and Sciences*, 15 (May 1985): 3. Ellis offers a fascinating approach to Kempe's life and text, exploring her work in the context of the imagery of the medieval household and her life in the context of the realities of medieval housewifery.

5. THE RAGGED ROUT OF SELF: MARGARET CAVENDISH'S
TRUE RELATION AND THE HEROICS OF
SELF-DISCLOSURE

1. Paul Delany, *British Autobiography in the Seventeenth Century* (New York: Columbia Univ. Press, 1969), p. 160. Although Delany admits that Cavendish's preoccupation with herself "ensures that we come into unobstructed contact with her, instead of being blocked by the multiple defences erected by so many male autobiographers," he nevertheless finds this preoccupation "tedious," which may explain why, after making such interesting claims for the work, he does not bother to analyze it. Since he does not, he has not the opportunity to reconsider his easy dismissal of the defenses she does erect.

2. Wayne Shumaker, *English Autobiography: Its Emergence, Materials, and Form* (Berkeley and Los Angeles: Univ. of California Press, 1954), p. 92. But, having said this, he too moves on without further exploring the intricacies of the work.

3. Cynthia S. Pomerleau, "The Emergence of Women's Autobiography in England" in *Women's Autobiography: Essays in Criticism*, ed. Estelle C. Jelinek (Bloomington: Indiana Univ. Press, 1980), p. 22. Pomerleau's article draws general comparisons among women's autobiographies of the seventeenth and eighteenth centuries; she does not consider Cavendish's *True Relation* in any detail either. Bottrall briefly discusses the works by women of the seventeenth century, but only alludes in passing to Cavendish's life in Margaret Bottrall, *Every Man a Phoenix* (London: John Murray, 1958). The historian Hilda L. Smith discusses the life and works in Hilda L. Smith, *Reason's Disciples: Seventeenth-Century English Feminists* (Urbana: Univ. of Illinois Press, 1982). Two literary critics have, however, given the work serious and more detailed consideration: Patricia Meyer Spacks, *The Female Imagination* (New York: Knopf, 1975), esp. ch. 6; and Mary C. Mason, "The Other Voice: Autobiographies of Women Writers," in *Autobiography: Essays Theoretical and Critical*, ed. James Olney (Princeton: Princeton Univ. Press, 1980), pp. 207–235. Though I do not always agree with the details of Spacks's analysis, I do agree with the general outlines of her reading of the autobiography. Mason's essay, although it offers an interesting theoretical framework, is ultimately too limited.

4. Virginia Woolf, "The Duchess of Newcastle," in *The Common Reader: First Series* (New York: Harcourt, Brace & World, 1925), p. 79.

5. This biographical material comes from *Dictionary of National Biography*, ed. Sir Leslie Stephen and Sir Sidney Lee (London: Oxford Univ. Press, 1917), vol. 3, pp. 1264–65.

6. The fact that a good many of the English autobiographies written during the seventeenth century remained unpublished for as long as two hundred years suggests one reason why the autobiographer, especially the secular one, confronted, as Delany notes, a "difficult and confusing task, for he had to organize his 'performance' without much help from literary tradition, unless he was using a particular religious convention" (p. 115). See also Waldo H. Dunn, *English Biography* (New York: E. P. Dutton, 1916), pp. 139–40; and Donald A. Stauffer, *English Biography before 1700* (Cambridge: Harvard Univ. Press, 1930), pp. 175–76.

7. See chapter two above for further discussion of the historical forces encouraging the emergence of these modes of self-representation.

8. Delany, pp. 17–18.

9. Shumaker, p. 57.

10. Pomerleau, p. 28.

11. Stauffer, p. 209.

12. For an analysis of the difference of men's and women's rhetorical style in biographies, Cavendish's biography of the duke included, see Patricia A. Sullivan, "Female Writing beside the Rhetorical Tradition: Seventeenth Century British Biography and Female Tradition in Rhetoric," *International Journal of Women's Studies* 3 (March/April 1980): 143–60.

13. Lucy Hutchinson, *Memoirs of the Life of Colonel Hutchinson* (London: Oxford Univ. Press, 1973). The work was written about 1670–1675 and first printed in 1806.

14. *Memoirs of Anne, Lady Halkett and Ann, Lady Fanshawe*, ed. John Clyde Loftis (Oxford: Oxford Univ. Press, 1979). The work was first published in 1907.

15. Ibid. The work was written in 1678.

16. Smith, pp. 75–76.

17. Ibid., p. 76.

18. As Smith remarks, "She wanted to be read, to be popular, to be remembered. Her social position brought her attention, but the duchess wanted the world to admire her for her own talents and works, not because she married well. This desire for personal recognition inspired her repetitious defense of the originality of her work. Her writings, she reiterated, came not from her husband nor others, but solely from her own rational powers" (p. 78).

19. Sandra M. Gilbert and Susan Gubar, *The Madwoman in the Attic: The Woman Writer and the Nineteenth-Century Literary Imagination* (New Haven: Yale Univ. Press, 1979), p. 20. See also Spacks, *The Female Imagination*, pp. 190–92.

20. For their discussion of the "anxiety of authorship" the woman writer must inevitably experience in patriarchal culture, see Gilbert and Gubar, ch. 2. Spacks explores the struggle in Cavendish's *Life* between "the desire to assert and the need to deny the self" in Spacks, *The Female Imagination*, p. 195; and Patricia Meyer Spacks, "Reflecting Women," *Yale Review* 63 (Autumn 1973): 36–37. While I, too, pose this general thematics in the work, I see other complexities and emphasize other entanglements in her self-representation.

21. *The Lives of William Cavendish, duke of Newcastle, and of his wife, Margaret, duchess of Newcastle. Written by the thrice noble and illustrious princess, Margaret, duchess of Newcastle*, ed. Mark Antony Lower (London: J. R. Smith, 1872), p. 309. Subsequent citations appear in the text. Smith suggests that "[t]his emphasis on her family status may have grown from her resentment toward those who cautioned the duke against marrying beneath himself." "Yet," she goes on to note, "the emphasis was similar to that which she was to pursue in her own life and writings; socially granted status mattered little compared to that which was awarded for intellectual contribution or personal merit. Her literary labors and her desire for fame grew out of a belief that merited worth, of the kind she believed her parent possessed, mattered more than the titled position her marriage brought her" (p. 86).

22. Discussing recurrent themes in Cavendish's plays, poetry, and prose pieces, Delores Paloma suggests that "the ideals and ambitions Cavendish sought to realize in her own life were appropriated from and expressed in terms borrowed from the heroic ethic of the masculine world" (Delores Paloma, "Margaret Cavendish: Defining the Female Self," *Women's Studies: An Interdisciplinary Journal* 7 [1980]: 55–56).

23. Mason, p. 223.

24. Delany, p. 169.

25. Pomerleau, p. 23.

26. Smith, p. 202.

27. As Smith suggests, "Practical accomplishment, which her mother inherited with widowhood, the daughter pursued in a less socially accepted form during the life of her husband" (p. 86).

28. *Natures Pictures*, 2d ed. (London, 1168), sig. Cv.

29. "If . . . female creativity has had to express itself within the confines of domesticity (in part because of the emphasis on the personal in female socialization), women could at least paint their own faces, shape their own bodies, and modulate their own vocal tones to become the glass of fashion and the mold of form. To make up, for such women, means not only making up stories but making up faces. In terms of the Pygmalion myth with which I began, the woman who cannot become an artist can nevertheless turn herself into an artistic object" (Susan Gubar, "'The Blank Page' and the Issues of Female Creativity," *Critical Inquiry* 8 [Winter 1981]: 249).

30. Suzanne Juhasz, "Towards a Theory of Form in Feminist Autobiography: Kate Millet's *Flying* and *Sita*; Maxine Hong Kingston's *The Woman Warrior*," in *Women's Autobiography*, ed. Jelinek, p. 230.

31. Mason is only partially accurate when she claims that "for all her singularity, for all her strong individuality and distinctiveness of personality, for all her fantasticalness, Margaret Cavendish required a substitute figure or other—an alter ego really—with and through whom she might identify herself. . . . [She] found in the Duke of Newcastle both her husband and her Lord, but remarkably enough she succeeds in making this of him without ever dimming the bright light of her own personality" (p. 222). Actually the duke functions much like the woman in Freud's male daydreams. He becomes a kind of male muse who sanctions and even inspires her writing.

32. For a discussion of the dynamics of male and female daydreams and writing, see Nancy K. Miller, "Emphasis Added: Plots and Plausibilities in Women's Fiction," *PMLA* 96 (January 1981): 40.

33. Stephen Jay Greenblatt, *Renaissance Self-Fashioning: From More to Shakespeare* (Chicago and London: Univ. of Chicago Press, 1980), p. 257.

34. Spacks, *The Female Imagination*, p. 194.

6. *A NARRATIVE OF THE LIFE OF MRS. CHARLOTTE CHARKE:* THE TRANSGRESSIVE DAUGHTER AND THE MASQUERADE OF SELF-REPRESENTATION

1. *A Narrative of the Life of Mrs. Charlotte Charke (Youngest Daughter of COLLEY CIBBER, Esq.), Written by HERSELF*, ed. Leonard R. N. Ashley (Gainesville: Scholars' Facsimiles & Reprints, 1969), pp. iii–iv. Subsequent citations appear in the text.

2. As Patricia Meyer Spacks notes in her discussion of Charke's autobiography, the dedication is added to her story after Charke's father refuses to send his word of forgiveness in response to the early installments (Patricia Meyer Spacks, *Imagining a Self: Autobiography and Novel in Eighteenth-Century England* [Cambridge: Harvard Univ. Press, 1976], p. 82).

3. Ibid., p. 87.

4. Ibid., p. 78.

5. Ibid.

6. The autobiography was written in weekly installments over the course of eight weeks, from about March 1 to April 19, 1755. The letter to her father is dated March 8.

7. Spacks emphasizes this story of victimization and vulnerability. As will become clear, I place emphasis elsewhere.

8. For a discussion of the late eighteenth century's critical response to the impact the new novel might have on women, see John Tinnon Taylor, *Early Opposition to the English Novel: The Popular Reaction from 1760 to 1830* (New York: King's Crown Press, 1943), pp. 87–101.

9. Spacks briefly alludes to Charke's "ceaseless efforts to make her utility equivalent to that of a boy" (p. 76).

10. For discussion of the rogue in eighteenth-century literature, see such works as Frank Wadleigh Chandler, *The Literature of Roguery*, 2 vols. (New York: Burt Franklin, 1958); Richard Bjornson, *The Picaresque Hero in European Fiction* (Madison: Univ. of Wisconsin Press, 1977); and Jerry C. Beasley, *Novels of the 1740s* (Athens: Univ. of Georgia Press, 1982).

11. Cynthia Merrill notes that Charke's choice of the male name "Mr. Brown" serves a double purpose (Cynthia Merrill, "Autobiography as Cross-Dressing: 'A Narrative of Mrs. Charlotte Charke,'" paper presented at "Autobiography and Biography: Gender, Text and Context," conference, Stanford University, April 11–13, 1986 [subsequent references are to "the Stanford conference"]). Obviously the name is masculine. But it is also the married name of the sister who opposes her. Thus in the name is captured her desire to masquerade as a man and her desire to be reconciled as a dutiful daughter. Merrill's analysis of Charke's text, similar to my own, emphasizes the "masculine" storytelling at the expense of the "feminine" storytelling in Charke's autobiography.

12. Terry Castle served as the respondent to Merrill's paper on Charke at the Stanford conference. In a flurry of provocative comments, Castle established certain questions that remain central in considering the phenomenon of cross-dressing for women of earlier centuries.

13. See Terry Castle, "The Carnivalization of Eighteenth-Century English Narrative," *PMLA* 99 (October 1984): 905. In her eloquent essay on the masquerade in eighteenth-century literature, Castle argues that the scene of masquerade functions subversively on three levels. While Castle specifically explores the psychological, ideological, and narrative impact of such scenes in the century's fiction, the insights she offers about fictive scenes provide interesting ways of approaching Charke's autobiographical masquerade.

14. Paul John Eakin, *Fictions in Autobiography: Studies in the Art of Self-Invention* (Princeton: Princeton Univ. Press, 1985), p. 226.

15. I refer here, à la Eakin, to the title of James Olney, *Metaphors of Self: The Meaning of Autobiography* (Princeton: Princeton Univ. Press, 1972).

16. Eakin, p. 226.

17. Donald A. Stauffer, *The Art of Biography in Eighteenth Century England* (Princeton: Princeton Univ. Press, 1941), p. 109. Spacks also comments on Stauffer's description.

18. Avrom Fleishman, *Figures of Autobiography: The Language of Self-Writing in Victorian and Modern England* (Berkeley and Los Angeles: Univ. of California Press, 1983), p. 88.

19. Paul J. Korshin, "The Development of Abstracted Typology in England, 1650–1820," in *Literary Uses of Typology from the Late Middle Ages to the Present* (Princeton: Princeton Univ. Press, 1977), ed. Earl Miner, p. 148, quoted in Fleishman, p. 87.

20. For a discussion of the attraction of the century to stories of criminality, see Lennard J. Davis, *Factual Fictions: The Origins of the English Novel* (New York: Columbia Univ. Press, 1983), ch. 7.

21. Beasley, p. 99.

22. Davis, pp. 126–31.

23. Castle, p. 905.

24. Interestingly, in September 1746 a certain Mary Hamilton was tried for fraud in a series of events similar to those narrated by Charke. Hamilton, dressed as a man, had proposed to and married a Mary Price in July 1746. Within two months the fraud was discovered, but not before, as court records and news accounts reveal, Hamilton had sexually violated "her" wife. The bizarre story was apparently common knowledge, for Henry Fielding wrote a pamphlet entitled "The Female Husband" based on Hamilton's story. We can only speculate about the effect that this previous story might have had on the perceived sensationalism of Charke's life story in the minds of her readers and in her own mind. For a discussion of the Hamilton case and of Fielding's authorship of "The Female Husband," see Sheridan Baker, "Henry Fielding's *The Female Husband:* Fact and Fiction," *PMLA* 74 (June 1959): 213–24.

25. For a discussion of the relationship of self-fashioning to self-cancellation, see Stephen Jay Greenblatt, *Renaissance Self-Fashioning: From More to Shakespeare* (Chicago: Univ. of Chicago Press, 1980), esp. ch. 1.

26. In her comments at the Stanford conference, Castle asked how the literary critic could "penetrate the seemingly impenetrable sexuality" of the cross-dressed subject.

27. Castle, commentary at the Stanford conference.

28. Spacks, p. 83.

29. Charlotte Charke, *A Narrative of the Life of Charlotte Charke, Youngest Daughter of Colley Cibber, Esq.* (London: Hunt and Clarke, 1827), pp. vi–vii.

30. Ibid., p. 167.

7. HARRIET MARTINEAU'S *AUTOBIOGRAPHY:* THE REPRESSED DESIRE OF A LIFE LIKE A MAN'S

1. *Harriet Martineau's Autobiography*, 2 vols., ed. Maria Weston (Boston: James R. Osgood, 1877), vol. 1, p. 1. Subsequent citations appear in the text.

2. Critics who discuss Martineau's *Autobiography* comment on the importance of the new understanding of individual psychological development that emerged during the century. See, for instance, R. K. Webb, *Harriet Martineau: A Radical Victorian* (New York: Columbia Univ. Press, 1960); Mitzi Myers, "Harriet Martineau's Autobiography: The Making of a Female Philosopher," in *Women's Autobiography: Essays in Criticism*, ed. Estelle C. Jelinek (Bloomington: Indiana Univ. Press, 1980), pp. 53–70; Valerie Kossew Pichanick, *Harriet Martineau: The Woman and Her Work* (Ann Arbor: Univ. of Michigan Press, 1980); Gillian Thomas, *Harriet Martineau* (Boston: Twayne, 1985), p. 123; and Gaby Weiner, "New Introduction" to *Harriet Martineau's Autobiography* (London: Virago Press, 1983), pp. ix–xx.

3. Mary Poovey, "*Persuasion* and the Promises of Love," in *The Representation of Women in Fiction: Selected Papers from the English Institute, 1981*, ed. Carolyn G. Heilbrun and Margaret R. Higonnet (Baltimore: Johns Hopkins Univ. Press, 1983), p. 153.

4. Linda H. Peterson, *Victorian Autobiography: The Tradition of Self-Interpretation* (New Haven and London: Yale Univ. Press, 1986), p. 126.

5. *The Works of Hannah More* (New York: Harper and Brothers, 1854), vol. 1, p. 367, quoted in ibid., p. 127.

6. Peterson, p. 136.

7. Martineau wrote her autobiography at furious speed in 1855, thinking death was near. She lived another twenty years but never revised or supplemented her text.

8. Sir Edward Boyle, *Biographical Essays, 1790–1890* (London: Oxford Univ. Press, 1936), p. 182; E. Boyle, "Miss Martineau's Monthly Novels," *Quarterly Review* 49 (April 1833): 136.

9. Richard N. Coe, *When the Grass Was Taller: Autobiography and the Experience of Childhood* (New Haven: Yale Univ. Press, 1984), p. 12.

10. Ibid., p. 38.

11. Luann Walthur, "The Invention of Childhood in Victorian Autobiography," in *Approaches to Victorian Autobiography*, ed. George P. Landow (Athens: Ohio Univ. Press, 1979), p. 65.

12. For an extensive discussion of Martineau's willful mother, see Mitzi Meyers, "Unmothered Daughter and Radical Reformer: Harriet Martineau's Career," in *The Lost Tradition: Mothers and Daughters in Literature*, ed. Cathy N. Davidson and E. M. Broner (New York: Ungar, 1980), pp. 70–80.

13. On Martineau's powerful evocation of the quality of childhood experience, see Meyers, *"Harriet Martineau's Autobiography,"* pp. 58–60.

14. Walthur, p. 71.

15. Paul John Eakin, *Fictions in Autobiography: Studies in the Art of Self-Invention* (Princeton: Princeton Univ. Press, 1985), p. 226.

16. Wilhelm Dilthey, *Das Erlebnis und die Dichtung* (Leipzig, 1913), p. 394, quoted in *The Voyage In: Fictions of Female Development*, ed. Elizabeth Abel, Marianne Hirsch, and Elizabeth Langland (Hanover: Univ. Press of New England, 1983), pp. 5–6.

17. Pichanick, p. 197.

18. Peterson (pp. 138–43) also explores the hermeneutical framework of Martineau's self-narrative.

19. Karl Joachim Weintraub, "Autobiography and Historical Consciousness," *Critical Inquiry* 1 (1975): 846. See also Eakin's discussion of Weintraub's analysis (pp. 203–204).

20. For a discussion of the fictive pattern established by Augustine's *Confessions* and rewritten through later spiritual autobiographies, see Avrom Fleishman, *Figures of Autobiography: The Language of Self-Writing in Victorian and Modern England* (Berkeley and Los Angeles: Univ. of California Press, 1983), esp. ch. 1 and 2.

21. See Peterson, pp. 130–32.

22. *The Positive Philosophy of Auguste Comte*, 3 vols., trans. Harriet Martineau (first pub. 1853), with intro. by Frederic Harrison (London: George G. Bell, 1965), vol. 2, pp. 284–85, quoted in Pichanick, p. 196.

23. "[S]he was able to ignore those aspects of Comtean theory which were not congenial and to derive strength and satisfaction from those elements of the philosophy which answered her purpose" (Pichanick, p. 198).

24. Peterson, p. 150.

25. During the nineteenth century, propriety emerged as the governing ideology of women's lives and rhetorical possibilities. Precisely because, ideologically, woman was described as sexually voracious, naturally lascivious, she must, as Mary Poovey argues, "display no vanity, no passion, no assertive 'self' at all." Poovey emphasizes the fundamental paradox permeating discussions of female virtue: "At the heart of the explicit description of 'feminine,' Angelic women, superior to all physical appetite, resides the 'female' sexuality that was automatically assumed to be the defining characteristic of female nature" (p. 19).

26. Walthur argues that such self-criticism was characterstic of Victorian representations of childhood: "Victorians did not wish to think of themselves as having been 'overamused' as children," she suggests, since "childhood suffering was bracing; it was good for you" (p. 72.) From that point of view, the vagaries of parents could be "rationalized" by the child's culpability and justified as potentially edifying.

27. It is easy when considering Martineau's life story to attribute to her a psychosomatic personality. Certainly the onslaught of deafness "fits" her experience in a clearly symbolic way. If the world turned a deaf ear to the suffering, lonely child who lived in a world of silenced desire, then the child could turn a deaf ear to the world, literally. If those around her took her for a slow learner and talked of her as "dumb," then the child could become dumb to that world.

28. Thomas, p. 129.

29. Philip Davis, *Memory and Writing: From Wordsworth to Lawrence* (Liverpool: Liverpool Univ. Press, 1983), p. 244. Davis discusses the impact of this vision of authorship on Martineau's writing.

30. For a discussion of the ideology of woman's proper sphere in the mid-nineteenth century, see Judith Newton, "Making—and Remaking—History: Another Look at Patriarchy," in *Tulsa Studies in Women's Literature* 3 (1984): 125–42.

31. The energy Martineau invests in presenting herself as the ideal woman evidences an underlying uneasiness about her position as a woman who has lived and written a life like a man's. Rumors circulate throughout her text, haunting her very storytelling: "It occurs to me that my life ought indeed to be written by myself or some one else who can speak to its facts; for, if the reports afloat about me from time to time were to find their way into print after my death, it would appear the strangest life in the world" (I:164). She even catalogs the apocryphal stories (I:164–65). Ultimately, her autobiographical posture becomes defensive as she uses her official autobiography to set the record straight, to answer for posterity the lies and half-truths, to respond to the personal indictments.

32. Margaret Homans, *Bearing the Word: Language and Female Experience in Nineteenth-Century Women's Writing* (Chicago and London: Univ. of Chicago Press, 1986), pp. 29–33.

33. Davis, p. 240.

34. Ibid., pp. 242–44.

35. Ibid., p. 241.

36. Ibid., p. 244.

37. "In proportion as the taint of fear and desire and self-regard fell off, and the meditation had fact instead of passion as its subject, the aspiration became freer and sweeter, till at length, when the selfish superstition had wholly gone out of it, it spread its charm through every change of every waking hour,—and does now, when life itself is expiring" (I:88).

38. Davis, p. 244.

39. For a discussion of the conflict between Harriet's and James's representations of their mother, see Myers, "Unmothered Daughter."

40. Davis, p. 243.

8. MAXINE HONG KINGSTON'S *WOMAN WARRIOR*: FILIALITY AND WOMAN'S AUTOBIOGRAPHICAL STORYTELLING

1. Albert E. Stone comments that Kingston's autobiography joins others in "this terrain of contemporary autobiography which abuts the continent of fiction" (Albert

E. Stone, *Autobiographical Occasions and Original Acts* [Philadelphia: Univ. of Pennsylvania Press, 1982], p. 25).

2. For a review article on recent literature on mothers and daughters, see Marianne Hirsch, "Mothers and Daughters," *Signs: Journal of Women in Culture and Society* 7 (Summer 1981): 200–222. See also Adrienne Rich, *Of Woman Born* (New York: Norton, 1976), esp. ch. 9.

3. Maxine Hong Kingston, *The Woman Warrior: Memoirs of a Girlhood among Ghosts* (New York: Random House, 1977), p. 3. Subsequent citations appear in the text.

4. At this moment the female body, emitting the menstrual flow and promising the subsequent discharge of childbirth portended in the blood, becomes one powerful and primary source of pollution in the community: The blood emitted reaffirms the association of woman with the dangerous powers of life and death, those two events that bring into play the processes of disintegration and integration within the patrilineal group and the forces of disorder and order in the community. See Emily M. Ahern, "The Power and Pollution of Chinese Women," in *Women in Chinese Society*, ed. Margery Wolf and Roxane Witke (Stanford: Stanford University Press, 1975), pp. 193–214. See also Mary Douglas, *Purity and Danger: An Analysis of Concepts of Pollution and Taboo* (New York: Praeger, 1966), esp. pp. 114–28.

5. For a discussion of the subversive power of woman's womb, see Susan Hardy Aiken, "Dinesen's 'Sorrow-acre': Tracing the Woman's Line," *Contemporary Literature* 25 (Summer 1984): 165–71.

6. For a discussion of *The Woman Warrior* with an attention to certain dynamics in the work that is similar to my own, see Paul John Eakin, *Fictions in Autobiography: Studies in the Art of Self-Invention* (Princeton: Princeton Univ. Press, 1985), pp. 255–75. As Eakin comments on this first "cautionary" tale, he focuses on the relation of woman to her community. I find Eakin's analysis throughout stimulating. Although we read the work in similar ways, we often give different emphases to the details.

7. Margery Wolf, "Women and Suicide in China," in *Women in Chinese Society*, ed. Wolf and Witke, p. 112. Why, for instance, was this married aunt living with her own parents rather than with her in-laws? And who had been the stranger, or was he a stranger, who had entered her house/womb? Kingston notes that a woman pregnant by someone near to, perhaps even in, her natal family would lay bare the vulnerability of the patrilineage to violations by incest.

8. Aiken, p. 167. See also Gayle Rubin, "The Traffic in Women: Notes on the 'Political Economy' of Sex," in *Toward an Anthropology of Women*, ed. Rayna R. Reiter (New York: Monthly Review Press, 1975), pp. 157–210; and Tony Tanner, *Adultery in the Novel: Contract and Transgression* (Baltimore: Johns Hopkins Univ. Press, 1979), pp. 58–66.

9. See Ahern, pp. 199–202.

10. See Wolf, pp. 113–14.

11. See Ahern, p. 198.

12. See ibid., p. 113.

13. Florence Ayscough, *Chinese Women: Yesterday and Today* (Boston: Houghton Mifflin, 1937), pp. 214–22.

14. Suzanne Juhasz makes this point also in her essay, "Towards a Theory of Form in Feminist Autobiography: Kate Millet's *Flying* and *Sita*; Maxine Hong Kingston's *The Woman Warrior*," in *Women's Autobiography: Essays in Criticism*, ed. Estelle C. Jelinek (Bloomington: Indiana Univ. Press, 1980), p. 234.

15. She does not succumb to the agoraphobia that presses so heavily upon her no-name aunt. Indeed, despite cold and hunger, she prospers in the midst of illimitable space and possibilities.

16. Kingston/Fa Mu Lan recognizes that her very life depends on this successful erasure of her true identity: "Chinese executed women who disguised themselves as soldiers or students, no matter how bravely they fought or how high they scored on the examination" (46). In that way traditional Chinese culture effectively denied women access to the power signified by the sword and the power signified by the surrogate sword, the pen and the knowledge it inscribed.

17. In the original legend Mu Lan remains chaste during her years as the woman warrior. Kingston does make a space in her interpretation and her text for female sexuality, but, as I note above, it remains suppressed in the larger community.

18. Josette Féral, "Antigone or the Irony of the Tribe," *Diacritics* 8 (Fall 1978): 4.

19. The baron whom Kingston/Fa Mu Lan finally slays mistakes her for this kind of warrior. In response to his query about her identity, she tells him she is "a female avenger." His response—" 'Oh, come now. Everyone takes the girls when he can. The families are glad to be rid of them' " (51)—suggests that he understands her to be an avenger of the wrongs of woman. Kingston/Fa Mu Lan specifies that the crime she seeks to avenge is, however, his impressment of her brother.

20. Her heroic space is far larger than that which provided the canvas for Fa Mu Lan's adventures: "Nobody in history has conquered and united both North America and Asia" (58). The public gestures of heroism she attempts are not uttered in a dazzling display of swordsmanship but in a self-effacing, tentative, "squeaky" voice that identifies her, not with the woman warrior, but with the "wives and slaves" tucked into the interstices of the mythical narrative. In her modern American space, the martial arts are not the grandiose gestures of heroic action; they are merely exercises "for unsure little boys kicking away under flourescent lights" (62). Moreover, in Communist China her relatives, instead of being identified with the exploited peasants, are identified as exploiting landowners and punished as the barons in the myth.

21. As the daughter knows, "all heroes are bold toward food" (104). They demonstrate by their gustatory feats their power over the natural world, their high degree of aristocratic cultivation, and their association with the sacred. See Claude Lévi-Strauss, *The Raw and the Cooked*, trans. John and Doreen Weightman (New York: Harper & Row, 1969).

22. See Mary Daly, *Gyn/Ecology: The Metaethics of Radical Feminism* (Boston: Beacon Press, 1978), pp. 153–77.

23. For a brief biography of Ts'ai Yen, see Wu-chi Liu and Irving Yucheng Lo, eds., *Sunflower Splendor: Three Thousand Years of Chinese Poetry* (Garden City: Anchor, 1975), pp. 537–58.

24. For a discussion of the narrative rhythms of identification and differentiation in *The Woman Warrior* and *China Men*, see Suzanne Juhasz, "Maxine Hong Kingston: Narrative Technique and Female Identity," in *Contemporary American Women Writers*, ed. Catherine Rainwater and William J. Scheik (Lexington: Univ. Press of Kentucky, 1985), pp. 173–89.

25. See Aiken, pp. 175–84.

Index